Reconceptualising Unaccompanied Child Asylum Seekers and the Law

Unaccompanied child asylum seekers are amongst the world's most vulnerable populations, and their numbers are increasing. The intersection of their age, their seeking asylum, and separation from their parents creates a specific and acute triple burden of vulnerability. Their precariousness has long been recognised in international human rights law. Yet, human rights-based responses have been subordinated to progressive global securitisation of irregular migration through interception, interdiction, extraterritorial processing and immigration detention. Such an approach necessitates an urgent paradigm shift in how we comprehend their needs as children, the impact of punitive border control laws on them, and the responsibility of States to these children when they arrive at their borders seeking asylum.

This book reconceptualises the relationship between unaccompanied child asylum seekers and States. It proposes a new conceptual framework by applying international human rights law, childhood studies and vulnerability theory scholarship in analysing State obligations to respond to these children. This framework incorporates a robust analysis of the operation and impact of laws on vulnerable populations, a taxonomy for articulating the gravity of any consequent harms and a method to prioritise recommendations for reform.

The book then illustrates the framework's utility using Australia's treatment of unaccompanied children as a case study. This book illuminates key learnings from human rights law, childhood studies and vulnerability theory and transforms them into a new roadmap for law reform. As such, it will be a valuable practice-based resource for practitioners, non-government organisations, advocates, policy-makers and the general public interested in advocating for the rights of vulnerable populations as well as for academics, researchers and students of human rights law, refugee law, childhood studies and vulnerability studies.

Jennifer L. Whelan is a practising human rights lawyer and academic.

Routledge Research in Asylum, Migration and Refugee Law

Available titles in this series include:

Migrant Rights at Work
Law's Precariousness at the Intersection of Immigration and Labour
Laurie Berg

Unaccompanied Children in European Migration and Asylum Practices
In Whose Best Interests?
Edited by Mateja Sedmak, Birgit Sauer, and Barbara Gornik

European Asylum Law and the Rights of the Child
Ciara Smyth

Asylum Law in the European Union
Francesco Cherubini

The Socio-Economic Rights of Asylum Seekers
Liam Thornton

Serious International Crimes, Human Rights, and Forced Migration
Edited by James C. Simeon

Migration Law, Policy and Human Rights
The Impact of Crisis in Europe
Rachael Dickson

Reconceptualising Unaccompanied Child Asylum Seekers and the Law
Jennifer L. Whelan

For more information about this series, please visit: https://www.routledge.com/Routledge-Research-in-Asylum-Migration-and-Refugee-Law/book-series/MIGRATION

Reconceptualising Unaccompanied Child Asylum Seekers and the Law

Jennifer L. Whelan

Routledge
Taylor & Francis Group
LONDON AND NEW YORK

First published 2023
by Routledge
4 Park Square, Milton Park, Abingdon, Oxon OX14 4RN

and by Routledge
605 Third Avenue, New York, NY 10158

Routledge is an imprint of the Taylor & Francis Group, an informa business

British Library Cataloguing-in-Publication Data
A catalogue record for this book is available from the British Library

Library of Congress Cataloging-in-Publication Data
A catalog record has been requested for this book

ISBN: 978-1-032-19629-9 (hbk)
ISBN: 978-1-032-19630-5 (pbk)
ISBN: 978-1-003-26013-4 (ebk)

DOI: 10.4324/9781003260134

Typeset in Galliard
by Deanta Global Publishing Services, Chennai, India

For Thomas and Mercedes, child refugees at a time when global responses provided them with protection and enabled them to flourish, and for all children and adults seeking asylum now – you deserve the same.

Contents

Figures

Tables

Acknowledgement

Thank you to Emeritus Professor Terry Carney and Associate Professors Laurie Berg and Karen O'Connell for your patient assistance, guidance and exacting observations as supervisors of the PhD that was the foundation of this book. I would also like to thank my PhD examiners, Associate Professor Dr Savitri Taylor and Professor Lenni B. Benson, whose thoughtful comments improved that body of work.

Thank you also to Dr Tanya Muscat and Zoë Whelan-Young for your thoughtful, meticulous and generous editing assistance.

Lastly, thank you to my friends and family, and especially Mike, Tom, Max and Zoë, for supporting and encouraging the writing of this book.

Introduction

This book contends for the reconceptualisation of State obligations to do no (further) harm to unaccompanied children seeking asylum by sea by developing scholarship from childhood studies, vulnerability theory and international human rights law. It ultimately proposes an urgent paradigm shift in how we comprehend children, the impact of punitive border control laws on them and the responsibility of States. The book offers a new child-centred, harm-remediation conceptual framework ('a mitigating vulnerability framework') that has global application and is drawn from international human rights law, childhood studies and vulnerability theory scholarship. This framework facilitates a robust analysis of the operation and impact of laws on vulnerable populations. It integrates both a taxonomy for articulating the gravity of any consequent harm and a method to prioritise advocacy for reform based on harm minimisation.

Unaccompanied child asylum seekers are amongst the world's most vulnerable populations, and their numbers are increasing. Unlike child refugees, whose claims have been accepted by the receiving State, their asylum claims have not yet been considered, and their arrival is unauthorised. The scope of their humanitarian crisis has been extensively documented as well as their ongoing susceptibility to abuse, assault, trafficking and labour and sexual exploitation whilst their asylum claims are determined.[1] So too has the causal connection between their exposure to pre-flight traumatic events and their separation from, or loss of, parents and other family members and significant psychological trauma.[2] They present with this trauma when they arrive at the borders of destination countries,[3] and it can persist for many years.[4]

I explicitly acknowledge unaccompanied children's resilience and agentic capacity. However, this book focuses on the need for States to better comprehend and attend to these children as well as the necessity to enact laws and policies that increase their resilience and ameliorate their dependence on the State. In this context, notwithstanding their capacities for resilience and agency, all unaccompanied children experience an acute and intertwined 'triple burden' of vulnerability: they are children, asylum seekers whose entry is unauthorised, and separated from their parents or guardians. They have distinct needs that correlate with each of these sites. First, as children, they need to be cared for and given opportunities to develop and to be protected from physical or mental violence and foreseeable

DOI: 10.4324/9781003260134-1

harm and neglect. Second, their legal precariousness and unauthorised presence as asylum seekers generate a distinct need not to be refouled or refused access to a Refugee Status Determination (RSD) procedure. Finally, their separation from their parents gives rise to a specific need for the provision of a legal guardian with legislative and functional responsibilities to act in their best interests.

The existing normative response to these acute vulnerabilities is grounded in States' extensive human rights obligations in international law. These establish substantive and unambiguous obligations on States to protect, assist and act in unaccompanied children's best interests and provide for their development.[5] States' human rights obligations *ought* to provide an effective counterbalance to securitisation rhetoric and punitive laws and policies. Yet, despite the adequacy of human rights, in principle, to meet these children's needs and address their vulnerabilities, the protection they provide, in practice, has not lived up to their promise. Global rhetoric regarding border securitisation has increasingly become the norm in many countries' domestic public and political discourse. Over the past two decades especially, the progressive global securitisation of the irregular migration of displaced people through interception, interdiction, extraterritorial processing and immigration detention has subordinated humanitarian and human rights-based responses to asylum seekers.[6] This is particularly so in legal systems in which treaty ratification does not create domestic legal obligations unless the provisions are incorporated into domestic law.

Globally, unaccompanied children seek asylum by land, air and sea. This book uses Australia's treatment of unaccompanied children seeking asylum by sea as a case study because boat arrivals have been the focus of Australian law and policy regulating the flow of asylum seekers to the country. This case study is also selected based on the extent of the disconnect between Australia's extensive human rights obligations under international law and its domestic law and policy and because of the interest other States have shown in adopting Australia's approach.

The numbers of unaccompanied children seeking asylum who arrive in Australia by sea are exceptionally low compared to global figures. The highest annual number of unaccompanied children by sea was 1,788 in 2011–2012. The Labor and subsequent Liberal/Coalition governments responded with a series of rapid amendments to the law regulating the treatment of asylum seekers in Australia (the *Migration Act 1958* (Cth) (*Migration Act*)) to progressively utilise offshore processing and Boat Turnbacks and Takebacks to prevent asylum seekers arriving by boat from being eligible to claim asylum in Australia. They also amended the law regulating the availability and provision of a statutory guardian (the *Immigration (Guardianship of Children) Act 1946* (Cth) (*IGOC Act*)) to effectively remove unaccompanied children arriving in boats from its operation. As such, Australian contemporary law and policy deliberately disowns the abject vulnerability of these children.

Australia's policies of mandatory immigration detention, deterrence through offshore processing and Boat Turnbacks and Takebacks have subjected unaccompanied child asylum seekers to grievous harm and critical human rights abuses, including physical and psychological abuse, torture and inhumane treatment and exposure to refoulement. Reports have thoroughly documented the predictable, egregious and long-term harm of both onshore and offshore immigration detention on children and have catalogued the legion of human rights abuses inflicted on them by these policies.[7] International human rights bodies have repeatedly found that Australia's detention policies are in breach of its obligations under international law.[8] The High Court has upheld the legality of the detention of asylum seekers in offshore detention centres under the Australian Constitution.[9] An analysis of the extensive and egregious human rights breaches caused by Australia's harsh, punitive and rejecting response to these children in successive regressive changes in law and policy illuminates just how starkly human rights law has not provided the necessary break for these children from the excesses of securitised responses.

Despite the widespread condemnation of Australia's human rights breaches, alarmingly, other States are adopting aspects of Australia's approach. Denmark, the first European country to do so, amended its *Aliens Act* on 3 June 2021, authorising the removal of asylum seekers to a third country to process their claims. Pursuant to the amendment, regardless of whether asylum seekers are determined to be refugees, they will not be resettled in Danish territory.[10] The United Kingdom also considered sending asylum seekers to the South Atlantic Ascension or St Helena Islands for offshore processing before introducing the *Nationality and Borders Bill 2021 (UK)* in July 2021. That Bill proposed implementing 'offshore' asylum hubs for processing asylum claims, giving restricted access to the UK asylum system and inferior immigration rights if granted permission to stay for anyone arriving by 'an illegal route', and introducing new provisions relating to the powers of border and immigration personnel to stop and redirect boats carrying asylum seekers in 'pushback' operations.[11]

Australia's harsh treatment, in contravention of international human rights law, and the apparent interest of other States in adopting Australia's approach must catalyse action. A human rights approach provides a universal, indivisible and aspirational *standard* for asylum seeker rights in all legal systems. But human rights compliance takes time. Advocacy will, and should, continue to compel legal and policy changes that balance border control priorities with human rights obligations. Yet, urgent interim changes to law and policy are required to respond to the particular vulnerability of unaccompanied asylum-seeking children and the substantive evidence of the considerable and lasting harm that domestic laws and policies are causing them. Behind the catalogues of breaches of State human rights obligations are children whose lives have been, and will continue to be, indelibly marked unless there is a radical change in approach.

The quest for a radical shift in approach generates the central question interrogated by this book that arises both from Australia's particular approach and those of countries seeking to emulate it: how ought States better respond to unaccompanied asylum-seeking children? In answering that broad question, this book asks the following ones as well. Are unaccompanied children vulnerable in a way that generates a moral obligation that supplements international law obligations to respond to, not exacerbate, their vulnerability? How effectively could international human rights law respond to their vulnerability if it were applied in practice? How did the series of amendments to Australian laws and policies post-2012 impact the complex vulnerabilities of these children? What risks do Australian law and policy approaches that are being adopted by other States pose to children? Finally, what approaches to making laws and policies should States adopt to appropriately respond to the vulnerability of unaccompanied asylum-seeking children who arrive by sea?

Reconceptualising State obligations to do no (further) harm to unaccompanied child asylum seekers

Answering the questions posed in this book requires a reconceptualisation of the way we comprehend these children and the impact of State practice on them, of the ways that we understand the relationship between the State and children seeking asylum and States' accountability for the impact their practices have on children because of that relationship.

As noted earlier, international human rights law is the current normative response that encapsulates the rights of these children and States' accountability for their treatment. Scholars have written extensively on the human rights of migrants[12] and child refugees[13] and on international and regional protection frameworks for child migrants.[14] Human rights scholars have also examined the human rights implications of specific legal challenges faced by child and adolescent unaccompanied asylum seekers, such as age assessment procedures,[15] family reunification and participation in decision-making,[16] and what constitutes best practice in the management of children seeking asylum.[17] However, holistic analysis of the ways in which State human rights obligations correlate with unaccompanied child asylum seekers' sites of vulnerability remains under-theorised.

Childhood studies scholarship offers significant insights into how the law ought to better comprehend these children and the impact of State practice on them. This scholarship has significantly advanced the importance of understanding childhood holistically as a period in which children are simultaneously 'being' and 'becoming'.[18] Michael Freeman, a human rights scholar, began the case for a holistic understanding of children in human rights law in 2010, arguing that '[i]t is important to recognise that children are more than pre-adult becomings'.[19] Nevertheless, the holistic comprehension of childhood and children in rights scholarship, and what this means for a State's human rights obligations, generally remains under-developed, particularly where unaccompanied asylum-seeking children are concerned.[20]

Understanding that 'childhood' is simultaneously a period and a state, that a 'child' is simultaneously a becoming person and an extant being, is central to properly comprehending the rationale for, and determining the proper extent of, States' obligation to respond to unaccompanied children. Viewing childhood holistically brings into sharp focus that children need care and protection both for their current selves to be psychologically well in the present and, simultaneously, to develop age-appropriate developmental benchmarks and psychological maturity milestones in their futures. Unaccompanied children arrive in States at their specific stage of development, with their specific care and protection needs, and the embodiment of all the potential for growth and development they possess. Whether their care, protection and development needs are adequately responded to, for example, by providing appropriate custodial care, appropriate psychological care to enable recovery from past trauma or additional educational services to remediate disruptions to education, is crucially important.

Vulnerability studies offer critical insights into reconceptualising the relationship between the State and the child seeking asylum and States' accountability for the impacts of State practice on the child because of that special relationship. As articulated by Martha Fineman in 2008, vulnerability theory provides a normative framework for holding States to account for their role in ameliorating or exacerbating people's vulnerabilities. It identifies both the universality of vulnerability as an inevitable and enduring aspect of the human condition and the significance of the role of the State in responding to and alleviating vulnerability or, conversely, in compounding it.[21] Its focus on the relationship between people's inherent shared vulnerability and social and State responsibility[22] makes it a promising yet under-utilised frame to analyse the adequacy of State responses to this cohort of children. While there are early signs that scholarship is beginning to attend to the application of vulnerability theory in practice,[23] it has an untapped potential as a supplementary approach to human rights to articulate the needs of non-citizen children and the requisite State response to them. There is also theoretical work to be done to sharpen vulnerability theory as a tool for legal analysis in concrete settings.[24] Fineman's vulnerability theory does not reach to determining what constitutes a response that neither exacerbates nor generates new vulnerabilities in practice. Further, taxonomies of vulnerability that distinguish between different types and sources of vulnerabilities that have been utilised in the social sciences remain under-theorised in law.[25]

After briefly examining the historical treatment of unaccompanied child asylum seekers in Australian law and policy in Chapter 1, as the necessary background for readers unfamiliar with this material, this book develops the platforms for the requisite reconceptualisation in five stages.

First, Chapter 2 explores how, regardless of their immigration and citizenship status, unaccompanied child asylum seekers are first and foremost children. In doing so, it applies childhood scholarship to law, arguing that a holistic conception of childhood – as a period in which all children are being children and becoming adults – is necessary to comprehend the complexity and actuality of children's lives. Drawing on key literature from childhood studies about the nature and needs of children, it identifies and examines how unaccompanied child asylum seekers share a compound triple burden of intersecting sites of vulnerability, notwithstanding variances in their age, cultural background, prior experiences of displacement, persecution or trauma, variances in their past and present family circumstances, and differences in their personalities, cognitive abilities and life circumstances. This triple burden of vulnerability – their age (minority), their asylum-seeking and unauthorised presence in the territory (alienage), and their separation from their parents or guardians (family separation) – provides the frame used in the book. This frame exposes their specific and heightened dependence on the State to respond to their overlapping care, protection and development needs and for analysing the impact of State practice on these children in the immediate and longer term.

Second, Chapter 3 evaluates the promise and limitations of human rights law in responding to the compound triple vulnerability of unaccompanied child asylum seekers. It identifies several deficiencies in the international human rights framework, including how the dispersal of States' obligations to unaccompanied child asylum seekers across the core international human rights legal instruments and the Refugee Convention, rather than being contained in a single human rights treaty, obscures a holistic conception of their extensive nature. It addresses this first by synthesising the precise scope of States' obligations to unaccompanied children seeking asylum that are dispersed across multiple treaties and related jurisprudence into a single framework. It then maps these obligations against the three sites of vulnerability of unaccompanied children (their minority, alienage, and separation from their parents) and examines the scope and content of the obligations to enable systematic analysis of how international human rights law requires States to respond to these children. This analysis demonstrates that if these rights were fully realised in practice, they ought to amply protect these children from serious harm.

However, using Australia's responses to these children as a case study, this chapter reveals the protection gap between the promise of human rights and implementation, the unfulfilled potential of human rights law and its failure to provide the necessary check on securitisation policies to prevent egregious harm. The Australian Government's progressive, degrading treatment of unaccompanied children seeking asylum by boat in the past two decades reflects a global phenomenon requiring urgent interim changes to, and a reconceptualisation of, global law and policy approaches regulating the deterrence of unaccompanied child asylum seekers to halt the perpetration of egregious harm on these children.

In the third stage of the book, Chapter 4 proposes a solution: that States continue to be pressed to move towards human rights compliance but, in the interim, that State attention be drawn to the fact they have a supplementary moral obligation not to exacerbate or generate new vulnerabilities for these children. Here, the book identifies the utility of vulnerability theory pioneered in law by Martha Fineman to reconceptualise the scope of State responsibility to vulnerable cohorts. Vulnerability theory is conceptually grounded in the universality of people's right to care and protection. It recognises, as a consequence, a response by the State that eliminates and does not create sites of vulnerability. Vulnerability theory offers a new way of delineating the precise nature of the vulnerabilities of particular groups, the significance of the impact of State practice, the State's role in ameliorating or exacerbating those vulnerabilities and the changes required to laws and policies to redress vulnerability. This chapter argues for an expanded and radical application of vulnerability theory, outside the traditional context of nation-state obligations to citizens, to include unaccompanied children based on their acute dependency on and proximity in the State. It contends that unaccompanied child asylum seekers, as 'proximate vulnerable children', have a sufficient 'other connection' required by vulnerability theory to hold States to account for responses that exacerbate or generate new vulnerabilities in these children. It then argues that, so extended, vulnerability theory provides the necessary normative justification for a supplementary framework that grounds States' domestic obligation to respond to their vulnerability without displacing the broader framework of human rights.

This chapter also proposes a novel universal three-stage mitigating vulnerability framework that can be utilised in practice to determine the appropriate mitigating vulnerability framework in different contexts. This is necessary because Fineman's vulnerability theory does not reach to the level of specificity required to distinguish between types of vulnerabilities in practice or identify a method to determine the necessary State response to vulnerability that can be applied in different contexts. Stage 1 requires an examination of the basis and operation of laws and policies governing the relationship between the subject(s) of the inquiry and the State in a specified context and period. Stage 2 investigates the impact of those laws and policies on the subject(s) of the inquiry by applying an embedded vulnerability taxonomy drawn from feminist philosophy to distinguish between types of vulnerabilities: dispositional, occurrent, inherent, situational and pathogenic.[26] This stage facilitates a characterisation of interactions between an individual or group and the relevant social, political and legal structures that ameliorate or worsen vulnerability by increasing or decreasing dependencies or that create or exacerbate harm and delineates sources of vulnerabilities. Finally, Stage 3 identifies the impacts that legislative and policy change can address and proposes the content of those changes and priorities for reform based on a gravity of consequences rationale in which the laws that generate new harms are remedied first.

In the fourth stage of the book, Chapters 5, 6 and 7 demonstrate the utility of an expanded and modified vulnerability theory and how the proposed mitigating vulnerability framework can be applied in practice to examine the effects of laws and policies on vulnerable populations. It does so by applying it to evaluate the impact of successive legislative and policy changes in the Australian context regulating the care and protection of unaccompanied child asylum seekers, their access to RSD, and the provision of guardianship arrangements. Applying the mitigating vulnerability framework in these chapters illuminates, from a child-centric perspective, what is at stake when States fail to have adequate regard for vulnerability and clarifies the imperative for, and the components of, necessary urgent response adjustments.

Chapter 5 assesses the effects of the legislative changes on the environments of care provided to unaccompanied children detained in immigration and community detention, Offshore Transferees, and children subject to Boat Turnbacks and Takebacks. It demonstrates how initial mandatory immigration detention generates new vulnerabilities that would not be adequately cared for or protected against whilst in detention, exacerbates existing trauma and generates new trauma that persists post-release. It contends that the vulnerabilities of the unaccompanied children released into community detention on the Australian mainland were largely not exacerbated by the care arrangements provided for them but that the manifestly inadequate environment of care for unaccompanied children transferred to Nauru generated new pathogenic vulnerabilities for this cohort.

Chapter 6 evaluates the effects of the legislative changes on unaccompanied children's vulnerability arising from their alienage. It establishes how the progressive restriction of access to RSD on the mainland, the winding back of Australia's non-refoulement obligations and, ultimately, the restriction on entry generated increasingly serious occurrent and pathogenic vulnerabilities.

Chapter 7 assesses the effects that the amendments to Australian legislation regulating the guardianship of unaccompanied children have had on their vulnerabilities generated by their separation from their parents. It contends that these children were vulnerable to not having their best interests represented because of the pre-existing conflict of interest inherent in the Minister being both their sole legal statutory guardian and responsible for enforcing Australia's migration laws. It further argues that the trajectory of legislative changes generated profound new pathogenic vulnerabilities for unaccompanied children subject to offshore processing. This included that the individual best interests of unaccompanied children in the Boat Turnback and Takeback cohorts would not be considered or be provided with any of the core protections guardians are mandated to extend to their wards. Chapters 5 to 7 each conclude with recommendations for reform.

Chapter 8 draws together the key findings and theoretical questions in the fifth and final stage of the book. It proposes a roadmap for urgent responsive action by the Australian Government that at least prevents these children from being subjected to further harm because of Australian law and policy until Australia fully realises the obligations it has voluntarily assumed as part of international law. It also contends for the application of the mitigating vulnerability framework in different jurisdictions and contexts, including forced migration due to climate change or internally displaced refugee children in conflict corridors. In so doing, it illustrates the framework's utility beyond the examination of Australia's treatment of unaccompanied children and its potential application to illuminate the effects of laws and policies that generate harm to children and identify priorities for reform in other contexts.

Notes

1 International Federation of Red Cross and Red Crescent Societies reported in 2018 that travelling without an accompanying adult renders unaccompanied minors vulnerable to being assaulted, sexually abused, raped, trafficked into sexual exploitation or forced into 'survival sex'. See International Federation of Red Cross and Red Crescent Societies, *Alone and Unsafe: Children, Migration and*

Sexual and Gender-Based Violence (IFRC, 2018). See also Elina Sarantou and Angeliki Theodoropoulou, *Children Cast Adrift: The Exclusion and Exploitation of Unaccompanied Minors (UAMs) in Greece, Spain and Italy* (Rosa Luxemburg Stiftung, 2019).

2 Tine Jensen et al., 'Long-Term Mental health in Unaccompanied Refugee Minors: Pre- and Post-Flight Predictors' (2019) 28(12) *European Child & Adolescent Psychiatry* 1671.

3 Ilse Derluyn and Eric Broekaert, 'Different perspectives on emotional and behavioural problems in unaccompanied refugee children and adolescents' (2007) 12(2) *Ethnicity & Health* 141.

4 See for example, Serap Keles et al., 'Resilience and acculturation among unaccompanied refugee minors' (2016) 42(1) *International Journal of Behavioural Development* 52; Tine Jensen et al., 'Development of mental health problems – a follow-up study of unaccompanied refugee minors' (2014) 8 *Child Adolescent Psychiatry Mental Health* 29.

5 States' extensive human rights obligations to unaccompanied child asylum seekers are examined fully in Chapter 3.

6 Anthea Vogl, 'Seeking asylum: human smuggling and bureaucracy at the border' (review) (2012) 27(1) *Canadian Journal of Law and Society* 159, 159.

7 Human Rights and Equal Opportunity Commission, *Those Who've Come Across the Seas: Detention of Unauthorised Arrivals* (Commonwealth of Australia, 1998); UNHCR, *Mission to the Republic of Nauru 3 to 5 December 2012: Report* (UNHCR, 2012); UNHCR, *Monitoring Visit to the Republic of Nauru 7 to 9 October 2013* (UNHCR, 2013c); Australian Human Rights Commission, *The Forgotten Children: National Inquiry into Children in Immigration Detention* (Commonwealth Government, 2014); UNHCR, *Returns to Sri Lanka of Individuals Intercepted at Sea* (Media Release, 7 July 2014) http://www.unhcr.org/afr/news/press/2014/7/53baa6ff6/returns-sri-lanka-individuals-intercepted-sea.html.

8 UN Human Rights Committee, *A v Australia Communication No. 560/1993 UN Doc. CCPR/C/59/D/560/1993* (30 April 1997); UN Human Rights Committee, *C v Australia UN Doc. CCPR/C/76/D/900/1999* (13 November 2002); UN Human Rights Committee *Baban v Australia, UN Doc. CCPR/C/78/D/1014/2001* (18 September 2003).

9 In *Plaintiff M68-2015 v Minister for Immigration and Border Protection* (2016) 257 CLR 42, the High Court of Australia rejected a challenge to the legality of the immigration facility on Nauru. The case was brought by a Bangladeshi detainee on Nauru who was brought to Australia for medical treatment. In a six to one decision, the High Court of Australia held that s 198AHA of the *Migration Act* authorised the Commonwealth's participation, to the extent that the Commonwealth did participate, in the plaintiff's detention.

10 *Law Amending the Aliens Act and the Return Act (Introduction of the Possibility of Transferring Asylum Seekers for Asylum Proceedings and Possible Subsequent Protection in Third Countries)* (Denmark) 3 June 2021.

11 *Nationality and Borders Bill 2021 (UK)*, as Amended in Public Bill Committee. Access at Nationality and Borders Bill – Parliamentary Bills – UK Parliament.

12 Vincent Chetail, 'The Human Rights of Migrants in General International Law: From Minimum Standards to Fundamental Rights' (2013) 28(1) *Georgetown Immigration Law Journal* 225.

13 Jeanette Lawrence et al., 'The Rights of Refugee Children and the UN Convention on the Rights of the Child' (2019) 8(3) *Laws* 20.

14 For example, see Mary Crock and Lenni Benson (eds), *Protecting Migrant Children: In Search of Best Practice* (Edward Elgar Publishing, 2018).

15 For example, see Mary Anne Kenny and Maryanne Loughry, '"These Don't Look Like Children to Me": Age Assessment of Unaccompanied and Separated Children' in Mary Crock and Lenni Benson (eds), *Protecting Migrant Children: In Search of Best Practice* (Edward Elgar Publishing, 2018).

16 Jacqueline Bhabha and Nadine Finch, *Seeking Asylum Alone: United Kingdom* (Harvard University Press, 2006). The lack of focus on guardianship may be attributed to the fact that guardianship necessarily entails the consideration of the content and limits of parental and State responsibility for children's upbringing, and this is necessarily more contentious than, for example, a child's right to family reunification. Similarly, in the succession of NGO, NHRI and UN reports regarding Australia's treatment of child asylum seekers, guardianship is scarcely ever mentioned.

17 Mary Crock et al., *Children and Young People in Asylum and Refugee Processes: Towards Best Practice in the Management of Children Seeking Asylum* (Federation Press, 2020).

18 Nick Lee, *Childhood and Society* (Open University Press, 2001); Nicola Ansel, *Children, Youth, and Development* (Routledge, 2005); Emma Uprichard, '"Children as Being and Becomings": Children, Childhood and Temporality' (2008) 22 *Children & Society* 303; Ancus Gheaus 'Unfinished Adults and Defective Children: On the Nature and Value of childhood' (2015) 9(1) *Journal of Ethics & Social Philosophy* 21.

19 Michael Freeman (ed), *Children's Rights: Progress and Perspectives* (Martinus Nijhoff, 2011) 13–15.

20 An exception is Noam Peleg's scholarship that examined how an incomplete conception of childhood leads to a skewed understanding of the child's right to development. See Noam Peleg, 'What Do We Mean When We Speak about Children's Right to Development?' in Farhad Malekiam and Kerstin Nordlöf (eds), *The Sovereignty of Children in Law* (Cambridge Scholarly Publishing, 2012) 134–156. Peleg argues the case for a right to development and rejects the 'human becomings' idea, which interprets the child's right to development as a means to an end (merely a right to ensure that the child 'survive' the time of childhood and become an adult). His hybrid conception of childhood is the foundation of his holistic theory of the child's right to development, which respects the child's wishes for what he or she is now and for what he or she can be, but also includes what he or she would like to be in the future.

Recently, Jeanette Lawrence et al., in 'The Rights of Refugee Children and the UN Convention on the Rights of the Child' 2019 8(3) *Laws* 20, acknowledged the significance of the inextricable intertwining of the child's present being and lifetime becoming to understanding how past events of trauma are reiterated in children's present happenings: at 22–23.

21 Martha Albertson Fineman, 'The Vulnerable Subject: Anchoring Equality in the Human Condition' (2008) 20(1) *Yale Journal of Law and Feminism* 1 ('Anchoring equality'); Martha Albertson Fineman, 'The Vulnerable Subject and the Responsive State' (2010) 60(2) *Emory Law Journal* 251 ('The Responsive State').

22 Martha Albertson Fineman, 'The Responsive State' (n 21) 267, 273.

23 See, for example, Jonathan Herring, *Vulnerable Adults and the Law* (Oxford University Press, 2016); Beverley Clough, 'Disability and Vulnerability: Challenging the Capacity/Incapacity Binary' (2017) 16 *Social Policy and Society* 469; Terry Carney, 'Vulnerability: False hope for vulnerable social security clients?' (2018) 41(3) *University of New South Wales Law Journal* 783; Laurie Berg, *Migrant Rights at Work: Law's Precariousness at the Intersection of Immigration and Labour* (Routledge, 2016); Mikaela Heikkilä, Hisayo Katsui and Maija Mustaniemi-Laakso, 'Disability and Vulnerability: A Human Rights Reading of

the Responsive State' (2020) 24(8) *The International Journal of Human Rights* 1180.

24 Terry Carney, in particular, has argued that 'vulnerability theory remains too capacious and ill-defined to provide more than false hope in substantive reform of social security law': Terry Carney (n 23) 786.

25 Catriona Mackenzie, Wendy Rogers and Susan Dodds, 'Introduction: What is Vulnerability and Why Does it Matter for Moral Theory?' in Catriona Mackenzie, Wendy Rogers and Susan Dodds (eds), *Vulnerability: New Essays in Ethics and Feminist Philosophy* (Oxford Publishing, 2014).

26 See Catriona Mackenzie, Wendy Rogers and Susan Dodds (n25) 32. Mackenzie, Rogers and Dodds distinguish between two states of vulnerability: dispositional (individual attributes that render an individual at risk of sustaining a particular harm) and occurrent (circumstances in which individuals are acutely at risk of sustaining harm). They characterise sources of vulnerability as inherent, situational and pathogenic. Inherent vulnerability arises from 'sources of vulnerability that are inherent to the human condition and that arise from our corporeality, our neediness, our dependence on others, and our affective and social natures'. Situational vulnerability arises in a context and is 'caused or exacerbated by the personal, social, political, economic or environmental situations of a person or social group'. In contrast, pathogenic vulnerability is a state of being at risk of having situational or inherent vulnerabilities increased or created because of ongoing relationships or socio-political situations that have negative or harmful effects.

1 The historical context of Australia's treatment of asylum seekers, including unaccompanied child asylum seekers

Australia's migration policies over the past three decades have a lengthy and controversial history.[1] Australia has essentially had five legal responses to asylum seekers arriving by boat. In chronological order, these have been regulation (1980s), mandatory onshore immigration detention (1990s), deterrence by utilising offshore processing of RSDs with prospects of being settled in Australia while also implementing boat turnback and takeback policies (2002–2007), a humane 'New Direction' response (2008–2011) and a return to deterrence by utilising offshore processing of RSD but with no prospect of being settled in Australia while implementing comprehensive boat turnback and takeback policies (2012–present). All but the New Direction response broadly correlate with four waves of arrivals of asylum seekers by sea.

Australia's relationship with asylum seekers occurs in a global context in which refugee regimes in the Global North are fundamentally based on the principle of deterrence rather than human rights protection.[2] Gammeltoft-Hansen and Tan's analysis of the development of deterrence policies by Western States in the past 30 years, including interdiction at sea, concluded that 'restrictive migration control policies are today the primary, some might say only, response of the developed world to rising numbers of asylum seekers and refugees'.[3] Despite comparatively small numbers of people seeking asylum in Australia, Australia's response to boat arrivals has largely been deterrent based and in breach of its human rights obligations. In 2006, Gelber and McDonald characterised Australia's response as manifesting a 'right to exclude'.[4] An analysis of the legal responses to boat arrivals reveals a mostly bipartisan creep towards a brutal exclusionary legislative regime.

Australia's first wave of asylum-seeking boat arrivals comprised 2,059 asylum seekers from Vietnam between 1976 and 1981. The Fraser Liberal/National (Coalition) government responded by establishing a regulatory border control framework through the *Migration Act 1958* (Cth) (*Migration Act*) to conduct an individual RSD for persons arriving unauthorised by boat.[5] It gave the Minister for Immigration and Ethnic Affairs (the Minister) and the officers of the Department of Immigration and Ethnic Affairs (the Department)[6] a range of powers and duties. This included a discretion to detain asylum seekers until their claim was processed.[7] Following the second wave of approximately 300 asylum seekers a year from predominantly Cambodia, southern China and Vietnam

DOI: 10.4324/9781003260134-2

beginning in 1989,[8] the Hawke (Labor) government amended the *Migration Act.* Effectively, these amendments introduced a policy of 'administrative detention' for all people entering Australia without a valid visa while their immigration status was resolved.[9] The Keating (Labor) government amended the *Migration Act* in 1992[10] to mandate detention for up to 273 days of unauthorised non-citizens, including children, in Australia's migration zone[11] unless they were afforded temporary lawful status by being granted a bridging visa.[12] Subsequent amendments in 1994 permitted the indefinite detention of all unlawful arrivals, pending processing of their applications for asylum and final determination of their status.[13]

Between 1999 and 2002, the third wave of 11,430 asylum seekers arrived by boat, predominantly from the Middle East, fleeing the war in Afghanistan. These arrivals included at least 344 unaccompanied child asylum seekers.[14] The Howard (Coalition) government introduced a new tranche of punitive amendments to the *Migration Act*, which were known as 'the Pacific Solution'. The amendments excised outer Australian territory islands, where the boats most commonly arrived. Unauthorised arrivals who entered Australia at an 'excised offshore place' were deemed to be 'offshore entry persons' who were barred from making a visa application unless the Minister personally intervened to permit it.[15] Thus, they were deemed to be located outside Australia's migration zone,[16] ineligible to apply for a visa[17] and subject to removal to asylum claim processing centres on Nauru and Manus Island. As part of the amendments, the Defence Force was also used to intercept boats carrying asylum seekers. Operation Relex (3 September 2001–13 March 2002) and Operation Relex II (14 March 2002–16 July 2006) directed the Royal Australian Navy to intercept and board boats suspected of carrying people without a visa once they had entered Australia's contiguous zone.[18] They were then to return the asylum seekers to the edge of Indonesian territorial waters. Between 19 October 2001 and 8 November 2003, the Navy turned around five boats carrying 614 asylum seekers.[19]

With a near cessation in boat arrivals, the government briefly relaxed its immigration policies in 2005 with amendments to the *Migration Act.* Such amendments gave the Minister a broad discretionary power to grant detainees a visa without an application.[20] They also facilitated the ability to approve the placement of individuals in the community while their protection claims were processed (residence determinations)[21] and inserted a new principle in the *Migration Act* that 'a minor shall only be detained as a measure of last resort'.[22]

The incoming Rudd (Labor) government in December 2007 oversaw several years of reversal of the previous punitive trend. Its more humane approach, especially to children and families seeking asylum, included requiring justification for detention based on risk, ending the detention of children and ensuring administrative review of the length and conditions of detention. The Rudd government went on to dismantle the Pacific Solution by closing the detention centres on Nauru and Manus Island, resettling the final 21 of the 1,637 asylum seekers who had been detained offshore in Australia on 8 February 2008 and abolishing temporary protection visas.[23]

However, conditions in the global context shifted with a flare-up of hostilities in Afghanistan; the resumption of civil war in Sri Lanka; and crises in Myanmar, the Middle East and Africa. This meant the numbers of asylum seekers arriving in Australia by boat escalated: 161 arrived in 2008, 2,726 in 2009, 6,555 in 2010, 4,565 in 2011 and 17,202 in 2012.[24] The number of unaccompanied children also increased, from 470 in 2011 to 889 in 2012.[25] In response, the Abbott (Coalition) government was vocal and persistent in calling for a return to offshore processing on Nauru, Boat Turnbacks and Takebacks and the resumption of temporary protection visas. Advocates for Australia's responsibility to treat unaccompanied children as a 'special case' were marginalised by consistent and voluble domestic public and media disapprobation of asylum seekers and a political debate that narrowed to the point that governments seemed unelectable without policies that punished unauthorised boat arrivals and that 'stopped the boats'.

In an attempt to circumvent continued arrivals, the Gillard (Labor) government entered into an agreement with the Malaysian Government that Australia would transfer 800 asylum seekers to Malaysia for offshore processing. In return, Australia would accept 4,000 refugees as part of the humanitarian resettlement program.[26] In a successful challenge to the agreement in *Plaintiff M70/2011 & Plaintiff M106/2011 by his Litigation Guardian v Minister for Immigration and Citizenship* (*M70/2011*), the High Court declared the policy invalid.[27]

M70/2011 was a watershed moment that led to the establishment of the Expert Panel on Asylum Seekers by the Gillard (Labor) government in an attempt to resolve the political deadlock.[28] The panel, commissioned to examine and provide a roadmap for Australian refugee policy, recommended legislative amendments to the *Migration Act* so that boat arrivals anywhere on Australian territory would have the same legal status as those deemed to have arrived in an excised offshore place and be subject to the same bar on visa applications.[29] Another recommendation was that Nauru and Papua New Guinea (PNG) establish capacity as soon as practical to process the claims of Irregular Maritime Arrivals,[30] that people be transferred via regional processing arrangements as a matter of urgency[31] and that the 'Malaysia Agreement' be built on further rather than being discarded or neglected.[32] The panel also recommended that the regional transfers occur in ways consistent with Australian, Nauruan and PNG responsibilities under international law.[33] The panel noted that the existing 'conditions necessary for effective, lawful and safe turnback of irregular vessels carrying asylum seekers to Australia' were 'not currently met' but that the situation could change in the future 'if appropriate regional and bilateral arrangements' were implemented.[34]

The Gillard (Labor) government and then the second Rudd (Labor) government responded to the High Court decision and the report of the expert panel with a rapid series of amendments to the *Migration Act* in 2012 and 2013, and the Abbott (Coalition) government continued those amendments in 2014.[35] The amendments did not, contrary to the recommendations of the panel, incorporate Australia's adherence to its international obligations. Nor did they build on the

Malaysia Agreement or facilitate a comprehensive and integrated regional system of asylum processing. Instead, these amendments progressively implemented offshore processing (initially with, and subsequently without, an ultimate entitlement to settle in Australia), culminating in a right to exclude all unauthorised boat arrivals, including unaccompanied children, via Boat Turnbacks and Takebacks in December 2013.

These progressive amendments generated four distinct categories of asylum seekers, all of which included unaccompanied children, differentiated only by their date of arrival and not by their relative vulnerability, as demonstrated in Table 1.1 'Asylum seeker cohorts determined by date of arrival'.

Table 1.1 Asylum seeker cohorts determined by date of arrival

Date of arrival	*Processing of asylum claim*	*Cohort*
Prior to 13 August 2012	Asylum claim processed in Australia	Onshore claimants
After 13 August 2012 and prior to 19 July 2013	Transferred initially to a third country (Nauru or PNG) for asylum claim processing after 'transiting' in Australia on Christmas Island or processed on the Australian mainland/ awaiting finalisation of their claims Eligible to settle in Australia if found to be a refugee	Legacy Caseload (approximately 30,000)
After 19 July 2013	Transferred to a third country (Nauru or PNG) to have their asylum claim processed after 'transiting' in Australia (on Christmas Island) Ineligible to settle in Australia if found to be a refugee	Offshore Transferees (approximately 3,000)
After September 2013	Ineligible to make a claim for asylum in Australia, boats are returned to their departure port	Boat Turnbacks and Takebacks or transfer to a regional processing country

M70/2011 was also a watershed moment for unaccompanied child asylum seekers because it concerned the Minister's obligations as their guardian. Due to the legislative amendments that followed that decision, unaccompanied child asylum seekers are represented in each cohort in Table 1.1. Australia is unique amongst common law countries in having a Minister who is simultaneously these children's sole statutory legal guardian and responsible for enforcing border protection laws and policies. Since 1946, the *IGOC Act* automatically appointed the Minister with the Immigration portfolio as the legal guardian of unaccompanied children.[36] The *IGOC Act* was enacted to provide for the reception of predominantly British immigrant children whose arrival was authorised after World War II.[37] Although it appointed the Minister as the legal guardian, the Minister's powers and duties were never the subject of real consideration or focus. In reality, the children's immigration status was determined before they arrived in Australia. Once they arrived, the Minister delegated their custodial powers to state welfare organisations.

In 1958, when the Australian Parliament enacted the *Migration Act* to regulate 'in the national interest, the coming into, and presence in, Australia of non-citizens',[38] neither the *Migration Act* nor the *IGOC Act* contained a provision expressly providing how the Acts were to be read in relation to each other.[39] Nor did the *IGOC Act* expressly refer to unaccompanied refugees or asylum seekers. The first mention of unaccompanied refugee minors appears in Minister Ruddock's second reading speech on the 1994 Bill stating:

> Under the current provisions of the Immigration (Guardianship of Children) Act 1946 the Minister for Immigration and Ethnic Affairs has guardianship of non-citizen children, including those entering Australia for adoption, **and unaccompanied refugee minors**. In practice, the minister immediately delegates his powers, as has been said, of guardianship of adoptive non-citizen children to the relevant state or territory welfare administrator (emphasis added).[40]

That Bill proposed the transfer of guardianship powers of non-citizen children entering Australia for adoption from the federal minister to state and territory governments. Although Minister Ruddock explained at length why the inter-country adoption provisions were being introduced, there was no mention whatsoever of refugee children, their unique needs or his role as their guardian.

Section 6 of the *IGOC Act* provides that the Minister shall have the rights, powers, duties, obligations and liabilities of a natural guardian of unaccompanied children under common law but does not identify the corresponding rights of the child wards. In common law, guardianship encompasses the full range of rights and powers that an adult can exercise regarding the welfare and upbringing of a child.[41] These include the duty to protect the child from harm and the right to make decisions relating to the child's long-term welfare.[42] Australian courts have held that Section 6 confers on the Minister all the usual incidents of guardianship, a set of rights and responsibilities analogous to those of a parent (or 'natural guardian').[43] They have also held that the concept of guardianship, for the purposes of the Act, confers a 'varying spectrum of powers and duties',[44] whose nature and extent must be assessed and evaluated from the language, scope and object of the applicable statute. Finally, they have distinguished the guardianship of a child from the care and custody of the child, noting that guardianship can involve duties that encompass 'the defence, protection and guarding of the child, or his property, from danger, harm or loss that may enure from without'.[45]

It was not until the 1990s that the Minister's duties as guardian under the *IGOC Act* were tested in litigation regarding unaccompanied children arriving without pre-authorisation who were claiming asylum. Subsequently, the courts have been reluctant to identify the corresponding rights held by unaccompanied child wards. One exception is the decision of *X v Minister for Immigration and Multicultural Affairs*.[46] North J accepted that the responsibilities of a guardian under s 6 included the responsibilities concerned with according fundamental human rights to children, which are the subject of the Convention on the Rights of the Child, and went on to find that:

> The guardian must therefore address the basic human needs of a child, that is to say, food, housing, health and education. Over the course of this century, attention to the needs has come to be recognised as a fundamental human right of children, including in various international instruments to which Australia is a party [at [34]].[47]

Unaccompanied children have been spectacularly unsuccessful in any litigation against the Minister, alleging a failure to diligently or fully discharge their guardianship obligations. Ironically, the only exception to this trend was *M70/2011*. The High Court held that the unaccompanied child asylum seeker could not be removed lawfully from Australia under the *Migration Act* unless the Minister, exercising a separate statutory power as guardian, gave written consent to the removal. The Court found that departmental officers had not 'shown any consideration of whether the Minister's consent was necessary or whether taking the second plaintiff [who was an unaccompanied child asylum seeker] from Australia would be in his interests'.[48] The Court granted an injunction restraining the Minister from removing the child from Australia without that consent.

The Gillard (Labor) government responded by making amendments to the *IGOC Act* between 2012 and 2014 that corresponded with the amendments to the *Migration Act* discussed above. These amendments progressively restricted the provision of meaningful guardianship to unaccompanied child asylum seekers in the Offshore Processing and Boat Turnback and Takeback cohorts by effectively nullifying the Minister's guardianship obligations when exercising powers to remove non-citizens under the *Migration Act*.[49] The establishment of offshore processing of protection claims removed altogether the previous *IGOC Act* requirement that the Minister consent in writing to remove a non-citizen child, bearing in mind their interests.[50] These amendments also stipulated that the *IGOC Act* does not affect the exercise of any function, duty or power of the Minister to remove an unaccompanied child asylum seeker to a place outside Australia or impose any obligation on the Minister to exercise a power conferred on them by migration law.[51]

Unaccompanied children have been subjected to Australia's punitive policy measures of mandatory immigration detention, deterrence through offshore processing and Boat Turnbacks and Takebacks, while also receiving compromised guardianship – their key potential source of legal protection – because their statutory guardian was, and remains, the Minister with the Commonwealth Immigration portfolio. The *IGOC Act* was not initially intended to apply to asylum-seeking children. Nor has it, subsequently, been adapted to resolve this critical conflict of interest for unaccompanied child asylum seekers in the onshore claimants and Legacy Caseload cohorts. Moreover, amendments to the *IGOC Act* post-*M70/2011* explicitly avoided the provision of even this compromised guardianship to unaccompanied child asylum seekers in the Offshore Transferee and Boat Turnback and Takeback cohorts.

As the analysis in Chapters 5, 6 and 7 will illuminate, since 2011, the increasingly punitive treatment of all asylum seekers arriving in Australia by boat, alongside the progressive dilution of guardianship for unaccompanied children seeking asylum in Australia by boat, has resulted in a very specific human rights crisis for these children. Australia has not 'welcomed' boat arrivals since the 1980s. However, the reintroduction of offshore processing and Boat Turnbacks and Takebacks for all asylum seekers who arrive in Australian waters or are intercepted at sea has effectively prevented anyone from seeking asylum in Australia if they arrived by boat. Since 2012, unaccompanied child asylum seekers have been increasingly dealt with in the same way as all other asylum seekers, with minimal concessions to their relative vulnerability. Their eligibility for processing their protection claim and settlement as a refugee in Australia is determined entirely by their date of arrival rather than their age or other relevant characteristics. As a result, the care and protection afforded to unaccompanied children arriving by boat under Australia's migration and guardianship regime is nugatory.

Notes

1 Academic literature has comprehensively canvassed successive Australian Governments' domestic law responses to asylum seekers. See Mary Crock and Ben Saul, *Future Seekers: Refugees and the Law in Australia* (The Federation Press, 2002); Don McMaster, *Asylum Seekers: Australia's Response to Refugees* (Melbourne University Press, 2001); David Marr and Marian Wilkinson, *Dark Victory: The Military Campaign to Re-Elect the Prime Minister* (Allen & Unwin, 2003).

2 Thomas Gammeltoft-Hansen and Nikolas Tan, 'The End of the Deterrence Paradigm? Future Directions for Global Refugee Policy' (2017) 5(1) *Journal on Migration and Human Security* 28.

3 Ibid 28.

4 Katherine Gelber and Matt McDonald, 'Ethics and Exclusion: Representations of Sovereignty in Australia's Approach to Asylum Seekers' (2006) 32(2) *Review of International Studies* 269. They argue that conceiving sovereignty as the right to exclude requires denying responsibility to the most vulnerable in global politics and that the Australian Government has garnered domestic support for this conception of sovereignty and ethical responsibility by marginalising alternative voices and emphasising asylum seekers' and refugees' otherness.

5 Commonwealth, *Parliamentary Debates*, House of Representatives, 16 March 1982, 991 (Ian Macphee, Minister for Immigration and Ethnic Affairs):

> We have a solemn humanitarian obligation to ensure that our limited program places are reserved for the genuine refugees. We must exclude those people whose claims for refugee status are suspect. This is a most difficult task … Australia will:
>
> Tighten refugee selection criteria and procedures for all programs with the particular objective of excluding from refugee entry those persons who do not meet the criteria allowed for in the United Nations Convention;
>
> … refugee determination will be made according to the application of these criteria on an individual basis.

6 The name of the portfolio of the Minister responsible for immigration in Australia and the corresponding Commonwealth Government department has changed regularly since the 1980s. In this book, for expediency and unless otherwise necessary for the context of the discussion, I refer to the Minister and the Department.

7 This and the second wave also precipitated amendments to the *Migration Act 1958* (Cth) (*Migration Act*) regulating asylum seekers' eligibility to apply for a protection visa in Australia.

8 Don McMaster, *Asylum Seekers: Australia's Response to Refugees* (Melbourne University Press, 2001) 73.

9 The *Migration Legislation Amendment Act 1989* (Cth). See also Janet Phillips and Harriet Spinks, 'Immigration Detention in Australia' *Parliamentary Library Research Paper* (Commonwealth Parliamentary Library, 2013) 3.

10 The *Migration Amendment Act 1992* (Cth). Prior to this amendment, unauthorised boat arrivals were detained on a discretionary basis only. See Janet Phillips and Harriet Spinks, 'Boat Arrivals in Australia since 1976', *Parliamentary Library Research Paper* (Commonwealth Parliamentary Library, 2017) 12.

11 The migration zone refers to any place in Australian territory where a person arriving without a valid visa can make a visa application.

12 Or alternatively, unless arrangements were made for their departure or for an application for an alternative visa.

13 The *Migration Reform Act 1992* (Cth) came into effect on 1 September 1994.

14 Based on the data regarding unaccompanied minors in detention contained in Janet Phillips and Harriet Spinks (n 9) 42.

15 The islands excised by the *Migration Amendment (Excision from Migration Zone) Act 2001* (Cth) and *Migration Amendment (Excision from Migration Zone) (Consequential Provisions) Act 2001* (Cth) included Ashmore and Cartier Islands, Christmas Island and Cocos (Keeling) Islands, where asylum seeker boats commonly arrived.

16 The *Migration Act* defines the migration zone as 'an area consisting of land that is part of the states and territories at mean low water, Australian resource installa-

tions and sea installations, sea within a port and piers or similar structures, but not including sea that is within the State or Territory limits but not within a port'.

17 Unless the Minister exercised a discretionary power to allow an application for protection by determining that their application was in the public interest.

18 This zone is 24 nautical miles from the Australian coast.

19 Janet Phillips, 'A Comparison of Coalition and Labor Government Asylum Policies in Australia since 2001' *Parliamentary Library Research Paper Series* (Commonwealth Parliamentary Library, 2013).

20 *Migration Act* s 195A, as inserted by *Migration Amendment (Detention Arrangements) Act 2005* (Cth) sch 1 item 10.

21 *Migration Act* pt 2 div 7 sub-div B, as inserted by *Migration Amendment (Detention Arrangements) Act 2005* (Cth) sch 1 item 11.

22 *Migration Act* s 4AA, as inserted by *Migration Amendment (Detention Arrangements) Act 2005* (Cth) sch 1 item 1. The amendments also introduced reporting requirements for the Commonwealth Ombudsman regarding persons who had been detained for more than two years. See *Migration Act* Part 8C, as inserted by *Migration Amendment (Detention Arrangements) Act 2005* (Cth) sch 1 item 19.

23 Janet Phillips and Harriet Spinks (n 9) 11. See also Alperhan Babacan and Hurriyet Babacan, 'Detention Down Under: New Directions in the Detention of Asylum Seekers in Australia' (2008) 4(15) *Review of International Law and Politics* 137.

24 Janet Phillips and Harriet Spinks (n 10) 22

25 Ibid.

26 Having first unsuccessfully attempted to enter into a regional agreement with East Timor to manage asylum seekers. See Janet Phillips and Harriet Spinks (n 10) 11. See also Angus Houston, Michael L'Estrange and Paris Aristotle, *Report of the Expert Panel on Asylum Seekers* (Commonwealth Government, 2012) (*Expert Panel Report*) 137.

27 (2011) 244 CLR 144. The High Court held, by majority, that the sole source of power under the *Migration Act* to take asylum seekers from Australia to another country for determination of their refugee status was conferred by Section 198A and that the declaration that Malaysia was a specified third country for the purposes of Section 198A was made without power. So far as that case related to unaccompanied child asylum seekers, solicitors for a 16-year-old Afghan unaccompanied child sought an injunction from the High Court restraining the Minister for Immigration and Citizenship (as he then was) from removing him to Malaysia. First, they challenged the lawfulness of Australia's proposed agreement with Malaysia and, second, whether the Minister was able to give a blanket direction that all unaccompanied child asylum seekers were to be transferred to Malaysia for processing of their asylum claim without the Minister's written consent under the *Immigration (Guardianship of Children) Act 1946* (Cth) (*IGOC Act*). The case, thus, involved consideration of whether and to what extent the Minister's obligations as guardian under the Act informed the conferral of power on immigration officers to take an unaccompanied child asylum seeker (as an 'offshore entry person') from Australia to a declared third country (Malaysia, in this instance) pursuant to the *Migration Act*.

28 Angus Houston, Michael L'Estrange and Paris Aristotle comprised the Expert Panel on Asylum Seekers.

29 *Expert Panel report* (n 26) [3.72–3.73].

30 Ibid [3.44–3.57].

31 Ibid [3.54, 3.57]. The panel further recommended [3.43] that this legislation should require that any future designation of a country as an appropriate place

for processing be achieved through a further legislative instrument that would provide the opportunity for the Australian Parliament to allow or disallow the instrument.

32 Ibid [3.58–3.70]. The panel recommended that this be achieved through 'high-level bilateral engagement focused on strengthening safeguards and accountability as a positive basis for the Australian Parliament's reconsideration of new legislation that would be necessary'.

33 Ibid [3.44–3.57].

34 Ibid [3.77–3.80].

35 See the *Migration Legislation Amendment (Regional Processing and Other Measures) Act 2012* (Cth), the *Maritime Powers Act 2013* (Cth), the *Migration Amendment (Unauthorised Maritime Arrivals and Other Measures) Act 2013* (Cth) and the *Migration and Maritime Powers Legislation Amendment (Resolving the Asylum Legacy Caseload) Act 2014* (Cth).

36 *IGOC Act* s 6. The Minister has the same rights, powers, duties, obligations and liabilities as a natural guardian of the child would have.

37 Significant research has been conducted about the history and impact on the lives of former unaccompanied child migrants, including Barry Coldrey, *Good British Stock: Child and Youth Migration to Australia* (National Archives, 1999); Philip Bean and Joy Melville, *Lost Children of the Empire* (Unwin Hyman, 1989); Margaret Humphreys, *Empty Cradles* (Transworld, 2009); and Alan Gill, *Orphans of the Empire: The Shocking Story of Child Migration to Australia* (Random House, 1998). Several state government inquiries and reports have added significantly to this scholarship, and an inquiry by the Senate Community Affairs References Committee, *Lost Innocents: Righting the Record* (Commonwealth Government, 2001), comprehensively investigated unaccompanied child migration to Australia under approved schemes during the twentieth century.

38 *Migration Act* s 4.

39 The courts subsequently acknowledged that the Minister's statutory obligations as the legal guardian of a non-citizen child may give rise to a potential 'conflict of roles' in respect of the performance of functions under the *Migration Act*. See *Odhiambo v Minister for Immigration and Multicultural Affairs* (2002) 122 FCR 29 at 47–48 [90].

40 Commonwealth, *Parliamentary Debates*, House of Representatives, 3 March 1994, 1694 (Phillip Ruddock).

41 Anthony Dickey, *Family Law* (Law Book Co, 2002) 341.

42 Ibid 344.

43 *Sadiqi v Commonwealth of Australia (No. 2)* (2009) FCA 1117 at [299].

44 Compare *Trevorrow v South Australia (No. 5)* (2007) 98 SASR 136 at 240–243 [439]–[450] and *South Australia v Lampard-Trevorrow* (2010) 106 SASR 331 at 376 [209], 378–379 [222]–[226].

45 *Wedd v Wedd* (1948) SASR 104 at 106–107, cited in *Trevorrow v South Australia (No. 5)* (2007) 98 SASR 136 at 241 [442].

46 (1999) 92 FCR 524 at 535–538 [34]–[43].

47 Ibid.

48 *M70/2011* (n 27) at [142].

49 The government first introduced the Migration Legislation Amendment (Offshore Processing and Other Measures) Bill 2011, which did not gain the support of the Coalition, Greens and the required number of Independents, in October 2011. On 13 October 2011, the government announced it would not pursue the amendments. See Julia Gillard, Prime Minister, 'Asylum Seekers; Malaysia Agreement; Commonwealth Ombudsman' (Transcript of press conference, 13 October 2011) <http://www.pm.gov.au/ press-office/transcript-joint-

press-conference-canberra-17>. However, it was subsequently reintroduced and passed as the *Migration Legislation Amendment (Regional Processing and Other Measures) Act 2012* (Cth) receiving royal assent on 18 August 2012.

50 *Migration Legislation Amendment (Regional Processing and Other Measures) Act 2012* (Cth).

51 Ibid.

2 Comprehending the specific vulnerability of unaccompanied child asylum seekers

I am a child and have not yet reached 17 years of age. I am living in Nauru for the last 2 months, and I was at Christmas Island for 8 months. You have not looked after those children who came from oppressing countries where there is no freedom, security and living. We have not seen from life except wars and killing. We fled the country seeking asylum and freedom but we did not find except harshness and bad treatment. I am alone here without my father, my mother, or my family. Where is the future? I have not found any future in Nauru.[1]

2.1 Introduction

Unaccompanied child asylum seekers experience layers of intersecting precariousness because of their minority, alienage, and separation from their parents. The opening quote hints at the relevance of the intersectional layering of the vulnerabilities, which will be further explored in this chapter. The excerpt, from a letter written by a 16-year-old, who had been detained in Nauru for 10 months according to Australia's policy of mandatory offshore processing of all asylum seekers arriving by boat, exposes glimpses of the complex vulnerability of unaccompanied asylum-seeking children.[2] He is a child with a lived experience of war and death. He is experiencing both the trauma that led him to seek asylum and the trauma of the process of seeking asylum without his parents. The conditions of his detention on Christmas Island and then Nauru have left him unable to imagine a future for himself.

This chapter situates the unaccompanied child asylum seeker at the centre point of this book's factual and conceptual landscape. It examines the sites where their dependencies and State responsibility interact to lay the foundations for the argument in the chapters that follow. I use the term 'vulnerability' in this chapter to describe unaccompanied child asylum seekers' susceptibility to harm as a matter of fact. I draw on this analysis in Chapter 3 to assess the adequacy of States' existing human rights obligations to address unaccompanied child asylum seekers and identify the protection gap between Australia's human rights obligations and its actual response. I also draw on this analysis in Chapter 4 to argue the imperative of utilising a modified version of vulnerability theory to

DOI: 10.4324/9781003260134-3

respond to these children. But first, I begin by considering the global geopolitical framework in which their vulnerability is produced.

2.2 The global context

Notwithstanding difficulties in accurately capturing comprehensive data on the number of unaccompanied and separated child migrants globally because their movements are mostly irregular and involve smuggling networks, the current worldwide displacement of children is the highest level ever recorded. In 2012, 50,000 unaccompanied and separated child migrants were in transit in 80 countries. By 2017, this had ballooned to an estimated 300,000 unaccompanied and separated child migrants in transit.[3] In this period, unaccompanied child asylum seekers have also grown significantly as a portion of this unaccompanied cohort. In 2014, 34,300 unaccompanied children lodged asylum applications worldwide, but by 2017, 75,000 unaccompanied or separated children had lodged applications for asylum in 70 countries.[4] Although the recorded number of applications in 2018 was 27,600, the actual number is likely to be much higher given that data recording is unreliable and incomplete. Furthermore, annual figures obscure the accumulation of backlogged unprocessed claims.

The impact of the humanitarian crisis generated by this displacement is difficult to overstate. A substantial body of literature has documented the acute vulnerability of unaccompanied child asylum seekers as survivors, as well as the victims of persecution and war, while their asylum claims are determined.[5] They also have a heightened risk of mental health problems, both upon[6] and after their arrival at the borders of destination countries.[7]

Most States appoint a guardian for unaccompanied child asylum seekers presenting in their jurisdiction in recognition of their specific and acute susceptibility to harm, although State asylum processes vary widely.[8] Typically, State-sponsored guardianship is afforded to these children.[9] Additionally, the acute impact of the separation of these children from their parents and the significance of the provision of effective guardianship is acknowledged in an extensive body of international soft law.[10] For example, the United Nations High Commissioner for Refugees (UNHCR) developed guidelines decades ago for the appointment of an independent guardian or adviser to promote decisions in the child's best interests.[11] In particular, European States have set clear practice standards to address the vulnerabilities of these children generated by their separation from their parents.[12]

2.3 Comprehending unaccompanied children's specific vulnerability

2.3.1 Acknowledging resilience

Scholarship regarding unaccompanied children frequently emphasises their vulnerability as survivors as well as victims of war and dislocation. It highlights their acute vulnerability to abuse, refoulement, susceptibility to trafficking and sexual and labour exploitation. Such research concentrates on vulnerability and victimhood more frequently than their independence and resilience. A focus of this book is the need for States to better comprehend and attend to these children. Underpinning this, I explicitly acknowledge the complex and nuanced relationship between the vulnerability and the agentic capacity of unaccompanied children. As noted in Section 2.2, the literature establishes that these children experienced deep traumas that forced them to flee alone and that their journeys seeking asylum entail varying degrees of uncertainty, fear, abuse or deprivation. But the literature also establishes that they, like all children, possess resiliencies and a desire to be agentic.[13] Therefore, we should not assume that they lack the capacity, agency or desire to rebuild their lives and pursue their own choices in environments free from persecution and violence. In fact, this deep and real tension between vulnerability and agency/resilience necessitates properly comprehending these children's complexity and defining the role of the State in attending to it in a way that maintains or develops their resilience without exacerbating existing or generating new vulnerabilities.

2.3.2 *The vulnerability of unaccompanied child asylum seekers: the triple burden*

Regardless of their immigration and citizenship status, unaccompanied child asylum seekers are, first and foremost, children. Just as there is no single universal experience of childhood, there is no single universal experience of being an unaccompanied child asylum seeker. Notwithstanding variances in their age, cultural background, prior experiences of displacement, persecution, trauma and family circumstances and differences in their personalities, cognitive abilities and life circumstances, these children all experience the simultaneous and intersecting 'triple burden' of minority, alienage, and family separation,[14] as captured in Figure 2.1.

Their location at the junction of the universal vulnerability of all children and their specific vulnerabilities makes unaccompanied child asylum seekers profoundly dependent on the State where they seek asylum. Recalling the extract that opens this chapter, the 16-year-old was grappling with fleeing a country where he had experienced war and murder. He was alone without his parents and was being detained by the State where he sought asylum on a remote outpost island, away from any services available to children on the Australian mainland. Additionally, without family support, he had to grapple with the fact that the State refused to process his claim and instead sent him to Nauru. A child is intellectually, psychologically, emotionally and physically distinct from an adult. Children's experience, understanding of, response to and recovery from war is different from that of adults. A child's fears and anxieties about being in immigration detention and being transferred to a State other than the one in which they sought asylum will be different from that of an adult. Thus, a child seeking asylum alone has distinct care and protection needs compared to adults or

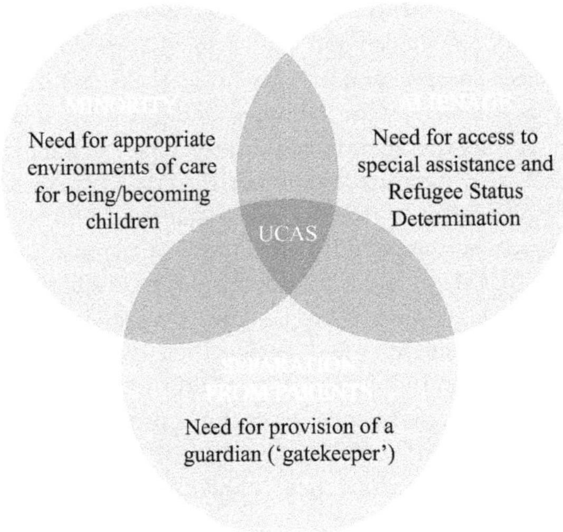

Figure 2.1 The triple vulnerability of unaccompanied child asylum seekers

family groups seeking asylum. Each of these attributes does not exist in isolation. Rather, they intersect with and affect the weight and depth of the impact of the other attributes.

2.3.3 *Minority*

In this section, I use 'minority' in its legal sense, referring to children under 18 years of age and capturing the complexities of childhood and being a child. Within the literature addressing the vulnerabilities of unaccompanied asylum-seeking children generated by their minority, the extent to which the meaning and function of 'childhood' itself causes vulnerability and ought to inform and impact legal and policy responses to them have been neglected. Social constructions of childhood vary across time and contexts.[15] It follows that the childhoods of unaccompanied child asylum seekers are not homogenous, with multiple factors – including a child's gender, race, ethnicity, class, (dis)ability and location – influencing every childhood. Still, the varying experiences of childhood do not preclude a common comprehension of the core objective realities of 'childhood' and of being a 'child'. These notions have been extensively theorised, as have notions of 'childhood' and 'the child'.

In particular, two different conceptions of childhood and the child have been acknowledged and debated in scholarship about children.[16] The first conception is the *becoming child*. In this construct, childhood is understood as the specific period between birth and the attainment of adulthood in a particular culture.[17] The 'child' is perceived as 'a becoming, an incipient being, a person in the process of formation'.[18] Childhood is construed as a time 'in which the individual, in both the physical and moral sense, does not yet exist, the period in which he is made, developed and is formed'.[19] In contrast, in the second conception, the *being child*, childhood is understood as significant for reasons beyond how it prepares a child to function fully as an adult.[20] For these scholars, because all children experience and have agency in their lives in the 'here and now', independently of the perspectives and concerns of adults,[21] the child is already:

> a person, a status, a course of action, a set of needs, rights or differences – in sum as a social actor. ... It does not have to be approached from an assumed shortfall of competence, reason or significance.[22]

Uprichard has neatly captured the problem generated by either binary construction:

> the notion of the being child in the world has been separated from that of the child becoming in the world to such an extent that each has generated its own childhood discourse ... whilst the discourse of the 'being' child accentuates the present, and that of the 'becoming' child stresses the future, both the present and the future interact together in the course of everyday life.[23]

I agree with the increasing cohort of scholars who argue that adopting either binary gives rise to a construction of children and childhood that is incomplete on its own.[24] Rather, a holistic conception of childhood as a period in which all children are being children and becoming adults[25] is necessary to comprehend the complexity and actuality of children's lives.

This holistic conception is relevant to properly comprehend the vulnerability of unaccompanied child asylum seekers arising from their minority. It has direct application to considering the nature and impact of States' obligations to them. Specifically, I argue that comprehending the complexity and actuality of the coexisting binaries generates distinct but overlapping State care and protection and development obligations to these children. Where States ignore these obligations, they impact these children both in the present and, potentially, over the course of their lives. Given the degree of vulnerability and trauma, it is very likely to create abiding harm if not addressed and ameliorated.

These obligations to protect and care for unaccompanied children as minors necessarily serve a double purpose: children need protection to reach adulthood and bring to fruition some of their childhood potential and also to protect and fully realise their current selves as children.[26] The 'child' has both current need and future potential simultaneously.[27] A State may be able to argue that it is adequately discharging its 'here and now' obligations to the 'being' child by providing minimal food, shelter and urgent medical care. However, it could not contend that it is meeting the needs of the 'becoming' child if it provides no mechanism for that child to develop by not delivering, for example, adequate access to education or to medical or psychological support to enable the child to recover from past trauma.

The 'child' stands in front of an adult decision-maker or caregiver at their specific stage of development and as the embodiment of the potential for growth and development possessed by that young person. So understood, these children, like all children, need the constant provision of food, shelter and adequate health care as well as the provision of appropriate education, training and opportunities to foster their expanding abilities. They are also likely to have specific care, protection and development needs as unaccompanied children who have fled war or persecution without their parents. Whether these needs are adequately responded to, for example, by providing additional educational services to remediate disruptions to education or appropriate psychological care to enable recovery from past trauma, is crucially important. The response determines whether the child can achieve age-appropriate developmental benchmarks compared to their peers, whether they can be psychologically well in the present and whether they can reach normal developmental and psychological maturity milestones in their futures. Construing 'childhood' simultaneously as a period and a state and 'the child' simultaneously as a becoming person and an extant being is, thus, essential to capture the complex actuality of children's lives and avoid responses to unaccompanied children that are unduly restricted by reference to only their care and protection vulnerabilities while neglecting their evolving capacities.[28]

Further, this holistic conception recognises the significance of the interacting biological, developmental and social processes that impact the life course of every human – there is no single biologically predetermined process of development for any child.[29] This is significant, as State choices about the quality of care and protection and opportunities for development afforded to unaccompanied children who seek asylum from the State impact directly and inexorably on that child's present physical and mental well-being as well as their biological, social and developmental processes in the present and in their future trajectory. States choose whether to enhance or inhibit each asylum-seeking child's development through the care, protection and development opportunities they provide. In balancing competing public policy objectives, States, thus, choose whether to meet the immediate interests and needs of unaccompanied children and whether to ensure that their potential for growth as becoming children into mentally and physically healthy adults is not thwarted.

Moreover, how we construe 'childhood' and 'the child' has a direct and material impact on the nature and scope of the State's obligations. The extent to which that child is also entitled to, for example, opportunities for play or freedom from adult responsibilities depends on whether the experience of childhood is seen as qualitatively different from that of adulthood and as a good in itself. Similarly, the extent to which the State comprehends the complexity of the lived experience of children impacts the responsiveness of policies to their particular vulnerabilities. For example, unaccompanied children assimilating into foreign cultures are negotiating deeply traumatic separations in their primary relationships as well as stark changes in cultural contexts, language, laws and social expectations while they are 'adjusting to changes within themselves and their close relationships'.[30]

Lastly, the holistic conception of childhood recognises that unaccompanied child asylum seekers anticipation of their futures contributes to forming their childhood and shaping their experiences in the present.[31] All children construct their own lives and their environment both in the present and with an eye to the future – their present choices are shaped by what they imagine their future possibilities are. As much as they are inexorably shaped by their traumatic circumstances, unaccompanied children are agents shaping their lives in response to their surroundings. Social scientists researching the perspectives of these children and young refugees have found that they 'are active in forming perspectives about ... what is expected of them and what they can expect for themselves'.[32] For all adolescents, goals and aspirations give their life meaning and direction and 'are endemic to feeling good about one's life in the present as well as in the future',[33] and future goals are particularly important for young people's well-being when they are living in challenging circumstances.[34] For unaccompanied child asylum seekers, in particular, having an orientation towards the future and a means of achieving future goals is particularly important to integrate their past experiences and reduce the extent of their particular vulnerabilities brought about by past trauma experiences.

Researchers working with asylum-seeking and refugee children have established how 'possibilities and hopes intertwine with other aspects of refugees' thoughts to help them "make sense" of events'.[35] This is particularly significant when punitive State laws and policies keep them held in detention or a prolonged state of stasis or uncertainty regarding their asylum applications. The literature highlights the correlation between their feelings of hopelessness and mental health issues where their future goals are thwarted. For the being/becoming child, the 'limitations on future possibilities detract from the quality of life in the present'.[36] The denial of their need for a future orientation to heal and continue developing transforms into a very specific vulnerability.[37] Although the receiving State is not accountable for the impact on unaccompanied children of their lived experience in the State from which they fled, it is responsible for the present experiences of that child *and* the psychological, emotional, physical and educational impact that those experiences have on the child's development into the future.[38]

This scrutiny of the complex actuality of unaccompanied child asylum seekers as simultaneously *becoming adults* and *child beings* not only illuminates why a holistic construction is instrumental in determining the proper scope of requisite State responses to them as children; it is also fundamental to comprehending the impact of State's hostile securitised responses to them on account of their alienage.

2.3.4 Alienage

Frequently, migration literature uses 'alienage' to refer to a person's legal status as a non-citizen. However, when examining the precarious 'alienage' of unaccompanied child asylum seekers in the analysis that follows, I use the term more expansively to encompass their particular condition of alienage: I include not only their non-citizenship but also their unauthorised presence and the fact that they are seeking asylum after fleeing persecution in their homeland.

Unlike citizen children who are conventionally understood as members of a politically and legally defined community within territorial boundaries, unaccompanied non-citizen children are legally and politically 'the other'.[39] Within citizenship studies, there is lively debate about the relevance and legitimacy of notions of citizenship that continue to presuppose the existence of a territorially bounded sovereign State impervious to transnational economic and communication exchanges and voluminous regular and irregular migration. This raises legitimate questions about States' moral right to accord differential work rights to citizens and non-citizens (many from poorer States).[40] The distinction between citizen and non-citizen is also pressing for unaccompanied child asylum seekers. They are dependent on the State for access to minimum education, health and social services. However, unlike citizen children, they may be ineligible to receive these basic services. Their precariousness is commonly compounded by their unfamiliarity with national culture, institutions or language in the country of asylum.

For unaccompanied children, the vulnerabilities generated by their unauthorised presence *and* their seeking asylum are particularly acute. Unlike unaccompanied refugee children whose claim has already been resolved, their dependence on the State to process their asylum claim and to not refoul them is absolute.[41] The heightened needs of unaccompanied child asylum seekers for special assistance in determining their refugee claims has long been acknowledged by international organisations with expertise in refugees and asylum seekers.[42] As far back as 1994, the UNHCR developed guidelines containing safeguards for status determinations regarding unaccompanied child asylum seekers.[43] The circumstances leading unaccompanied children to seek asylum are likely similar to, or even identical to, those of unaccompanied refugee children who have been authorised to reside in a country. State border control policies that concentrate on the control and deterrence of unaccompanied child asylum seekers, and not their heightened vulnerability, compound the trauma they have already experienced in their country of origin and the transit journey.[44] Yet, the practice of refugee regimes in the Global North are increasingly based on the principle of deterrence rather than human rights protection. Gammeltoft-Hansen and Tan's extensive analysis of the development of deterrence policies in the past 30 years concluded that 'restrictive migration control policies are today the primary, some might say only, response of the developed world to rising numbers of asylum seekers and refugees'.[45] State interventions have been increasingly justified by a political paradigm in which border control is 'unquestionably related to (if not determinative of) the safety of the state'.[46] The vulnerability that stems from unaccompanied children's unauthorised presence is, therefore, mainly dependent on the character of the State's political response to asylum seekers more generally.

In this context, space for the recognition of asylum seekers' common humanity and dignity, let alone recognition of children as 'special cases', has virtually disappeared. Vulnerability theorists concede, rightly, that humans' instinctive response to vulnerability does not necessarily lead to acts of tolerance or generosity.[47] Instead, apprehensions of vulnerability in others can 'motivate care, generosity, and retributive violence in equal measure'.[48] And so, refugees and asylum seekers are susceptible to a broad spectrum of responses ranging from disavowal and violence to nurture and care.[49] In Australia, *refugee* children, whose presence in the State has been both authorised and invited, ordinarily receive a caring and nurturing response. They are constructed as 'quintessential innocent civilians'.[50] In contrast, unaccompanied children are most often exposed to violence and disavowal[51] because they are seen as legally and morally culpable for the 'unauthorised' border crossing. Where domestic political and media disapprobation of asylum seekers is consistent and voluble, their arrival experience encompasses actual visceral experiences of exclusion as well as those that are imagined and feared.[52]

The vulnerability of these being/becoming children is further compounded and complicated by the fact that they must emotionally and logistically negotiate their legal precariousness as unauthorised asylum seekers without the care, support or protection of a parent or guardian.

2.3.5 Family separation

Unaccompanied child asylum seekers share all the inherent vulnerabilities of any other child who lacks parental support. However, unlike unaccompanied child refugees, whose asylum claim has been determined, they also lack an adult carer to assist them and represent their interests in staking a claim for asylum or non-refoulement. Moreover, unlike children who undertake unauthorised inter-country travel with their families, unaccompanied children experience these traumas alone. This is particularly concerning for the being/becoming child because the traumatic experiences of young asylum seekers are well outside the normal transitional experiences of childhood and adolescence, which puts 'at risk their present and long-term wellbeing'.[53] Further, these children commonly have enduring anxieties about the safety of the family they have left behind as well as the burden of expectation that they should be living a better life.[54] The ongoing impact of separation from their families who remain in dangerous environments and their sense of psychological isolation is succinctly captured in this quote from an unaccompanied child asylum seeker in Australia:

> We all spend time, a lot of time, thinking about our family – it's very important; that is part of our life. … It comes automatically to our minds because our families are not safe. [Our] people are actually murdered in the shops, every second a bomb blasts and its continuous. We are continually abused, bombs blast in shopping centres, our family members are not safe.[55]

> I don't say anything about my rejection to my family because they already have lots of problems. If I say it to them, it will just increase their problems, their tension, so I don't say anything.[56]

It is usually a parent's role to care for and foster the development of their child. However, where a child's parents die or are adjudged to be incapable of providing sufficient care and protection, States have long deployed the legal mechanism of guardianship. Guardianship provides for the appointment of an adult charged with protecting the child's interests and managing their property when their parents die[57] and for the appointment of a statutory guardian as a measure of last resort when the State determines that children need care and protection.[58] Contemporary common law recognises that guardianship encompasses the full range of rights and powers that an adult could exercise regarding the welfare and upbringing of a child.[59] This includes the duty to protect the child from harm, act for their benefit, make decisions relating to the child's long-term welfare and not profit from the relationship.[60] Guardians also owe a fiduciary duty in which 'one person is obliged, or has undertaken, to act in relation to a particular matter in the interests of another with a 'special vulnerability' and is entrusted with a power to affect those interests in a legal and practical sense'.[61]

Unaccompanied child asylum seekers have no parent to mediate their relationships with the State. Guardianship is the key legal mechanism for prescribing the legislative and functional responsibility to ensure that these children receive care and protection from harm in the present, the provision of circumstances that enable their development and access to, and realisation of, the processing of their asylum claims. For unaccompanied child asylum seekers, the State-appointed guardians become, in effect, the gatekeeper between the child and the State's legal and policy responses to them. It is here that comprehending the being/becoming child is vital. From the perspective of the being/becoming child, guardians have a dual protective and anticipatory obligation to address the child's vulnerability by virtue of their family separation. They have the legislative and functional responsibility to protect the child from harm and neglect in the present and protect their capacity to develop into the future. This includes advocating for the provision of emotional and psychological support to enable their recovery from past significant trauma[62] and ensuring that they receive adequate representation to prosecute their claim for asylum.

International law and best practice State models vest the guardian with the functions of advocating on behalf of an individual child to ensure that all decisions have their best interests as a primary consideration. Guardians must ensure that the child's views and opinions are sought and considered and that the child has suitable care, accommodation, education, language support and healthcare provision. They also have the functions of ensuring that the child is legally represented in procedures that will address protection claims and durable solutions and that possibilities of family tracing and reunification are explored where appropriate. In discharging these functions, the guardian consults with, advises and advocates on behalf of the child. They provide a link, ensure transparency and facilitate cooperation between the child and the various organisations that may provide them with services.

As noted in Section 2.2, the acute impact of the separation of these children from their parents and the significance of the provision of effective guardianship is acknowledged in an extensive body of international soft law, including UNHCR and European States' guidelines and practice standards, to address the vulnerabilities of these children generated by this separation.[63] These standards are consistent with the construction of the guardian as being in a relationship with the individual child – having dual protective and anticipatory inward-looking obligation to them – and as an outward-looking gatekeeper between the child and the State. As illustrated in Table 2.1, analysis of the ten Separated Children in Europe Programme 'Statement of Good Practice' guidelines reveals an almost even division in these two roles.

Five responsibilities pertain to the quality of the relationship between the child and the guardian to ensure that the being/becoming child is cared for and heard (the inward-looking role). The balance of the responsibilities seek to ensure that the child's legal interests and protection needs are realisable with the guardian being the gateway between the child, the legal system and State/civil society organisations services (the outward-looking role).

Table 2.1 Inward- and outward-looking responsibilities of guardians of unaccompanied child asylum seekers

Responsibilities of the guardian to develop a relationship with the individual unaccompanied child (the inward-looking role)	*Responsibilities of the guardian as gatekeeper to the unaccompanied child and the State (the outward-looking role)*
Ensure the children's views and opinions are considered in all decisions that affect them.	Ensure that all decisions have the child's best interests as a primary consideration.
Ensure that the child has suitable care, accommodation, education, language support and healthcare provision and that they can practice their religion.	Ensure the child has suitable legal representation to assist in procedures that will address protection claims and durable solutions.
Engage with the child's informal network of friends and peers.	Contribute to a durable solution in the child's best interests.
Consult with and advise the child.	Provide a link and ensure transparency and cooperation between the child and the various organisations who may provide them with services.
Explore, together with the child, the possibility of family tracing and reunification, and assist the child to keep in touch with his or her family where appropriate.	Advocate on the child's behalf.

For the being/becoming child, having a guardian that discharges both roles is critical. Without effective guardianship, the being/becoming child's susceptibility to harm and neglect in the present is increased. They are also unlikely to access the necessary specialist assistance to recover from trauma. The chances of them receiving representation and assistance for the proper determination of their refugee claim is remote. The vulnerabilities of children separated from their parents without effective guardianship are especially evident in States like Australia, where the statutory appointed guardian's independence from the State's border control machinery is compromised.

2.4 Conclusion

This chapter explored how, regardless of their immigration and citizenship status, unaccompanied child asylum seekers are, first and foremost, being/becoming children. Notwithstanding variances in their age, cultural background, prior experiences of displacement, persecution, trauma, variances in their past and present family circumstances and differences in their personalities, cognitive abilities and life circumstances, these children share a compound triple burden of vulnerability. My examination of their triple burden of vulnerability generated by the convergence of their minority, alienage, and family separation exposes their specific and heightened dependence on the State to respond to these vulnerabilities. In the next chapter, I evaluate the promise and limitations of human rights law in responding to these compound triple vulnerabilities.

Notes

1 Australian Human Rights Commission, *Anonymous Unaccompanied Child, Submission 146 to The Forgotten Children: National Inquiry into Children in Immigration Detention* (AHRC, 2014) 1.
2 Internationally, these children are variously called 'unauthorised unaccompanied minors', 'unaccompanied minor asylum seekers' or 'unaccompanied asylum-seeking children'. I prefer the term unaccompanied asylum-seeking children because the use of the term 'children' is, as I will argue, purposive.
3 UNICEF, *A Child Is a Child: Protecting Children on the Move from Violence, Abuse and Exploitation* (Geneva, 2017).
Even when such data is collected, it is 'rarely disaggregated by nationalities, risk category, gender or age'. See UNHCR, UNICEF, IOM, *Refugee and Migrant Children in Europe: Overview of Trends* (UNHCR, 2017) 6.
4 UNHCR, *Refugee Global Trends* (UNHCR, 2017) 3, 47 <http://www.unhcr.org/5943e8a34.pdf>. Moreover, the UNHCR states that this is likely to be an underestimate.
5 International Federation of Red Cross and Red Crescent Societies, *Alone and Unsafe: Children, Migration and Sexual and Gender-Based Violence* (IFRC, 2018) reported that travelling without an accompanying adult renders unaccompanied minors vulnerable to being assaulted, sexually abused, raped, trafficked into sexual exploitation or forced into 'survival sex', 112. See also Ilse Derluyn et al., 'Minors Travelling Alone: A Risk Group for Human Trafficking?' (2009) 48(4) *International Migration* 164; Jacqueline Bhabha et al., *Children*

on the Move: An Urgent Human Rights and Child Protection Priority (Harvard University, 2016); Tine Jensen et al., 'Stressful Life Experiences and Mental Health Problems among Unaccompanied Asylum-Seeking Children' (2013) 20(1) *Clinical Child Psychology and Psychiatry* 106; Matthew Hodes et al., 'Risk and Resilience for Psychological Distress amongst Unaccompanied Asylum Seeking Adolescents' (2008) 49(7) *Journal of Child Psychology and Psychiatry* 723.

6 See Marianne Vervliet et al., 'The Mental Health of Unaccompanied Refugee Minors on Arrival in the Host Country' (2014) 55(1) *Scandinavian Journal of Psychology* 33.

7 Tine Jensen et al., 'Long-Term Mental Health in Unaccompanied Refugee Minors: Pre- and Post-Flight Predictors' (2019) 28(12) *European Child & Adolescent Psychiatry* 1671. See also Tammy Bean et al., 'Comparing Psychological Distress, Traumatic Stress Reactions and Experiences of Unaccompanied Refugee Minors with Experiences of Adolescents Accompanied by Parents' (2007) 195(4) *Journal of Nervous and Mental Disease* 288; Ilse Derluyn and Eric Broekaert, 'Different Perspectives on Emotional and Behavioural Problems in Unaccompanied Refugee Children and Adolescents' (2007) 12(2) *Ethnicity & Health* 141.

8 European Union Agency for Fundamental Rights, *Separated, Asylum-seeking Children in European Union Member States: Comparative Report* (Austria, 2011) 49–53.

9 The exception is the United States, which has the largest number of unaccompanied child asylum seekers globally but does not appoint them a guardian. Instead, unaccompanied child asylum seekers who reach the United States and are not released quickly to relatives, without any formal legal process, remain in a pseudo-guardianship relationship with the federal agency within Health and Human Services.

10 Soft law refers to 'normative provisions contained in non-binding texts': Dinah Shelton (ed), *Commitment and Compliance: The Role of Non-binding Norms in the International Legal System* (Oxford University Press, 2000) 292.

11 UNHCR, *Refugee Children: Guidelines on Protection and Care* (United Nations, 1994), 101, 126 <http://www.unhcr.org/refworld/docid/3ae6b3470.html>; UNHCR, *Guidelines on Policies and Procedures in Dealing with Unaccompanied Children Seeking Asylum* (United Nations, 1997) [5.7] <http://www.unhcr.org/3d4f91cf4.html>.

The UNHCR, *Handbook on Procedures and Criteria for Determining Refugee Status* (United Nations, 2011) also reiterated the requirement that a legal guardian be appointed to promote a decision that is in the best interests of an unaccompanied or separated child. The UNHCR's *Guidelines on the Applicable Criteria and Standards Relating to the Detention of Asylum-Seekers and Alternatives to Detention* (United Nations, 2012) reaffirms the need for an independent and qualified guardian as well as a legal adviser to be appointed for unaccompanied or separated children.

12 These include the *Inter-Agency Guiding Principles on Unaccompanied and Separated Children* (International Committee of the Red Cross, 2004); Separated Children in Europe Programme, *Statement of Good Practice* (SCEP, 4th ed., 2009) and Defence for Children International, *Core Standards for Guardians of Separated Children in Europe* (DFCI, 2014). States in the Asia Pacific region are lagging far behind our European counterparts in agreeing on and articulating similar regional State guidelines for acknowledging the vulnerabilities of children generated by their separation from their parents.

13 See, for example, Jonathan Herring's *Vulnerability, Childhood and the Law* (Springer, 2018). He resists the broad construction of children as a vulnerable group who are particularly susceptible to harm and unable to look after themselves.

See also Serap Keles et al., 'Resilience and Acculturation among Unaccompanied Refugee Minors' 42(1) *International Journal of Behavioural Development* 52; Brit Oppedal and Thormod Idsoe, 'The Role of Social Support in the Acculturation and Mental Health of Unaccompanied Minor Asylum Seekers' (2015) 56(2) *Scandinavian Journal of Psychology* 203.

14 Jacqueline Bhabha, 'Independent Children, Inconsistent Adults: International Child Migration and the Legal Framework', *Innocenti Discussion Paper* (UNICEF Innocenti Research Centre, 2008). Bhabha references the 'triple burden' as a statement of fact, but she does not theorise its content.

15 A substantial body of literature has acknowledged the differences between childhood in the Global North and South. See, for example, Nicola Ansell, *Children, Youth, and Development* (Routledge, 2005) 8, 23–24.

16 This led to the emergence of parallel discourses about children and childhood and the evolution of binary constructions of the child as either a being or a becoming person in developmental psychology, social anthropology and sociology. Developmental psychologists – devising theories and explanations for how children develop specific competencies – have reinforced the construction of childhood as a period. Piaget's stages of childhood set premises for children passing through defined cognitive and moral stages to develop into competent adults. See Jean Piaget, *The Child's Conception of the World* (Routledge, 1929). Piaget's work remained the key lens through which parents, teachers, social workers and healthcare professionals (particularly in the Global North) socially constructed childhood until the early twenty-first century. Although, from the late 1970s, Piaget's stages of development were critiqued for their emphasis on children's lack of skills, knowledge and 'faulty reasoning'.

See Martin Woodhead, Dorothy Faulkner and Karen Littleton (eds), *Cultural Worlds of Early Childhood* (Routledge, 1998). They were also critiqued for their questionable applicability across contexts and cultures.

See Robert Serpell, 'How Specific are Perceptual Skills? A Cross-Cultural Study of Pattern Reproduction' (1979) 70(3) *British Journal of Psychology* 365, who argued that children's competencies and skills are heavily influenced by their daily experience in their particular contexts. In contrast, social anthropologists examining the experience of childhood across cultures had long recognised that childhood differs across time and place. Developments in social anthropology generated understandings of childhood that encompassed the inter-connections between childhood and adulthood in economic and social life. They also enabled analysis of how age, gender, class and race differentiate childhoods across different times and contexts and led to the inclusion of children's experiences in research and reports acknowledging the significance of children's voices. See, for example, Margaret Mead and Martha Wolfenstein (eds), *Childhood in Contemporary Cultures* (University of Chicago Press, 1955); Enid Schildkrout, *People of The Zongo* (Cambridge University Press, 1978).

17 Adulthood is marked by reaching the legal age of majority or satisfying cultural customary practices.

18 Emile Durkheim, 'Childhood' in William Pickering (ed), *Durkheim: Essays on Morals and Education* (Routledge, 1979) 150.

19 Ibid.

20 Loren Lomasky, *Persons, Rights and the Moral Community* (Oxford University Press, 1987), 202:

> If one were condemned … to remain a child throughout one's existence … it would be a personal misfortune of the utmost gravity.

See also Colin MacLeod, 'Primary Goods, Capabilities and Children' in Ingris Robeyn and Harry Brighouse (eds), *Measuring Justice: Primary Goods and*

Capabilities (Cambridge University Press, 2010); Ancus Gheaus, 'Unfinished Adults and Defective Children: On the Nature and Value of Childhood' (2015) 9(1) *Journal of Ethics & Social Philosophy* 21.

21 Allison James, Chris Jenks and Alan Prout, *Theorizing Childhood* (Teachers College Press, 1998) 8.

22 Ibid 207.

23 Emma Uprichard, 'Children as 'Being and Becomings': Children, Childhood and Temporality' (2008) 22 *Children & Society* 306, 308.

24 There has been increasing recognition, since Nick Lee's seminal work on constructions of childhood in 2001, that both children and adults are alike in their ongoing experience of the dual processes of being and becoming and that adults and children, in relationship to each other, are more and less competent at certain things over the course of their lives. See Nick Lee, *Childhood and Society* (Open University Press, 2001). Also, the becoming conception of children, for example, has been criticised for perceiving children as inadequate, incomplete or incompetent by virtue of focusing on adult capabilities that the child has not yet acquired and not on what the child can do differently to, or sometimes better than, adults. See Gareth Matthews, 'Philosophy and Developmental Psychology: Outgrowing the Deficit Conception of Childhood' in Harvey Siegel (ed), *The Oxford Handbook of Philosophy of Education* (Oxford University Press, 2009).

25 See Michael Freeman (ed), *Children's Rights: Progress and Perspectives* (Martinus Nijhoff, 2011) 13–15. Michael Freeman, a human rights scholar, began the case for the dissolution of the binary construction in human rights law in 2010:

> It is important to recognise that children are more than pre-adult becomings. But it is equally important to understand that appreciating that they are 'beings' does not preclude their also 'becomings'. ... The child is both a 'being' and a 'becoming' ... the being child will become an adult.

See Michael Freeman, 'The Human Rights of Children' (2010) 63 *Current Legal Problems* 1, 13.

26 Ancus Gheaus (n 20) 21.

27 Michael Freeman (ed), *Children's Rights: Progress and Perspectives* (n 25) 15. Accepting that childhood is simultaneously a period and a state and that children are simultaneously beings and becomings necessarily alters our understanding of the role and realities of childhood, provides significant challenges to established paradigms and has significant implications for children's rights scholarship.

28 This addresses John Tobin's concern that the 'characterisation of children as vulnerable carries the risk that they will be defined by their vulnerabilities. To address the unintended consequences of a vulnerability paradigm, there is a need to expand the conception of children in a way that recognises their evolving capacities and right to participation'. See John Tobin, 'Understanding Children's Rights: A Vision Beyond Vulnerability' (2015) 84 (2) *Nordic Journal of International Law* 155.

29 Harriet Nielson, 'The Arrow of Time in the Space of the Present: Temporality as Methodological and Theoretical Dimension in Child Research' (2016) 30 *Children and Society* 1, 7.

30 See Jeanette Lawrence et al., 'Understanding the Perspectives of Refugee Unaccompanied Minors Using a Computer-Assisted Interview' (2016) 17(2) *Forum: Qualitative Social Research* 1, 2.

31 Jens Qvortrup et al. (eds), *Childhood Matters: Social Theory, Practice and Politics* (Ashgate, 1994) 125–134, 269.

32 Jacqueline Goodnow, 'Refugees, Asylum Seekers, Displaced Persons: Children in Precarious Positions' in Gary Melton et al. (eds), *The Sage Handbook of Child Research* (Sage, 2014) 339–360.

33 Sarah Johnson, Robert Blum and Tina Cheng, 'Future Orientation: A Construct with Implications for Adolescent Health and Wellbeing' (2014) 26(4) *International Journal of Adolescent Medicine & Health* 459, 468.

34 Rachel Seginer, *Future Orientation: Developmental and Ecological Perspectives* (Springer, 2009). See also Thomas Weisner, 'Culture, Context, and Well-Being' in Asher Ben-Arieh et al. (eds), *Handbook of Child Well-Being* (Springer, 2014) 87–103.

35 See Mark Brough et al., 'Unpacking the Micro–Macro Nexus: Narratives of Suffering and Hope among Refugees from Burma Recently Settled in Australia' (2012) 26(2) *Journal of Refugee Studies* 207.

36 Guy Coffey et al., 'The Meaning and Mental Health Consequences of Long-Term Immigration Detention for People Seeking Asylum' (2010) 70 *Social Science & Medicine* 2070.

37 See Elizabeth Grosz, *The Nick of Time: Politics, Evolution and the Untimely* (Duke University Press, 2004) 184, who argues that 'the past is the condition of every future; however, the future that emerges is only one of the possibilities that was given by the past'.

38 Related to children's own construction of their lives and their futures is the relationship between vulnerability and the agentic capacity of unaccompanied children as minors. This relationship is complex and nuanced. Much research about unaccompanied child asylum seekers emphasises their vulnerability and passivity more frequently than their independence and resilience as the survivors, as well as the victims, of war and dislocation. However, acknowledging their vulnerability as minors does not negate that they also, like all children, possess resiliencies and a desire to be agentic. Many unaccompanied asylum seekers have experienced deep traumas that forced them to flee alone, and their journeys seeking asylum entail varying degrees of uncertainty, fear and deprivation. Yet, this vulnerability coexists alongside capacity, agency or desire to rebuild their lives and pursue their own choices in environments free from persecution and violence. See Muireann Ní Raghallaigh, 'The Causes of Mistrust amongst Asylum Seekers and Refugees: Insights from Research with Unaccompanied Asylum-Seeking Minors Living in the Republic of Ireland' (2013) 27(1) *Journal of Refugee Studies* 82.

39 Linda Bosniak's *The Citizen and the Alien: Dilemmas of Contemporary Membership* (Princeton University Press, 2006) explores the exclusion of transnational migrants in liberal democratic societies, especially the United States, with a status short of full citizenship.

40 See Rainer Bauböck, 'Stakeholder Citizenship: An Idea Whose Time Has Come?' in Bertelsmann Stiftung, European Policy Centre and Migration Policy Institute (eds), *Delivering Citizenship. The Transatlantic Council on Migration* (Gütersloh, 2008) 31.

41 This is particularly so in States such as Australia, where unaccompanied children seeking asylum by boat are treated distinctly from unaccompanied refugee children whose claim has already been determined elsewhere and who are brought to Australia for settlement under its Unaccompanied Humanitarian Minor program.

42 See for example, Conclusions on the International Protection of Refugees, adopted by the UNHCR Executive Committee, No. 47 (XXXVIII), 'Refugee Children', 1987; Council of the European Union, Resolution on 'Unaccompanied Minors Who are Nationals of Third Countries', *Official Journal of the European Communities* C 221, 19 July 1997, 23–27.

43 UNHCR, *Refugee Children: Guidelines on Protection and Care* (United Nations, 1994) 101, 126; UNHCR, *Guidelines on Policies and Procedures in Dealing with Unaccompanied Children Seeking Asylum* (United Nations, 1997) [5.7].

44 As noted in Chapter 1, my book is focused on unaccompanied child asylum seekers as Australia's current Boat Turnback laws – by intercepting vessels and returning them to sea and potentially refouling unaccompanied children – exacerbates their vulnerability in breach of Australia's most basic international human rights obligation. However, I do not assert that *only* unaccompanied child asylum seekers are so vulnerable as to enliven the mitigating vulnerability framework contended for in Chapter 4. Instead, provided the requisite 'sufficient connection' can be established, a mitigating vulnerability framework ought to be able to be made out for different cohorts.

45 Thomas Gammeltoft-Hansen and Nikolas Tan, 'The End of the Deterrence Paradigm? Future Directions for Global Refugee Policy' (2017) 5(1) *Journal on Migration and Human Security* 28, 28.

46 Anthea Vogl, 'Seeking Asylum: Human Smuggling and Bureaucracy at the Border' (2012) 27(1) *Canadian Journal of Law and Society* 159, 159.

47 See Judith Butler for further discussion of the inter-relationship between the relative security of some lives and the abuse of the precariousness of others' lives. Judith Butler, *Frames of War: When Is Life Grievable?* (Verso, 2009) 2, 48.

48 Ann V. Murphy, 'Corporeal Vulnerability and the New Humanism' (2011) 26 (3) *Hypatia* 575, 583.

49 Ibid 578.

50 Ibid.

51 J. Marshall Beier (ed), *The Militarization of Childhood* (Palgrave Macmillan, 2011) 8–9.

52 See Ćetta Mainwaring and Noelle Brigden, 'Beyond the Border: Clandestine Migration Journeys' (2016) 21(2) *Geopolitics* 243, who discuss the concept of the journey of clandestine migrations using a similar frame at 244.

53 Elaine Chase, 'Security and Subjective Wellbeing: The Experiences of Unaccompanied Young People Seeking Asylum in the UK' (2013) 35(6) *Sociology of Health & Illness* 858.

54 *Anonymous Unaccompanied Child, Submission No. 146* (n 1) 1.

55 Ilan Katz, Geraldine Doney and Effie Mitchell, *Evaluation of the Expansion of the Community Detention Program: Final Report SPRC 12/13 to the Department of Immigration and Citizenship* (DIAC, 2013) 47.

56 Ibid 48.

57 Antonio Buti, 'The Early History of the Law of Guardianship of Children: From Rome to the Tenures Abolition Act 1660' (2003) 7(1) *University of Western Sydney Law Review* 92. The evolution of the law of guardianship from 449 BC Rome up to modern times has been comprehensively chronicled. In addition to Buti's article, see R. H. Helmholz's 'The Roman Law of Guardianship in England, 1300–1600' (1978) 52 *Tulane Law Review* 223; John Seymour, '*Parens Patriae* and Wardship Powers: Their Nature and Origins' (1994) 14 *Oxford Journal of Legal Studies* 159.

58 Where a statutory guardian is appointed, they are commonly the head of a government department who then delegates their functions to department officers or not-for-profit organisations accredited to provide care.

59 Anthony Dickey, *Family Law* (Law Book Co, 2002) 341.

60 The English common law since medieval times recognised the separate duty of the sovereign as *parens patriae* (parent of the country) to provide care for those who were not able to take care of themselves, protect persons deemed incapable of managing their own affairs, assume responsibility for such property or assets as they possessed and assist those who were unable to obtain redress from the ordinary courts because of their position. The promulgation of *De Praerogativa Regis* in 1324 formalised the king's duty to take custody of the person and lands

of infants without carers and with 'incompetent', 'idiot' or 'lunatic' adults. Accordingly, guardianship was distinct in law from the broader *parens patriae* jurisdiction of the English courts of chancery to take custody of, and responsibility for, both infants (minors under 18) and adults assessed to be lacking capacity by making an order declaring them a 'ward of the Court'.

61 *Hospital Products Ltd v United States Surgical Corporation* (1984) 156 CLR 41.

62 Ulika Wernesjö, 'Unaccompanied Asylum-Seeking Children: Whose Perspective?' (2011) 19(4) *Childhood* 495.

63 Notably, European States have developed clear practice standards to address the vulnerabilities of asylum-seeking children generated by their separation from their parents. See, for example, the *Statement of Good Practice* (n 12) that endorses minimum guardianship standards at 21–22.

3 The unfulfilled potential of human rights for unaccompanied child asylum seekers

3.1 Introduction

Human rights law holds out the promise of protecting unaccompanied children seeking asylum but is ultimately deficient in delivering on it. The universal human rights norms governing States' treatment of unaccompanied child asylum seekers, discussed in this chapter, are extensive. Yet, they have failed to sufficiently influence domestic legislative responses to unaccompanied child asylum seekers in a way that adequately responds to their vulnerabilities. Chapter 2 set out the triple vulnerability of these children and the critical significance of guardianship systems in responding to their needs. This chapter examines the potential of human rights law's promise of universal and aspirational standards to address these compound vulnerabilities. Presently, the human rights framework is the only available legal mechanism to limit State responses to these children focused primarily on border security. By detailing the extent of that framework and correlating State human rights obligations with the triple vulnerabilities of these children, this chapter illustrates that effective implementation of these rights in domestic law and policy would amply address the acute vulnerabilities of these children. However, using Australia as a case study, analysis of three key moments in the trajectory of recent Australian law (see Section 3.4) demonstrates a legislative closing down of human rights through successive pieces of legislation. The failure of the human rights framework to prevent the awful impact of these three moments on these children provides the impetus for the supplementary mitigating vulnerability framework proposed in Chapter 4.

3.2 State legal obligations towards unaccompanied child asylum seekers in international human rights law

States have extensive obligations to unaccompanied child asylum seekers in international human rights and refugee law specifically set out in treaties. It is a fundamental principle of international treaty[1] law that 'every treaty in force is binding upon the parties to it and must be performed by them in good faith',[2] with State parties held accountable for the realisation of these obligations in law, policy, and practice. The international human rights system holds States to a legal standard

DOI: 10.4324/9781003260134-4

for the treatment – either by State action or inaction – of its citizens and others within its jurisdiction under national, regional or international laws. It enables the identification of the source and nature of human rights violations. It also provides mechanisms for holding the State accountable to national or international bodies for the actions they take that cause, continue or worsen people's ability to attain minimum civil, political, economic, social and cultural rights and for laws and policies that fail to address patterns of preventable human rights deprivations. The system also obliges States to continue reporting on the extent to which they are realising the totality of their international human rights obligations. State policies, legislation and regulations ought to align with, but at least must not undermine, the fundamental normative human rights standards in global human rights instruments, conventions and other internationally agreed commitments of the State. In practice, however, there is regular non-alignment, which is discussed further in this chapter.

Answering the research question 'How effectively does international human rights law respond to their vulnerability?' first requires an examination of the content of States' human rights obligations to unaccompanied child asylum seekers. This examination is not straightforward because States' human rights obligations to them are generated across all the core international human rights treaties and the Refugee Convention rather than being contained in any single core treaty. This is because international human rights were initially broadly classified in the *Universal Declaration of Human Rights* in 1948. Subsequently, the *International Covenant on Civil and Political Rights* (ICCPR)[3] and the *International Covenant on Economic, Social and Cultural Rights* (ICESCR),[4] respectively, codified in greater detail the core civil and political and economic, social and cultural rights of all persons in international law treaties. Since 1954, thematic treaties have applied and extended these core rights to specific groups of people. Six of these thematic treaties generate State obligations to unaccompanied children: the *Convention on the Rights of the Child* (CRC);[5] the *Convention on the Elimination of All Forms of Discrimination Against Women* (CEDAW);[6] the *Convention on the Elimination of All Forms of Racial Discrimination* (CERD);[7] the *Convention on the Rights of Persons with Disabilities* (CRPD);[8] the *Convention against Torture and Other Cruel, Inhuman or Degrading Treatment or Punishment* (CAT);[9] the *Convention Relating to the Status of Refugees* (the Refugee Convention) and the 1967 *Protocol Relating to the Status of Refugees.*[10]

To address this dispersal, Table 3.1, 'A comprehensive synthesis of States' extensive legal obligations to unaccompanied child asylum seekers', groups State obligations arising from the provisions of each of the relevant core treaties and the Refugee Convention. Table 3.1 illustrates clearly how specific State obligations are generated across multiple treaties.[11] It identifies 26 core State obligations to unaccompanied child asylum seekers, including obligations to all asylum seekers (Column 1) and additional specific obligations to them as children (Column 2). The 26 substantive State obligations identified comprise 15 obligations to all asylum seekers and 11 additional obligations to asylum-seeking children. That 11 State obligations specifically relate to children reflects international human rights

Table 3.1 A comprehensive synthesis of States' extensive legal obligations to unaccompanied child asylum seekers

State obligation to all asylum seekers	*Additional obligations owed only to children*
	Best interests of the child must be a primary consideration CRC 3(1); CRPD 7(1) *Provision of guardianship taking into account the best interest of the child as their basic concern* CRC 18(1), 20 *Take all appropriate legislative and administrative measures to ensure children have such protection and care as is necessary for their well-being* CRC 3(2) *Right of asylum-seeking children to special protection and assistance including to fair and effective RSD* CRC 20, 22 *Right to development* CRC 6(2)
Right to life and to not be removed to a country where life or freedom would be threatened (non-refoulement) Refugee Convention 33; ICCPR 6, 7; CAT 3, 16 *Right to not be penalised or discriminated against for arriving in Australia without authorisation* Refugee Convention 31	CRC 6, 37
Right to equality and respect for human rights without discrimination ICCPR 2(1), 26; ICESCR 2(2); CERD 5; CEDAW 2; CRPD 5; 12; Refugee Convention 3.	CRC 2
Freedom of movement ICCPR 12; Refugee Convention 26; CERD 5(i)	CRC 10
Freedom from arbitrary detention ICCPR 9(1).	CRC 37(b)
	The right of children to be detained only as a measure of last resort and for the shortest period of time CRC 37(b)

(*Continued*)

Table 3.1 Continued

State obligation to all asylum seekers	*Additional obligations owed only to children*
Freedom from torture and other cruel, inhuman, or degrading treatment or punishment while in detention ICCPR 7, 10; CAT 2, 16; CRPD 15; ICERD 5(b).	CRC 37(a)
Right to liberty and security of the person and to protection from violence ICCPR 7, 9, 10; ICESCR 12; CAT 2, 16 CERD 5(b); CRPD 14, 16.	*Right to protection from sexual exploitation, abduction, trafficking and other abuse and exploitation* CRC 3(3), 19, 33, 34, 35, 36, 38
Humane treatment and respect for dignity while in detention ICCPR 7, 10; CAT 16; ICESCR 11, 12; CRPD 9, 14(2), 15.	CRC 3, 37(c)
Right to privacy ICCPR 17; CRPD 22.	CRC 17
Right to enjoy the highest attainable standard of mental and physical health ICESCR 12; CRPD 7, 25; CEDAW 12; CERD 5(e)(iv).	CRC 3, 5, 6, 9, 12, 18, 19, 23(3), 24, 25, 37(c)
	Child victim's right to rehabilitation CRC 39
Right to adequate standard of living ICESCR 11; CRPD 28; Refugee Convention 21, 23	CRC 6, 24, 27
Right to education ICESCR 13, 14; CEDAW 10; CRPD 24; CERD 5(e)(v); Refugee Convention 22.	CRC 28, 29
Right to have family protected from arbitrary or unlawful interference ICCPR 17, 23; CRPD 23	CRC 8(1), 9,10(1)
	Right to rest, recreation and play CRC 31
Right to practice culture, language and religion ICCPR 27; ICESCR 15(1)(a); CRPD 30; Refugee Convention 4	CRC 8(1), 30
	Right to a name, nationality and identity CRC 7,8
Right to freedom of speech, association, thought, conscience and religion ICCPR 18, 19, 21 22; CRPD 21; CERD 5(d)(vii), (viii)	CRC 13, 14, 15
	Right to express views and participate in decision-making CRC 12; CRPD 7(3)

law's longstanding recognition of the need for State standards to respond to the acute needs of unaccompanied minors.[12]

It is crucial to identify and comprehend the scope and content of each of these State obligations. Every time a State turns back an asylum-seeking child on a boat or transfers them to an offshore processing centre, that State is potentially breaching a multitude of these obligations. These breaches are primarily invisible in domestic political rhetoric that demonises asylum seekers as 'illegals', but in reality, every breach is a significant derogation of the rights of the being/becoming child who is being turned away or transferred.

3.3 Correlating States' human rights obligations with the triple burdens of vulnerability of unaccompanied child asylum seekers

States' extensive human rights obligations to unaccompanied child asylum seekers can, therefore, be extensively traced across multiple treaties. Cataloguing State obligations does not properly answer the question of how effectively international human rights law responds to the vulnerabilities of unaccompanied child asylum seekers. To illuminate the relationship between State obligations to these children in human rights law and the three sites of their vulnerability, Table 3.2, 'Correlation between State human rights obligations to unaccompanied children and their triple vulnerability', correlates the 26 human rights obligations (Section 3.2) with their vulnerabilities generated by their minority, alienage, and separation from their parents. As Table 3.2 exhibits, these can be logically characterised, for clarity, as principal (in normal text) and ancillary (in italicised text) obligations.[13] Ancillary obligations are those necessary to achieve the principal obligation.

Having delineated a framework for comprehending how States' human rights obligations correlate with the specific vulnerabilities of unaccompanied children, this section now articulates the scope and content of those obligations to determine how effectively international human rights law does or does not respond to those vulnerabilities. The analysis stipulates with precision the legal standards to which States have bound themselves by drawing on relevant treaty provisions; General Comments;[14] relevant State Reports to treaty monitoring committees;[15] relevant complaints jurisprudence of applicable treaty bodies; United Nations High Commissioner for Human Rights (UNHCHR), United Nations High Commissioner for Refugees (UNHCR) and Office of the United Nations High Commissioner for Human Rights (OHCHR) guidelines; and academic scholarship.

This section argues that States' full implementation of their international legal obligations would be an adequate response to the vulnerability of these children. Although rarely fully realised in practice, understanding their full scope is necessary to comprehend the extent of the disconnect between State's international legal obligations and their actual treatment of unaccompanied children under domestic border control laws and policies. As I argue in Section 3.4, Australia has a gaping rift between the promise of human rights protection and implementation

Table 3.2 Correlation between State human rights obligations to unaccompanied children and their triple vulnerability

Minority	*Alienage*	*Separation from parents*
Consider the best interests of the child as a primary consideration	Not refoul the child *Right to not be removed to a country where their life or freedom would be threatened (non-refoulement)*	Provide unaccompanied asylum seekers with special protection and assistance, including ensuring that their legal guardian considers their best interests as their basic concern
Provide the child with humane treatment and respect for their human dignity *Right to a name, nationality and identity*	Provide special protection and assistance, including to fair and effective RSD	
Provide the child with care, protection and assistance	Treat them without discrimination	
Right to an adequate standard of living *Freedom from arbitrary detention* *Detention as a last resort and for the shortest period of time* *Freedom from torture and cruel, inhuman and degrading treatment* *Right to liberty and security of the person* *Right to freedom of movement unless restrictions are necessary for regularising status* *Right to privacy* *Right to rehabilitation*	*Right to not be penalised or discriminated against for arriving without authorisation*	
Facilitate the child's participation in decision-making		
Realise their right to development		
Right to education *Right to enjoy the highest attainable standard of mental and physical health* *Right to have family protected from arbitrary or unlawful interference* *Right to rest, recreation and play* *Right to practise culture, language and religion* *Right to freedom of speech, association, thought, conscience and religion*		

in practice. The magnitude of that divide leads me to argue in this book for an alternative normative basis for urgently attending to the vulnerabilities of unaccompanied asylum-seeking children.

3.3.1 Human rights law and children's minority

As illustrated in Table 3.2, States have five human rights obligations that correlate with the vulnerabilities generated by the minority of unaccompanied child asylum seekers. Although the construct of the being/becoming child is a very recent one in human rights law, the provisions of human rights laws do encompass the notion that a child has both current needs and future potential.[16] As discussed below, the five obligations cumulatively require States to care for, protect and fully realise the current personhood of these children while also addressing their need for care and protection to reach adulthood and bring to fruition their childhood potential. These are:

- considering the child's best interests as a primary consideration;
- treating children humanely and respecting their dignity;
- caring for, protecting and assisting them (which includes protecting them from violence and cruel, inhuman and degrading treatment); and
- realising their right to development; and
- facilitating their participation in decision-making.

3.3.1.1 Consider the unaccompanied child's best interests as a primary consideration

International human rights law firmly establishes States' obligation to consider the best interests of each child as a primary consideration in all actions concerning the child, whether by public or private social welfare institutions, courts, administrative authorities or legislative bodies.[17] This foundational 'best interests' principle has existed for nearly 60 years,[18] and despite it having no enshrined definition, authoritative guidance explicitly stipulates the scope and content of States' best interest obligations to children, the necessary underlying legal framework and the necessary measures to secure proper representation of a child's best interests.[19] By requiring States to actively consider the best interests of each individual child[20] and take that interest into account as a primary consideration[21] in the operation of private or public institutions and judicial and administrative proceedings that impact children, this obligation responds holistically to the being/becoming child's care and protection and development needs.[22]

Implementation of this obligation requires States to develop a Best Interest Assessment legal framework where States document their regard to the particular needs of individual unaccompanied children wherever a decision by a State authority has a major, continuing[23] or fundamental impact on the child's life.[24] These assessments must:

- involve a clear and comprehensive evaluation of an individual child's specific circumstances;[25]

- be done in a friendly and safe atmosphere by qualified professionals who are trained in age and gender sensitive related interviewing techniques;[26]
- be determined individually, on a case-by-case basis, before competing interests are taken into account;[27]
- provide reasons stating the child's factual circumstances, the relevant considerations, how they have been weighted to determine the child's best interests and whether the decision differs from the child's views;[28] and
- provide formal mechanisms to appeal and revise the decision to address procedural or substantive decision-making errors,[29] including where best interest assessment requirements have not been complied with.[30]

In requiring best interest assessments to include a clear and comprehensive evaluation of the unaccompanied child's nationality, upbringing, ethnic, cultural and linguistic background, particular vulnerabilities and protection needs,[31] this obligation requires States to respond comprehensively to the vulnerability of the individual being/becoming child.

3.3.1.2 Humane treatment and respect for their dignity

As captured in Table 3.1, States' duties to treat people humanely and with respect for their dignity is a distinct right recognised in nearly every international human rights convention. Dignity, like 'equality', is an amorphous concept that lies at the heart of international human rights law. It is also aligned conceptually with vulnerability theory in its appeal to the recognition of core attributes that compose the common humanity of all peoples regardless of their culture, legal status, age, or the character of their human embodiment. States' duty to treat children humanely and with respect for their dignity is also central to the realisation of other rights in those treaties.[32] It encompasses the prohibition of inhumane treatment, humiliation or degrading treatment; facilitating the conditions for individuals' self-fulfilment, autonomy or self-realisation; the protection of group identity and culture; and the creation of the necessary conditions for an individual's essential needs to be satisfied.[33] States' obligation to treat unaccompanied child asylum seekers with humanity and respect for their dignity responds to their vulnerability by creating explicit parameters for their permissible treatment.

3.3.1.3 Care, protection and assistance

States' obligation to care for, protect and assist unaccompanied children requires States to take all appropriate legislative and administrative measures to ensure such protection and care as is necessary for their well-being.[34] The State's obligation regarding well-being includes ensuring that the child has an adequate standard of living by meeting the child's needs for water, nutrition, shelter and clothing. But it also entails far more than meeting the child's basic physical and material needs. It encompasses the being/becoming children's sense of the quality of their lives and includes psychological and social dimensions, such as feeling secure in their care arrangements and feeling respected.

International human rights law also explicitly establishes States' extensive obligations to protect all children from all forms of physical or mental violence,[35] injury or abuse, neglect or negligent treatment, maltreatment or exploitation prejudicial to any aspect of their welfare.[36] The duty 'leaves no leeway for the discretion of States parties ... [they] are under strict obligation to undertake 'all appropriate measures' to fully implement this right for all children'.[37] It prohibits States from subjecting unaccompanied child asylum seekers to torture or other cruel, inhuman or degrading treatment or punishment, including during the RSD process.[38] States are specifically prohibited from placing unaccompanied child asylum seekers in immigration detention other than as a measure of last resort and for the shortest appropriate period of time.[39] This is even if the detention is lawful under the domestic legislation of the State party.[40]

International human rights law responds directly, comprehensively and proportionately to the acute care and protection needs of unaccompanied children. It requires States to implement obligations to proactively prevent and explicitly prohibit laws, policies and practices that perpetrate physical or mental violence or abuse on children[41] and to protect these children from arbitrary and cruel, inhuman or degrading treatment or punishment in the present. In addition, States have clear obligations not to compound the distress of any child that is already 'seriously distressed as a result of past events, such as serious violations of his or her fundamental rights'.[42] They are also required to promote these children's physical and psychological recovery as well as social reintegration when they have been victims of any form of neglect, exploitation, abuse or torture or any other form of cruel, inhuman or degrading treatment or punishment.[43] It is especially relevant for understanding the effectiveness of international human rights law in responding to this aspect of the vulnerability of the being/becoming child that these obligations require contemporaneous, forward-looking and remedial State responses.

3.3.1.4 Development

As illustrated in Table 3.1, the international human rights framework imposes extensive obligations on States to ensure that every unaccompanied child has a standard of living adequate for their physical, mental, spiritual, moral and social development.[44] Consistently conceiving of the being/becoming child holistically to ensure the child's abilities to fulfil their human potential to the maximum during childhood and adulthood alike, States must meet the child's concrete physical needs *as well as* their psychological needs for emotional and intellectual development and their social needs.[45] States are also obliged to ensure that all children:

- have access to compulsory primary school education and secondary schooling;[46]
- have opportunities for rest and leisure and to engage in play and recreational activities appropriate to their age;[47]

- can practise their culture, language and religion;[48]
- can enjoy the highest attainable standard of health; and[49]
- have their identity, including nationality, name and family relations preserved.[50]

In particular, for unaccompanied child asylum seekers, States must have regard for the 'desirability of continuity in the child's upbringing and to the child's ethnic, religious, cultural and linguistic background'.[51]

3.3.1.5 Realising unaccompanied child asylum seekers' right to participate in decision-making

As part of the general principle of respect for the views of the child, which underpins the CRC, international human rights law requires States to establish the legal and policy framework for children's views to be given due weight, in accordance with their age and maturity, in all settings, including judicial or administrative proceedings affecting them.[52] Consistent with the being/becoming child, the right to participate is not static or fixed. Instead, the expression of the right to participate expands with the increasing maturity of the child; therefore, States must adapt the processes enabling participation according to the child's evolving capacity.[53]

The CRC requires decision-makers to do two things in all matters affecting unaccompanied children. First, to perceive the child as possessing both the capacity and the right to agency. Second, to put in place mechanisms or processes to facilitate participation by the child when negotiating access to the personnel and bureaucracies responsible for implementing State policies, processes and facilities responsible for the refugee determination process. In practical terms, the State's obligation to realise the right to participate requires ongoing attention to the conditions necessary for meaningful participation, including opportunities for participation and the provision of adults with expertise to hear them, particularly concerning guardianship arrangements and legal representation.

States have unambiguous obligations to consider these children's best interests as a primary consideration, treat them with humanity, respect their dignity, care for them, protect them (including from violence and cruel, inhuman and degrading treatment), realise their right to development and facilitate their participation in decision-making. If implemented in practice, these five core obligations would systematically care for, protect and fully realise the current personhood of these children while also addressing their need for assistance to bring to fruition their childhood potential into adulthood.

3.3.2 Human rights law and children's alienage

This section identifies the scope and content of States' human rights obligations that respond to unaccompanied children's alienage, arguing that States' full implementation of these obligations would adequately respond to this area of their vulnerability. As examined in Chapter 2, unaccompanied child asylum seekers' vulnerability because of their alienage encompasses at least two sites of legal precariousness: first, engaging in the process of seeking asylum after fleeing persecution from their country of nationality, and second, their unauthorised presence as non-citizens in the State. As illustrated in Table 3.2, States have three principal human rights obligations that correlate with these vulnerabilities: non-refoulement; to provide them with special protection and assistance, including a fair and effective RSD; and to not discriminate against them.

3.3.2.1 Non-refoulement

The duty of non-refoulement, like that of acting on the child's best interests, is a bedrock principle of international law.[54] The Refugee Convention, CAT, ICCPR and CRC all forbid States from sending/removing a refugee or asylum seeker[55] to territories where their life or freedom would be threatened; where they have a well-founded fear of persecution on account of their race, religion, nationality, membership of a particular social group or political opinion; or where they face a real risk of significant harm either in the country to which they are removed or any other place to which that country might send them.[56] States are also prohibited from removing anyone to a country where they are in danger of death, torture or other cruel, inhuman or degrading treatment, including arbitrary detention.[57]

There is an absolute duty upon States to not return a child to a country where there are substantial grounds for believing that there is a real risk of irreparable harm to the child. This cannot be overridden by other general policy considerations, including national security or deterring maritime migration.[58] States' non-refoulement obligations to children also include ensuring the child's right to life, survival and development are not violated and that children are not subjected to torture, cruel, inhuman or degrading treatment, punishment or arbitrary detention. The obligation applies in the country to which they will initially be removed, as well as in any country to which the child may subsequently be removed.[59]

International human rights law provides adequate protection against refoulement if, whenever a State is considering moving an asylum seeker to another State's territory, the State first conducts an individualised refoulement assessment. This includes when States intercept asylum seekers on the seas. Although, under the international law of the sea, the distance of the boat from the State's coastline determines what State actions are permissible,[60] international human rights law requires States to observe their non-refoulement obligations before pushing back boats containing unaccompanied children. This includes conducting an RSD.[61] While in exceptional circumstances, initial screening at sea may be undertaken to proactively identify people with protection needs and expedite their access to a full RSD process, State obligations of non-refoulement require appropriate pre-transfer risk and vulnerability assessment processes.[62]

3.3.2.2 Access to asylum procedures and interim care and protection until their refugee status is determined

International human rights law requires States to ensure that unaccompanied child asylum seekers receive appropriate protection and humanitarian assistance to enjoy their rights under the CRC and the other international human rights or humanitarian instruments to which the State is a party.[63] This includes the Refugee Convention. While the Refugee Convention defines who it confers protection on and establishes key principles, such as non-penalisation for illegal entry and non-refoulement,[64] it does not set out procedures for RSD, leaving this to individual States to determine. However, there are settled guidelines regarding the minimum standards for realising a fair RSD procedure that complies with the CRC, Refugee Convention and ICCPR provisions.[65] These guidelines require State RSD processes to ensure that all asylum-seekers, regardless of how they arrive within the jurisdiction of a State:

- have access to fair, non-discriminatory and appropriate claim adjudication procedures before a competent authority, fully qualified in asylum and refugee matters;[66]
- have access to legal counsel and receive guidance and advice on all stages of the procedure;
- have the opportunity to present evidence concerning their personal circumstances and conditions in the country of origin;
- receive written decisions; and
- have the opportunity for formal review of a negative RSD by a fair and independent tribunal.[67]

States have a heightened obligation to give unaccompanied or separated children access to appropriate asylum procedures, which recognise that 'certain vulnerable asylum-seekers require particular attention, understanding and sensitivity, especially if accelerated or otherwise curtailed procedures are introduced'.[68] Specifically, unaccompanied children must not be refused entry, returned at the point of entry, or subjected to detailed interviews alone by immigration authorities at the point of entry.[69] Instead, as soon as a separated child is identified, 'a suitably qualified guardian or adviser should be appointed to assist them at all stages' and interviews be carried out by specially trained personnel.[70]

Additionally, the CRC imposes positive obligations on States to ensure that they receive access to appropriate interim care and protection until their refugee status is determined and a strategy for their ongoing care has been settled.

3.3.2.3 Equality and non-discrimination

States' duty to ensure the equal enjoyment of rights without any discrimination, remove obstacles to equality and act against discrimination by public and private agencies[71] are foundational human rights recognised in the ICCPR,[72] the ICESCR[73] and the CRC.[74] However, the right to equality and non-discrimination does not necessitate identical treatment, and differential treatment is not discriminatory so long as 'the criteria for differentiation [are] reasonable and objective and the aim is to achieve a purpose which is legitimate'.[75] Accordingly, it is permissible for State asylum laws and policies to treat asylum seekers who arrive by boat differently (and this treatment will not constitute discrimination under the ICCPR) only if the State can establish that such treatment is reasonable and objective and that the differential treatment aims to achieve a legitimate purpose under the ICCPR.[76] Border securitisation policies that distinguish between arrivals by boat and air, for example, are impermissible if the State cannot establish that the differentiation is both reasonable and objective as well as achieving a legitimate ICCPR purpose.

States' human rights obligations should provide unaccompanied child asylum seekers with the legal framework necessary to protect them from refoulement, give them access to asylum procedures and interim care and protection until their refugee status is determined and protect them from illegitimate discrimination (particularly that based on their mode of arrival). In addition, States that implement these three principal human rights obligations would comprehensively respond to their vulnerabilities generated by their alienage examined in Chapter 2.

3.3.3 *Human rights law and unaccompanied children's separation from their parents*

This section identifies the scope and content of States' human rights obligations that respond to unaccompanied children's separation from their parents. As captured in Table 3.2, States' human rights obligations that correlate with this vulnerability require them to provide unaccompanied children with special protection and assistance, including ensuring that their legal guardian considers their best interests as their basic concern. This section illustrates that if States implemented these human rights law obligations, they would adequately respond to the vulnerabilities generated by unaccompanied children's separation from their parents examined in Chapter 2.

3.3.3.1 *State obligations to provide special protection and assistance, including guardianship*

There is no special provision in the Refugee Convention regarding the refugee status of unaccompanied minors or the provision of guardianship. However, the Final Act of the Conference that adopted the Refugee Convention recommended that governments take the necessary measures for 'the protection of refugees who are minors, in particular unaccompanied children and girls, with special reference to guardianship and adoption'.[77] The CRC, far more unequivocally, affirms the right of asylum-seeking children to appropriate protection and assistance, including through the provision of guardianship.[78]

The CRC explicitly provides for the provision of care and protection of refugee children and children deprived of their family environment. Article 20(1)[79] recognises the special vulnerability of children temporarily or permanently deprived of their family environment and their entitlement to 'special protection and assistance provided by the State'. Further, Article 22(1) requires States to take appropriate measures to ensure that every child seeking refugee status receives proper protection and humanitarian assistance in the enjoyment of the rights contained in the CRC and such other human rights instruments ratified by the State.[80]

Articles 18(1) and 20(2) of the CRC explicitly provide for the provision of guardianship. Article 18(1) of the CRC provides:

> States Parties shall use their best efforts to ensure recognition of the principle that both parents have common responsibilities for the upbringing and development of the child. Parents or, as the case may be, legal guardians, have the primary responsibility for the upbringing and development of the child. The best interests of the child will be *their basic concern* (emphasis added).

Article 20(2) then obliges the State to 'ensure alternative care for such a child', including through the appointment of a guardian. Note that, for the guardian, the child's best interests are to be **their basic concern**, not simply to be taken into account as **a primary consideration**. This is significant as Article 3 of the CRC requires an administrative authority, legislative body or court taking action regarding a child to give active consideration to that child's best interests, among other considerations. However, for the child's guardian, Article 18(1) requires them to have the child's best interests as their basic concern. The balancing of best interest considerations permitted by the State under Article 3 is not permitted by a parent or guardian under Article 18(1). They are held to a higher standard.[81] UNHCR guidelines also make manifestly clear that governments should refer unaccompanied children seeking asylum to 'an independent and formally accredited organization [and] appoint a guardian or adviser as soon as the unaccompanied child is identified'.[82] They also require that 'unaccompanied children should have a legal guardian in any legal proceedings that is able to advocate for the child's interests or to make decisions on their behalf'.[83] The United Nations Committee on the Rights of the Child has noted that 'the appointment of an independent guardian for unaccompanied child asylum seekers is the key procedural safeguard to ensure the child's best interests is respected'.[84]

The CRC does not define guardianship or establish specific procedural safeguards for the appointment of a guardian or decisions on alternative care for children deprived of their family environment. Nor does the Refugee Convention.[85] Recalling the discussion in Chapter 2, Section 2.3.5 about the significance of the provision of effective guardianship to the child's welfare, apart from the CRC provisions relating directly to the provision of guardianship, an extensive body of international soft law articulates State obligations to appoint a legal guardian to unaccompanied or separated children to safeguard the child's interests.[86]

General Comment No. 6 on the Treatment of Unaccompanied and Separated Children Outside Their Country of Origin also provides authoritative guidance on the six requirements for States to discharge their guardianship duties to unaccompanied children.[87] States are required to:

- create the legal framework and take necessary measures to secure proper representation of, and safeguard, an unaccompanied child asylum seeker's best interests;
- ensure the guardian has the necessary childcare expertise to ensure their legal, social, health, psychological, material and educational needs are met in a continuum of care;
- ensure agencies or individuals whose interests could potentially be in conflict with those of the child's are ineligible for guardianship;
- monitor the quality of the exercise of guardianship to ensure the best interests of the child are represented throughout the decision-making process and to prevent abuse;
- provide unaccompanied children involved in asylum procedures or administrative or judicial proceedings with legal representation in addition to the appointment of a guardian; and
- ensure unaccompanied children are informed of arrangements with respect to guardianship and legal representation and that their opinions are taken into consideration.[88]

International human rights law also acknowledges the critical importance of the guardian's dual role as gatekeeper mediating the child's relationship of proximity with the State and as an individual in relationship with the child. By requiring the guardian to be independent of any agency or individuals whose interests could potentially conflict with the child's,[89] guardians can advocate for the child's best interests as their basic concern. In the context of the RSD process, guardians ensure that the child has access to free legal assistance and representation,[90] interviews are conducted fairly, all relevant information is presented and considered and there is no procedural injustice. Since they are specifically vulnerable to both inadequate custodial care and poor representation in the RSD process, fully compliant State practice would also implement review mechanisms. These would monitor the quality of the provision of guardianship arrangements in place from their reception in the State until the finalisation of their asylum claim to ensure their best interests are represented throughout the decision-making process and to specifically prevent abuse.[91]

Human rights-compliant State practice requires that the guardian be appropriately qualified and have the requisite interpersonal competencies to engage with the child. In addition, the child's effective participation is required to discharge the best interests, development, legal representation and accountability obligations of the guardian.[92] In implementing these human rights obligations, it is clear that the guardian is not only a conduit between the child and the State's border control machinery or State service providers but also that the guardian is required to be in a relationship with the child. Effective engagement with affected children capable of expressing their views and opinions is required for guardians to be able to determine the child's capacity to perceive and articulate their own best interests. It is also necessary for the guardian to determine what is in the child's best interests in decision-making about them (e.g., their care, accommodation, education, language support or healthcare needs) and to communicate these needs to their day-to-day carers and service providers.

A State guardianship framework that implemented these human rights obligations in practice would methodically respond to the vulnerabilities of unaccompanied child asylum seekers generated by their separation from their parents examined in Chapter 2.

3.4 The failure to implement human rights protections in practice: Australia as a case study

So far, this chapter has illustrated that States' extensive human rights obligations to unaccompanied child asylum seekers would, if realised in practice, amply address their acute vulnerabilities generated by their minority, alienage, and separation from their parents. These obligations ought to provide a legal and normative counterbalance to securitisation rhetoric and punitive laws and policies that aggravate the vulnerability of these children. Human rights have been the dominant counter-narrative to securitised responses in the past 30 years. Yet, notwithstanding the growth of the number of States ratifying human rights conventions, refugee regimes in the Global North are increasingly practically based on the principle of deterrence through restrictive migration control policies rather than human rights protection. Asserting States' human rights obligations to unaccompanied children has, to date, been insufficient to change State practice towards them in a way that balances their acute needs against State border control priorities. Instead, human rights obligations are demonstrably displaced by restrictive migration control laws in practice.[93] This is particularly so in Australia, despite it having ratified all the treaties discussed in this chapter.

Under Australian law, ratification by the executive does not automatically lead to binding domestic obligations. Instead, a treaty must be explicitly legislated to be binding,[94] and there has been negligible incorporation of relevant obligations into the *Migration Act* or the *IGOC Act*. However, as identified in Table 3.1, 23 of the State obligations to unaccompanied child asylum seekers are contained in the provisions of the CRC, and 11 of the State obligations are contained in the ICCPR. The CRC and the ICCPR are scheduled to the legislation that prescribes the functions of Australia's National Human Rights Institution – the Australian Human Rights Commission (AHRC). The *Australian Human Rights Commission Act 1986* (Cth) provides the AHRC with a mandate to inquire into allegations of human rights abuses by the Commonwealth, including in relation to child asylum seekers, make findings and recommendations and report to Parliament. Moreover, the AHRC has powers to investigate alleged violations of the ICCPR, to monitor Australia's compliance with the ICCPR, including the power to examine whether federal legislation complies with Australia's obligations under the ICCPR.[95] However, the AHRC has no penalty or enforcement powers when it finds human rights violations or makes remedial or compensatory recommendations. There is also limited provision in Australian domestic law for the incorporation of human rights into the common law.[96]

And so, notwithstanding Australia's human rights obligations, the lack of a compelling mechanism in international human rights law to close the gap between obligation and enforcement has enabled successive Australian governments, as discussed in Chapter 1, to progressively amend the *Migration Act* to respond to asylum seekers arriving by boat in a way that takes these children further from human rights standards, not closer. Three examples illustrate this in particular: the persistence of mandatory onshore immigration detention and offshore immigration detention, the implementation of boat turnback and takeback policies that have practically prevented boat arrivals since December 2013[97] and contemporaneous amendments to the *IGOC Act* that subordinated the Minister's guardianship obligations to these children to border control measures. The trajectory of these legislative changes has been a turning away from Australia's human rights obligations with respect to these children.

3.4.1 The persistence of the practice of onshore mandatory immigration detention and offshore immigration detention, despite repeated findings of the harm immigration detention inflicts on children

Australia has persisted with its practice of legislatively mandating potentially indefinite mandatory immigration detention since 1994, apart from the brief New Directions hiatus between 2005 and 2009.[98] The introduction of mandatory immigration detention in 1994 breached Australia's obligations under the ICCPR that prohibit arbitrary detention, which Australia had ratified on 13 August 1980, and the CRC that prohibit the mandatory detention of child asylum seekers other than for the shortest possible period of time, which Australia had ratified on 17 December 1990. The 1994 amendment initiated the deliberate bifurcation between Australian domestic migration law and international human rights obligations. It set the tone for the pre-eminence of securitisation over care and protection as a defining feature of the relationship between Australian and asylum-seeking children.

The terrible impacts of Australia's policies of mandatory onshore immigration detention and offshore immigration detention on children have been thoroughly documented in reports of national inquiries conducted by Australia's National Human Rights Institution published in 2004 and 2014.[99] Both reports provided graphic evidence of the damaging impact of immigration detention on children. They found that it perpetuated a multitude of human rights breaches, including exposing them to arbitrary detention and inhumane and cruel treatment and punishment. They also found that mandatory immigration detention, specifically, can never be in a child's best interest and that Australia's immigration detention law and policy framework was fundamentally inconsistent with the CRC.[100] The first report vividly captured how the length, indeterminacy and inhospitable conditions of detention, until 2004, precipitated pervasive unrest and periodic rioting, particularly in the centres that were very remote from urban locations. Numerous child detainees sewed their lips together, drank shampoo and attempted suicide.[101]

Human rights advocates and academics have also been highly critical of the extensive human rights abuses suffered by asylum seekers because of their prolonged detention in unsuitable conditions in Australia's onshore immigration centres.[102] Although many States detain unauthorised arrivals in specific circumstances, Australia mandates immigration detention for all unauthorised arrivals.[103] These reports have highlighted the repeated abject failures of successive governments to relieve these children from the damaging impact of mandatory immigration detention, which, despite the New Directions hiatus, has been the norm in Australian law for asylum seekers arriving by boat for 30 years.

Although there are currently no unaccompanied child asylum seekers in onshore mandatory immigration detention or offshore detention, because those who arrived before the reintroduction of offshore processing and the Boat Turnback and Takeback policy have turned 18, the persistent practice of onshore mandatory detention illustrates the abject failure of human rights to prevent the acute harms to these children as a consequence of Australian law and policy. The practice continued despite substantiated reports of the human rights abuses it generated and notwithstanding growing sociological understandings of the significance of protecting, caring for and providing for the development of children and medical evidence about the devastating long-term impacts of immigration detention-related trauma.

3.4.2 *Return to offshore processing and Boat Turnbacks and Takebacks in 2012–2014*

The return to offshore processing and Boat Turnbacks and Takebacks between 2012 and 2014 further illustrates the ultimate ineffectiveness of human rights in practice to limit the worst excesses of Australia's securitised responses to unaccompanied child asylum seekers. This return occurred against a background of longstanding condemnation of Australia's earlier flouting of its human rights obligations to asylum seekers during the Howard (Coalition) government's earlier Pacific Solution. The transfer of asylum seekers to third countries under the first iteration of the Pacific Solution was comprehensively condemned for the extensive human rights breaches manifested by the arrangements.[104] The impact of offshore processing on the psychological well-being of asylum seekers was devastating. In figures provided by the Department in response to Questions on Notice at the 2006 Senate Legal and Constitutional hearings into the *Migration*

Amendment (Designated Unauthorised Arrivals) Bill 2006,[105] each of the 27 asylum seekers remaining on Nauru had mental health concerns by 2005, with ten taking anti-anxiety medication, four taking anti-psychotic medication and seven taking anti-depressants. Between 2002 and 2005, the Department itself had documented 11 incidents of self-harm, an attempted suicide, a hunger strike involving 45 detainees and incidents of adjustment disorder, acute stress reaction, anxiety, depression, reactive depression, severe depression, post-traumatic stress disorder, insomnia, obsessive-compulsive disorder and somatisation disorder.[106]

The utilisation of Boat Turnbacks and Takebacks was also extensively criticised for shirking Australia's international obligations to asylum seekers, including non-refoulement.[107] There were also credible reports that people lost their lives and were seriously injured because of these operations.[108] The reintroduction of these policies after 2012 was a flagrant breach of Australia's human rights obligations and contemptuous of the crippling impact of offshore immigration detention on asylum seekers. Australia turned back 29 boats carrying 740 asylum seekers between December 2013 and October 2016.[109] Beyond mandatory immigration detention, the UNHCR Special Missions and Monitoring Visits to Nauru and Manus Island reported devastating human rights abuses arising from the conditions in the offshore processing centres.[110] Once again, numerous reports from domestic human rights advocates and academics condemned the reintroduction of these policies and their deleterious impact, especially on children.[111] Still, there were no changes that addressed the harms perpetuated by these laws.

3.4.3 *The subordination of the Minister's guardianship obligations in the* IGOC Act *to his border control functions in the* Migration Act

The third legislative change that was determinative of Australia's closing down of its compliance with its human rights obligations to unaccompanied child asylum seekers was the subordination of the Minister's guardianship obligations in the *IGOC Act* to their border control functions in the *Migration Act* in 2012. Before this amendment, similarly to the two legislative changes already discussed, the inadequacy of Australia's existing arrangements to provide adequate guardianship for unaccompanied child asylum seekers consistent with its obligations under the CRC had been thoroughly documented.[112] In 2012, Australia was also the only State in which the government representative responsible for regulating migration was also the appointed guardian of unaccompanied children.[113] Again, notwithstanding the explicit human rights failings in the pre-2012 guardianship arrangements arising from the inherent conflict of interest, the 2012 amendments exacerbated the conflict. These amendments clearly breached Australia's obligations to provide an independent and effective guardian under the CRC. The breach had an instrumental impact in practice. There was no independent statutory guardian to represent the best interests of children subject to offshore processing by, for example, arguing that the immigration detention environment inhibits their recovery from past trauma and exposes them to ongoing stress and the threat of violence, or to contest the suitability of offshore processing because of their individual circumstances. These acutely vulnerable children were denied even a cursory response to their separation from their parents.

In sum, Australian migration law and policy regarding unaccompanied child asylum seekers has not, from its inception, been developed from first principles that are human rights compliant. Instead of being driven by human rights-informed responses to the acute vulnerability of unaccompanied child asylum seekers, Australian law and policy responses have been driven by political imperatives. The three key legislative moments examined in this section were instrumental in closing down Australia's domestic realisation of its human rights obligations to unaccompanied child asylum seekers. This reveals a political weakness of the human rights system in achieving justice for particularly vulnerable groups. There is no correlation between the egregiousness of breaches or the degree of vulnerability of the subject and the level of domestic accountability. Human rights norms have effectively created normative and legal change in different contexts across the globe. However, Australia illustrates that they have not been sufficient, at this stage, to prevent human rights abuses in the context of unaccompanied children seeking asylum in Australia by sea. Australia currently lacks an effective domestic mechanism to ensure adequate protection of these children's rights. Without legislation that more comprehensively enlivens Australia's international human rights obligations to unaccompanied asylum-seeking children, they remain unrealised aspirations. The chasm between Australia's obligations in international law and their realisation on the ground continues to widen as the government asserts its right to control its borders by such laws and policies as it sees fit. Unless or until Australia willingly incorporates its obligations into domestic law, or enforcement mechanisms for State human rights violations are strengthened, human rights law is inadequate to counter the progressive degrading of the treatment of unaccompanied children seeking asylum by boat under Australian law.

3.5 Conclusion

This chapter has argued that although States' human rights obligations provide the existing normative response to the acute vulnerability of these children, this response has been insufficient as a check on securitisation policies to prevent real harms from being perpetrated on them.

It argued that to comprehend how effectively international human rights law responds to the triple vulnerabilities of these children requires, first, an identification of States' human rights obligations and, second, the mapping of those obligations onto the three sites of vulnerability: their minority, alienage, and separation from their parents. In attending to the identification of State obligations, I argued that their dispersal across the core international human rights legal instruments and the Refugee Convention obscures their extensive nature and works against a holistic conception of the obligations. I addressed this by synthesising those dispersed obligations into 26 core obligations to these children. To illuminate the relationship between these obligations and the three sites of these children's vulnerability, I then correlated the obligations with each of the three sites of vulnerability. Having then articulated the full scope and content of State obligations to respond to each site, I concluded that States' full implementation would, if realised in practice, amply alleviate these sites of vulnerability of these children.

However, the acute human rights breaches consequent to Australia's harsh response to these children in successive regressive changes in law and policy illustrates how, in practice, human rights obligations have been manifestly inadequate as a limiting mechanism to curb the exacerbation of these children's vulnerabilities in domestic securitised responses to them. This dissonance between obligations and response generates a gap in which unaccompanied children are egregiously harmed. In this gap, I argue we must find another way to respond to the vulnerable unaccompanied child asylum seeker. Advocacy will, and should, continue urging legal and policy changes that give full effect to human rights obligations. Yet, an additional interim change to the way law and policy responds to these children that avoids exacerbating their vulnerability until States realise their human rights obligations is necessary to halt these grave breaches. This change requires a reconceptualisation of our understanding of the relationship between unaccompanied child asylum seekers and the State where they are seeking asylum and the obligations that arise because of that relationship.

In the following chapter, I argue that a vulnerability approach can step into the gap and provide the underpinning for a State response to unaccompanied minor asylum seekers that protects them as being/becoming children in the context of their triple vulnerability without displacing their ultimate human rights claims.

Notes

1 A treaty is 'an international agreement concluded between two States in written form and governed by international law, whether embodied in a single instrument or in two or more related instruments and whatever its particular designation', article 2(1)(a) *Vienna Convention on the Laws of Treaties*, opened for signature 23 May 1969, 1155 UNTS 331 (entered into force 27 January 1980) (*Vienna Convention*).
2 See Article 26 of the *Vienna Convention* (ibid).
3 *International Convention on Civil and Political Rights*, opened for signature 19 December 1966, 999 UNTS 171 (entered into force 23 March 1976) (ICCPR). Australia ratified the ICCPR on 13 August 1980.
4 *International Convention on Economic, Social and Cultural Rights*, opened for signature 16 December 1966, 993 UNTS 3 (entered into force 3 November 1976) (ICESCR). Australia ratified the ICESCR on 10 December 1975.
5 *International Convention on the Rights of the Child* opened for signature 20 November 1989, 1577 UNTS 3 (entered into force 2 September 1990) (CRC). Australia ratified the Convention on 17 December 1990.
6 *Convention on the Elimination of All Forms of Discrimination against Women*, opened for signature on 18 December 1979), 1249 UNTS 13 (entered into force 3 September 1981) (CEDAW). Australia ratified CEDAW on 28 July 1983.

7 *Convention on the Elimination of All Forms of Racial Discrimination*, opened for signature on 21 December 1965, 660 UNTS 195 (entered into force 4 January 1969) (CERD). Australia ratified CERD on 30 September 1975.

8 *Convention on the Rights of Persons with Disabilities*, opened for signature 13 December 2006, 2515 UNTS 3 (entered into force 30 March 2008) (CRPD). Australia ratified the CRPD on 17 July 2008.

9 *Convention against Torture and Other Cruel, Inhuman or Degrading Treatment or Punishment*, opened for signature 10 December 1984, 1465 UNTS 85 (entered into force 26 June 1987) (CAT). Australia ratified CAT on 8 August 1989.

The two core treaties that do not contain State obligations to unaccompanied child asylum seekers are the *International Convention on the Protection of the Rights of All Migrant Workers and Members of Their Families* and the *International Convention for the Protection of All Persons from Enforced Disappearance*.

10 *Convention Relating to the Status of Refugees*, opened for signature 28 July 1951, 189 UNTS 137, (entered into force 22 April 1954) (Refugee Convention). Australia acceded to the Convention on 22 January 1954.

The Refugee Convention contained both temporal and geographic limitations, referring to events before 1 January 1951 and focusing on events that had occurred in Europe. The 1967 Protocol lifted these restraints and extended the Convention protections to persons who became refugees as a result of events occurring on or after 1 January 1951. Hereafter, a reference to the Refugee Convention refers to the Refugee Convention and Protocol.

Relevantly, for the discussion about the treatment of unaccompanied child asylum seekers in Australian law that ensues in the remaining chapters, Australia has ratified all the relevant human rights treaties and the Refugee Convention.

11 For example, the right to health is protected in six treaties, the right to non-refoulement is protected in four, and the obligation to not subject persons to torture or to cruel, inhuman or degrading treatment or punishment while in immigration detention is found in eight articles in five treaties. See Articles 7 and 10 ICCPR (n 3); Articles 18 and 37(a) CRC (n 5); Articles 2 and 16 CAT (n 9); Article 15 CRPD (n 8); Article 5(b) CERD (n 7). Assessment of relevant rights becomes even more complicated when an unaccompanied child asylum seeker is situated at the intersection of multiple treaties. For example, an unaccompanied asylum-seeking girl with a disability may have a human rights claim under both the ICCPR and ICESCR in addition to the specific themed treaties, which may apply to her as well: the CRC, CEDAW, CRPD and the Refugee Convention.

12 See, for example, Conclusions on the International Protection of Refugees, adopted by the UNHCR Executive Committee, No. 47 (XXXVIII), 'Refugee Children', 1987. The same is true of soft law instruments; see in particular, UNHCR, *Refugee Children: Guidelines on Protection and Care* (Office of the UNHCR, 1994) (*Refugee Children Guidelines*) 101, 126; UNHCR, *Guidelines on Policies and Procedures in Dealing with Unaccompanied Children Seeking Asylum* (Office of the UNHCR, 1997) (*Unaccompanied Children Guidelines*) [5.7]; UNHCR, *Handbook on Procedures and Criteria for Determining Refugee Status UN Doc HCR/1P/4/ENG/REV. 3* (Office of the UNHCR, 2011) (*Refugee Status Determination Handbook*) [214].

13 In practice, these sites of vulnerability intersect, and States' human rights obligations will arise in more than one site. For example, the duty to act in the child's best interest by conducting Best Interest Assessments that comprehensively assess that child's nationality, upbringing, ethnic, cultural and linguistic background, particular vulnerabilities and protection needs responds to their cumulative vulnerability generated by their minority, separation from their par-

ents (particular vulnerabilities) and their alienage (nationality, upbringing, ethnic, cultural and linguistic background and protection needs).

14 General Comments are authoritative explanations published by treaty bodies about how the provisions of the treaties overseen by that body are to be interpreted and applied in practice.

15 For example, the Human Rights Committee, the Committee Against Torture, the Committee for the Rights of Persons with Disabilities, the Committee for the Elimination of Discrimination against Women and the Committee on the Rights of the Child.

16 Michael Freeman (ed), *Children's Rights: Progress and Perspectives* (Martinus Nijhoff, 2011) 15. Accepting that childhood is simultaneously a period and a state and that children are simultaneously beings and becomings necessarily alters our understanding of the role and realities of childhood, provides significant challenges to established paradigms and has significant implications for children's rights scholarship.

17 CRC (n 5) art 3(1). See also UN Committee on the Rights of the Child, *General Comment No. 14 The Right of the Child to Have His or Her Best Interests Taken as a Primary Consideration,* UN Doc CRC/C/GC/14 (29 May 2013) (*General Comment No. 14*) [15(a)].

18 The Best Interest Principle was previously recognised in the 1959 Declaration on the Rights of the Child, which was the precursor to the CRC.

United Nations General Assembly *Declaration of the Rights of the Child* (1959) G.A. res. 1386 (XIV), 14 U.N. GAOR Supp. (No. 16) at 19, U.N. Doc. A/4354:

> The child shall enjoy special protection, and shall be given opportunities and facilities, by law and by other means, to enable him to develop physically, mentally, morally, spiritually and socially in a healthy and normal manner and in conditions of freedom and dignity. In the enactment of laws for this purpose, the best interests of the child shall be the paramount consideration.

19 UN Committee on the Rights of the Child, *General Comment No. 14* (n 17).

20 Best interests will differ from child to child. Accordingly, an individualised assessment of children's best interests in their particular circumstances is required. See Rachel Hodgkin and Peter Newell, *Implementation Handbook for the Convention on the Rights of the Child* (UNICEF, 2002) 246.

21 Geraldine Van Bueren, *The International Law on the Rights* of *the Child* (Brill Nijhooff, 1995) 46; *Minister of Immigration and Ethnic Affairs v Teoh* (1995) 183 CLR 273 at 289 (Mason CJ and Deane J).

22 The UN Committee on the Rights of the Child has noted that 'The realisation of this obligation by State organs is key to ensuring "both the full and effective enjoyment of all the rights recognized in the Convention and the holistic development of the child"': UN Committee on the Rights of the Child, *General Comment No. 14* (n 17) [4].

23 Ibid [6(c)], [14(b)], [19].

24 UN Committee on the Rights of the Child *General Comment No. 6 (2005), Treatment of Unaccompanied and Separated Children Outside Their Country of Origin, UN Doc.CRC/GC/2005/6* (1 September 2005) (*General Comment No. 6*) [IV c].

25 *General Comment No. 14* (n 17) [49].

26 Ibid [20].

27 Ibid [1].

28 Ibid [97]. Note that reasons for decisions must explicitly state all the factual circumstances regarding the child, what elements have been found relevant in

the best interests assessment, the content of the elements in the individual case and how they have been weighted to determine the child's best interests. If the decision differs from the views of the child, the reason for that should be clearly stated. If, exceptionally, the solution chosen is not in the best interests of the child, the grounds for this must be set out to show that the child's best interests were a primary consideration despite the result.

29 Ibid [98].

30 Ibid [98].

31 Ibid [20].

32 For a comprehensive discussion of the genesis and meaning of the right to dignity, see Christopher McCrudden, 'Human Dignity and Judicial Interpretation of Human Rights' (2008) 19 *EJIL* 655.

33 Andrew Clapham, *Human Rights Obligations of Non-State Actors* (Oxford University Press, 2006) 545–546.

34 CRC (n 5) art 3(2).

35 ICCPR (n 3) arts 2, 7, 9, 10, 17; CAT (n 9) arts 2, 16; ICESCR (n 4) art 12.

36 CRC (n 5) arts 3(2), 3(3) 18(1), (2), 19, 20, 22, 19, 34, 35, 36, 37, 38, 39.

37 UN Committee on the Rights of the Child, *General Comment No. 13 The Right of the Child to Freedom from All Forms of Violence*, UN Doc CRC/C/GC/13 (18 April 2011) (*General Comment No. 13*) [37].

38 CRC (n 5) art 37(a).

39 CRC (n 5) 37(b) and ICCPR (n 3) art 9(1). The Refugee Convention Guidelines also require States to ensure that unaccompanied asylum-seeking children are not detained for immigration reasons. UNHCR, *Global Consultations on International Protection/Third Track: Asylum Processes, EC/GC/01/12* (31 May 2001) *(Fair and Efficient Asylum Procedures)* [46].

40 UN Human Rights Committee, *A v Australia, Communication No. 560/1993, U.N. Doc. CCPR/C/59/D/560/1993* (30 April 1997) [9.2]; UN Human Rights Committee, *Van Alphen v. The Netherlands, Communication No. 305/1988, U.N. Doc. CCPR/C/39/D/305/1988* (23 July 1990) [5.8].

41 UN Committee on the Rights of the Child, *General Comment No. 13* (n 37) [46].

42 UN Committee on the Rights of the Child, *Guidelines on Determining the Best Interests of the Child* (2008), 70.

43 CRC (n 5) art 39.

44 Ibid art 27.

45 Traditionally, in international law, the right to development was construed as encompassing the protection of children's socio-psychological development to secure their future as adults consistent with 'the human becomings' construction of childhood, as discussed in Chapter 2. However, since 2013, scholars, such as Noam Peleg, have advocated for a more comprehensive child's right to development framework. Peleg conducted a systematic analysis of the meaning of the child's legal right to development analysing UN Committee on the Rights of the Child's jurisprudence from 1993 and 2010 and concluded that, in that period, the Committee overlooked 'development' itself as a human right, focusing instead on the protection of children's socio-psychological development. Peleg's conception of the child's right to development is congruent with understandings of the being/becoming child, as it 'accommodates a hybrid conception of childhood, a respect for children's agency, recognition of the importance of the process of maturation ('development') as well as its outcome, and a cross-disciplinary understanding of "development"'.

See Noam Peleg, *The Child's Right to Development* (Doctoral Thesis, University College, London, 2013); Michael Freeman, 'The Human Rights of Children' (2010) 63 *Current Legal Problems* 1.

46 CRC (n 5) arts 28, 29; ICESCR (n 4) art 13.
47 CRC (n 5) art 31.
48 For children seeking asylum with their parents, States also have an obligation to protect children's families from arbitrary or unlawful interference: ibid arts 8(1), 9, 10.
49 Ibid art 24.
50 Ibid art 8.
51 Ibid art 20.
52 Ibid art 12.
53 See Anne Graham, Jenni Whelan and Robyn Fitzgerald, 'Progressing Participation: Taming the Space between Rhetoric and Reality' (2006) 16(2) *Children, Youth and Environments* 231, 252.
54 UNHCR, *Advisory Opinion on the Extraterritorial Application of Non-Refoulement Obligations under the 1951 Convention Relating to the Status of Refugees and Its 1967 Protocol*, 26 January 2007, [5]; UNHCR Executive Committee, *Conclusion No. 6 (XXVIII): Non-Refoulement*, 1977, [(c)].
55 Although the Refugee Convention explicitly refers to refugees in Article 31, the UNHCR has clarified that the duty of non-refoulement applies to asylum seekers also. UNHCR, *Advisory Opinion on the Extraterritorial Application of Non-Refoulement Obligations under the 1951 Convention Relating to the Status of Refugees and Its 1967 Protocol* (UNHCR, 2007) 3.
56 Refugee Convention (nl 0) art 33(1); CAT (n 9) arts 3, 16; CRC (n 5) arts 6, 37; ICCPR (n 3) arts 2, 6, 7. The prohibition is expressed in the Refugee Convention, CAT and CRC and implied in the ICCPR. See UN Human Rights Committee, *General Comment No. 31 [80]: The Nature of the General Legal Obligation Imposed on States Parties to the Covenant*, CCPR/C/21/Rev.1/Add.13, 26 May 2004 (*General Comment No. 31*), [12].
57 UNHCR, *Advisory Opinion on the Extraterritorial Application of Non-refoulement Obligations under the 1951 Convention Relating to the Status of Refugees and Its 1967 Protocol* (26 January 2007), [6]; UN Committee on the Rights of the Child, *General Comment No. 6* (n 24) [27].
58 The Refugee Convention contains an exception to the principle of non-refoulement in Article 33(2). A refugee will not be protected against refoulement if there are reasonable grounds for regarding them as a danger to the security of the State or if they have been convicted by a final judgment of a particularly serious crime that constitutes a danger to the community. However, as Jane McAdam and Guy Goodwin-Gill have argued, State non-refoulement obligations under the ICCPR and CAT apply to all people without exception, thus imposing a stricter non-refoulement obligation on States than Article 33(2) of the Refugee Convention. See Guy Goodwin-Gill and Jane McAdam, *The Refugee in International Law* (Oxford, 2007) 243–244.
59 UN Committee on the Rights of the Child, *General Comment No. 6* (n 24) [26]–[27].
60 See *United Nations Convention on the Law of the Sea*, opened for signature 10 December 1982, 1833 UNTS 396 (entered into force 16 November 1994); Natalie Klein, 'Assessing Australia's Push Back the Boats Policy under International Law: Legality and Accountability for Maritime Interceptions of Irregular Migrants' [2014] 15 *Melbourne Journal of International Law* 1; Ivan Shearer, 'Problems of Jurisdiction and Law Enforcement against Delinquent Vessels' (1986) 35 *International and Comparative Law Quarterly* 320, 330; Yoshifumi Tanaka, *The International Law of the Sea* (Cambridge University Press, 2012) 123; Donald R. Rothwell and Tim Stephens, *The International Law of the Sea* (Hart, 2010) 80.
61 Natalie Klein (n 60) 6.

62 UN High Commissioner for Refugees, *Protection Policy Paper: Maritime Interception Operations and the Processing of International Protection Claims: Legal Standards and Policy Considerations with Respect to Extraterritorial Processing* (UNHCR, 2010) [55].
63 CRC (n 5) art 22(1).
64 Refugee Convention (n 10) arts 1, 31, 33.
65 UNHCR *Refugee Status Determination Handbook* (n 12); UNHCR, *Unaccompanied Children Guidelines* (n 12); UNHCR, *Refugee Children Guidelines* (n 12). See also UNHCR, *Global Consultations on International Protection/Third Track: Asylum Processes (Fair and Efficient Asylum Procedures)* (n 39).
66 UNHCR, *Unaccompanied Children Guidelines* (n 12) [8.2].
67 Ibid [8.2]. See also UN Human Rights Committee, *General Comment No. 13* (n 37) [1], [17] regarding the correct interpretation of Article 14 of the ICCPR.
68 UNHCR, *Global Consultations on International Protection/Third Track: Asylum Processes (Fair and Efficient Asylum Procedures)* (n 39) [44], [50].
69 Ibid [46].
70 Ibid.
71 Human Rights Committee, *General Comment No. 18, Non-Discrimination, UN Doc CCPR/C/21/Rev.1/Add. 1* (1989), [5], [10].
72 ICCPR (n 3) arts 2(1) and 26.
73 ICESCR (n 4) art 2(2).
74 CRC (n 5) art 2.
75 Ibid [13].
76 A permissible purpose would be, for example, where differential treatment is required to protect the human rights of other persons.
77 UN Conference of Plenipotentiaries on the Status of Refugees and Stateless Persons, *Final Act of the United Nations Conference of Plenipotentiaries on the Status of Refugees and Stateless Persons, UN Doc A/CONF.2/108/Rev.1,* (25 July 1951) (*UN Conference of Plenipotentiaries*) para B(2).
78 CRC (n 5) arts 20, 22.
79 Ibid art 21: 'A child temporarily or permanently deprived of his or her family environment, or in whose own best interests cannot be allowed to remain in that environment, shall be entitled to special protection and assistance provided by the State'.
80 Ibid art 22: 'States Parties shall take appropriate measures to ensure that a child who is seeking refugee status or who is considered a refugee in accordance with applicable international or domestic law and procedures shall, whether unaccompanied or accompanied by his or her parents or by any other person, receive appropriate protection and humanitarian assistance in the enjoyment of applicable rights set forth in the present Convention and in other international human rights or humanitarian instruments to which the said States are Parties'.
81 Note that there are potentially additional obligations on States in which an unaccompanied minor is a victim of trafficking, has a disability or there are additional factors of vulnerability. Under Article 39 of CRC, States are obliged to take all appropriate measures to promote physical and psychological recovery and social reintegration of child victims of 'any neglect, exploitation, or abuse; torture or any other form of cruel, inhuman or degrading treatment or punishment; or armed conflicts'. The health, self-respect and dignity of the child should dictate the environment in which the recovery and reintegration takes place. Moreover, under Article 23 of the CRC, mentally or physically disabled children have the right to enjoy a full and decent life, in conditions which ensure dignity, promote self-reliance and facilitate active participation in the community and Article 1 of the CRPD obliges States to 'promote, protect and ensure the full and equal

enjoyment of all human rights and fundamental freedoms by all persons with disabilities and to promote respect for their inherent dignity'.

82 UNHCR, *Unaccompanied Children Guidelines* (n 12) [5.7].

83 UNHCR, *Refugee Children Guidelines* (n 12) 126.

84 *General Comment No. 6* (n 24) [21].

85 *UN Conference of Plenipotentiaries* (n 77) para B(2). Although the Final Act of the Conference that adopted the Refugee Convention recommended that governments take the necessary measures for 'the protection of refugees who are minors, in particular unaccompanied children and girls, with special reference to guardianship and adoption'.

86 UNHCR, *Refugee Children Guidelines* (n 12) 101, 126; UNHCR, *Unaccompanied Children Guidelines* (n 12) [5.7]; UNHCR, *Refugee Status Determination Handbook* (n 12) [214].

87 Besides *General Comment No. 6* (n 24), the *Refugee Children Guidelines* (n 12) and *Unaccompanied Children Guidelines* (n 12) provide further direction for States discharging guardianship obligations to unaccompanied children in accordance with international legal obligations.

88 UN Committee on the Rights of the Child, *General Comment No. 6* (n 24) [33]–[38].

89 Ibid [33].

90 Ibid [69]. This includes representation in proceedings implementing durable solutions, including any appeals or reviews.

91 Ibid [35].

92 Ibid [37].

93 This is despite the extensive obligations that persist even after these children have been transferred to offshore processing centres.

94 This reflects the principle in common law legal systems that agreeing to be bound by a treaty is the responsibility of the executive in the exercise of its prerogative power, while the parliament retains responsibility for law-making. Most common law countries require specific enabling legislation to be passed by the Commonwealth Parliament and/or state and territory parliaments to incorporate the provisions of treaties into domestic law for the provisions of a treaty to have domestic effect. In Australia, for example, Section 51(xxix) of the Australian Constitution, gives the Commonwealth Parliament the power to enact legislation that implements the terms of those international agreements to which Australia is a party. In contrast, in monist legal systems, States' international treaty obligations are automatically incorporated into domestic law.

95 See ss 11(1)(e)–(f).

96 For further explanation of Australia's implementation of its human rights obligations, see Michael Kirby, 'Domestic Implementation of International Human Rights Norms' [1999] 5(2) *Australian Journal of Human Rights* 109.

97 See Janet Phillips, 'Boat Arrivals and Boat "Turnbacks" in Australia Since 1976: A Quick Guide to the Statistics', *Parliamentary Library Research Paper Series 2016–2017*, 2 (Boat Arrivals Since 1976). In 2013, 300 boats arrived carrying 20,587 asylum seekers. The government has reported that one boat arrived in 2014 and none in 2015 or 2016. Phillips reports that 2014 arrivals 'include 2 medical transfers on 31 January and 2 February 2014 from SIEV 879 (this boat was reportedly 'turned back' and not counted as an arrival); 157 people on board a boat from India intercepted on 27 July 2014 – the passengers were subsequently transferred to Curtin Detention Centre and then to Nauru for processing (this boat was counted as an arrival, but 41 people on board another boat intercepted at the same time were returned to Sri Lankan authorities at sea); and one Sri Lankan national on board a boat intercepted on 15 November 2014, who was referred for refugee determination and transferred to Manus Island

for processing (the 37 other passengers were transferred at sea to Sri Lankan authorities and the boat was not counted as an 'arrival')'.

98 The *Migration Reform Act 1992* (Cth), which came into effect on 1 September 1994.

99 Human Rights and Equal Opportunity Commission, *A Last Resort? National Inquiry into Children in Immigration Detention*, (Commonwealth Government, 2004) *(A Last Resort?)*; Australian Human Rights Commission, *The Forgotten Children: National Inquiry into Children in Immigration Detention* (Commonwealth Government, 2014) (*The Forgotten Children Inquiry*).

100 Human Rights and Equal Opportunity Commission, *A Last Resort?* (n 99) 5, 283–356.

Australian Human Rights Commission, *The Forgotten Children Inquiry* (n 99), 29, 54, 62,151–169, 192–195.

Relevantly, *The Forgotten Children Inquiry Report* also found that the detention of all children who arrive without a visa as the first and only option without special considerations for unaccompanied children constituted a breach of Articles 37(b) and 20(1) of the CRC, 241.

101 Human Rights and Equal Opportunity Commission, *A Last Resort?* (n 99) 297.

102 See, for example, Mary Crock, '"You Have to be Stronger than Razor Wire": Legal Issues Relating to the Detention of Refugees and Asylum Seekers' (2002) 10 *Australian Journal of Administrative Law* 33; Tania Penovic, 'Immigration Detention of Children: Arbitrary Deprivation of Liberty' (2003) 7 *Newcastle Law Review* 56; Tania Penovic and Adiva Sifris, 'Children's Rights through the Lens of Immigration Detention' (2006) 20 *Australian Journal of Family Law* 12; Tania Penovic, 'The Separation of Powers: *Lim* and the 'Voluntary' Immigration Detention of Children' (2004) 29 *Alternative Law Journal* 222; Andreas Schloenhardt, 'Deterrence, Detention and Denial: Asylum Seekers in Australia' (2002) 22 *University of Queensland Law Journal* 54; Andreas Schloenhardt, 'To Deter, Detain and Deny: Protection of Onshore Asylum Seekers in Australia' (2002) 14 *International Journal of Refugee Law* 302.

103 Janet Phillips and Harriet Spinks 'Immigration Detention in Australia' *Parliament of Australia Background Note* (Department of Parliamentary Services, 2013), 2.

104 See for example, Kazimierz Bem et al., *A Price Too High: The Cost of Australia's Approach to Asylum Seekers: The Australian Government's Policy of Offshore Processing of Asylum Seekers on Nauru, Manus Island and Christmas Island* (A Just Australia and Oxfam Australia, 2007).

105 Figures provided in response to Questions on Notice, Senate Legal and Constitutional hearings into the Migration Amendment (Designated Unauthorised Arrivals) Bill 2006, 26 May 2006.

106 Kazimierz Bem et al. (n 104) 17.

107 Jane McAdam and Kate Purcell, 'Refugee Protection in the Howard Tears: Obstructing the Right to Seek Asylum' (2008) 27 *Australian Year Book of International Law* 87; Susan Kneebone, 'The Pacific Plan: The Provision of 'Effective Protection'?' (2006) 18 *International Journal of Refugee Law* 696; Savitri Taylor, 'The Pacific Solution or a Pacific nightmare?: The Difference between Burden Shifting and Responsibility Sharing' (2005) 6 *Asian-Pacific Law and Policy Journal* 1; Mary Crock, 'In the Wake of the Tampa: Conflicting Visions of International Refugee Law in the Management of Refugee Flows' (2003) 12 *Pacific Rim Policy Journal* 49; Penelope Mathew, 'Australian Refugee Protection in the Wake of the *Tampa*' (2002) 96 *American Journal of International Law* 661.

108 George Roberts, 'UNHCR Interviews Asylum Seekers over Forced Return to Indonesia', *AM* (online at 18 March 2014 <http://www.abc.net.au/am/content/2014/s3965710.htm>; Michael Bachelard, 'Investigation: 'Burned Hands'

on the High Seas', *Sydney Morning Herald* (online at 7 February 2014) <http://www.smh.com.au/world/investigation-burned-hands-on-the-high-seas-20140206-hvbdl.html#ixzz2salkUX2y>; Peter Alford, 'ABC Navy Brutality Reports Unravel', *The Australian* (online at 1 February 2014) <http://www.theaustralian.com.au/news/abc-navybrutality-reports-unravel/story-e6frg6n6-1226815392921>.

109 Janet Phillips, Boat Arrivals Since 1976 (n 97) 5–6.

110 See UNHCR, *Mission to the Republic of Nauru, 3 to 5 December 2012 report* (UNHCR, 2012) and UNHCR, *Monitoring Visit to the Republic of Nauru 7 to 9 October 2013* (UNHCR, 2013).

111 Australian Human Rights Commission, *The Forgotten Children Inquiry,* (n 99) Senate Legal and Constitutional Affairs Committee, *Conditions and Treatment of Asylum Seekers and Refugees at the Regional Processing Centres in the Republic of Nauru and Papua New Guinea* (Commonwealth Government, 2016); Philip Moss, *Review into Recent Allegations Relating to Conditions and Circumstances at the Regional Processing Centre in Nauru Final Report* (Department of Immigration and Border Protection, 2015); Amnesty International, *Nauru Offshore Processing Facility Review 2012* (Amnesty, 2012); Amnesty International, *Island of Despair: Australia's 'Processing' of Refugees on Nauru* (Amnesty, 2016); Human Rights Watch and Amnesty International, *Australia: Appalling Abuse, Neglect of Refugees on Nauru: Investigation on Remote Pacific Island Finds Deliberate Abuse Hidden Behind Wall of Secrecy* (online at 2 August 2016) <https://www.hrw.org/news/2016/08/02/australia-appalling-abuse-neglect-refugees-nauru>. The Australian Churches Refugee Taskforce, *All the Lonely Children: Questions for Policy Makers Regarding Guardianship for Unaccompanied Minors* (Australian Churches, 2013) reported on existing and emerging concerns regarding the guardianship of refugee and asylum-seeking children in 2012–2013. Wendy Bacon et al., *Protection Denied, Abuse Condoned: Women on Nauru at Risk*, (Australian Women in Support of Women on Nauru, 2016) (online 22 July 2016) <https://www.asrc.org.au/2016/07/22/protection-denied-abuse-condoned-women-on-nauru-at-risk-report/>. Lastly, see Paul Farrell et al., 'The Nauru Files: Cache of 2,000 Leaked Reports Reveal Scale of Abuse of Children in Offshore Detention', *The Guardian (Australia)*, (online at 10 August 2016) <https://www.theguardian.com/australia-news/2016/aug/10/the-nauru-files-2000-leaked-reports-reveal-scale-of-abuse-of-children-in-australian-offshore-detention>.

112 See the Australian Churches Refugee Taskforce (n 111). Mary Crock and Mary-Anne Kenny, 'Rethinking the Guardianship of Refugee Children after the Malaysia Solution' (2012) 34 *Sydney Law Review* 437 and legal practitioners including Julie Taylor, 'Guardianship of Child Asylum-Seekers' 34(1) (2006) *Federal Law Review* 204 and Maria O'Sullivan, 'The 'Best Interests' of Asylum-Seeker Children: Who's Guarding the Guardian?' (2013) 38(4) *Alternative Law Journal* 228. Also, the Australian Human Rights Commission, *The Forgotten Children Inquiry* (n 99) found that 'the Minister for Immigration and Border Protection does not meet the criteria set out by the Committee on the Rights of the Child (in para 33 of *General Comment No. 6*) to effectively perform the role of guardian for unaccompanied children)', 171.

113 The relevant guardianship case law in the context of unaccompanied children prior to the 2012 statutory amendments has been extensively examined by academics, notably Mary Crock and Mary-Anne Kenny (n 112) and legal practitioners, including Julie Taylor (n 112) and Maria O'Sullivan (n 112).

4 The potential of expanding vulnerability theory to prioritise State responses to unaccompanied asylum-seeking children

4.1 Introduction

This book, so far, has laid the foundation for a reconceptualisation of the way we respond to the vulnerabilities of unaccompanied asylum-seeking children. The extent and urgency of their need for State protection is made clear by examining their triple vulnerability. International human rights law establishes substantive and unambiguous obligations on States to protect, assist and act in unaccompanied children's best interests while their claims are processed, recognising that they are among the world's most vulnerable children. However, this does not necessarily create enforceable domestic legal obligations. Australia's extensive human rights obligations to these children would, if fully realised, be sufficient to address their triple vulnerability. Yet, domestic laws and policies do not adequately require the realisation of these obligations and have, in practice, been insufficient to prevent acute harms. We need a new approach that exposes what is at stake for unaccompanied child asylum seekers when laws and policies close off the possibility of human rights protections and prioritises responding to unaccompanied minors' most acute sites of vulnerability.

This chapter argues that vulnerability theory provides a compelling supplementary normative, ethical justification to hold States accountable domestically for the way they respond to unaccompanied asylum-seeking children. Its central utility is its alternative anchoring in vulnerability rather than human rights. Therefore, the theory is suited to arguing for an immediate State response to this triply vulnerable group without diminishing the significance of a human rights standard for all asylum seekers. But vulnerability theory, as traditionally conceived, excludes unaccompanied non-citizen children from its protective scope because scholars have implicitly restricted analysis of States' obligations on account of vulnerability to citizens.[1] I argue that while human rights and vulnerability theory both have gaps that currently prevent them from effectively responding to these children's urgent and acute needs, the gap in vulnerability theory can, and ought to, be closed by expanding its scope to encompass unaccompanied asylum-seeking children. In this chapter, I argue that, so extended, vulnerability theory provides the necessary normative justification for a supplementary framework that grounds States' domestic obligation to respond to

DOI: 10.4324/9781003260134-5

these children's triple vulnerability without displacing the broader framework of human rights.

4.2 The conceptual foundations of vulnerability theory

The notion of vulnerability is not new in law, having ancient origins in common law equitable jurisdictions and the provision of legal guardianship mechanisms. Discussions of the specific vulnerability of certain populations and groups and the adequacy of legal responses to those groups feature prominently and extensively in scholarly research on ethics, law and human rights.[2] As referenced in this book, vulnerability theory was articulated as an alternative to existing identity-based equality models in law by Martha Fineman in 2008. It is a distinct theory that captures and extends beyond general discussions of vulnerability.

Fineman's vulnerability theory essentially proposes a reconceptualisation of the relationship between the State and its subjects. The foundation for this reconceptualisation is recognition that actual and potential vulnerability is a universal and constant attribute of all humans. A key conceptual strength of vulnerability theory is that it highlights the normative relevance of embodied vulnerability and the ensuing inequalities deriving from distinct individual embodied experiences.[3] It exposes how all people, simply by virtue of their physical embodiment, require specific conditions for survival and are necessarily socially and relationally dependent on others at some points of their lives (including, at least, as babies/children and again in old age). People are also universally susceptible to dependency at other points because their embodiment makes them prone to illness and injury and susceptible to harm as a consequence of social, economic and political events.

By articulating our shared universal vulnerability, this theory challenges the classical liberal paradigm of the rational, free-choosing, autonomous and able-bodied person of equal standing in society in relation to others.[4] It rejects this invulnerable, disembodied and de-contextualised liberal subject in favour of a vulnerable subject.[5] Fineman and subsequent vulnerability theorists have resisted the restriction of the concept of vulnerability 'to defined groups of fledgling or stigmatized subjects'[6] as well as associations of vulnerability with 'victimhood, deprivation, dependency, or pathology'.[7] Rather, they posit vulnerability as a preferable and more authentic justification to protect classes and group identities (such as race and gender) for anchoring substantive equality and distributive justice in liberal democracies.[8]

Premising analysis on the vulnerable subject rather than the traditional liberal subject disrupts the persistence of inequality that flows from analysis being normatively premised on privileged white males. It also profoundly impacts on challenging assumptions underpinning the law in liberal democracies, which are equally premised on citizens as purportedly free-choosing, autonomous and able-bodied legal subjects of equal standing. Vulnerability theory unpicks the relationships between people's vulnerability and their social, political and economic positioning in society by examining the interconnectedness of individuals' distinct experiences and their accumulation of resilience. This approach challenges the liberal assumption that individuals have equal opportunities to accumulate resources or access social or institutional support.[9]

Grounded in the reality that humans are interdependent for the fulfilment of our needs, vulnerability theory highlights the ways that State action/inaction is either vulnerability-mitigating and resilience-building for these unequally positioned groups or resilience-degrading and dependency-increasing. It also reveals the structural biases and harms embedded in, and obscured by, political and legal institutions. Vulnerability theory ultimately tugs at the stitching of conventional liberal philosophy premised on limited State responsibilities to able-bodied legal subjects of equal standing and, instead, argues that the logical corollary of the vulnerable subject is what Fineman calls the responsive State.[10] Attending to the responsive State, as illustrated in Figure 4.1, 'The relationship between group vulnerability and the responsive State' enables interrogation of a causative relationship between State laws and policies and the resiliencies and dependencies of specified groups.

Governments are responsible for reducing, mediating and ameliorating the unequal burden on individuals whose vulnerabilities are generated by normative social, political and institutional inequalities by programmatic, structural and institutional reform.[11]

The remedy proposed by vulnerability theory is to premise any analysis of social institutions and socio-political structures on the vulnerable subject. This disrupts the inequality that necessarily flows when analysis is premised on the traditional liberal subject, on an individualistic conception of autonomy and the incorrect presumption that we are *a priori* equally positioned in society.[12] The

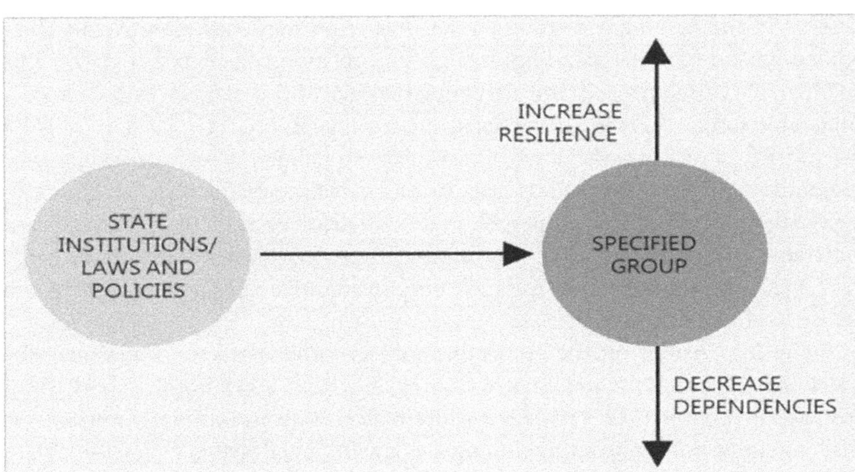

Figure 4.1 The relationship between group vulnerability and the responsive State

appropriate State response is to reduce the unequal burden on individuals with vulnerabilities generated by normative social, legal, political and institutional inequalities by assisting them to accumulate resiliencies (physical, human, social and environmental assets or resources). This will address the effects of vulnerability and gradually remedy it.

Vulnerability has been criticised for being 'slippery'.[13] Scholars have cautioned that vulnerability theory's perceived 'conceptual fluidity' impedes its clarity as an analytical tool and inhibits its practical application for interventions in law or public policy.[14] Indeed, Terry Carney has argued that while 'usages differ across disciplines, none pin down its meaning with much precision and law is no exception – vulnerability theory remains too capacious and ill-defined to provide more than false hope in substantive reform of social security law'.[15]

Legal scholars have begun work to address this lack of specificity in exploring the application of vulnerability theory to the law. These include Jonathan Herring in children's law as well as family and carers law,[16] Beverley Clough in disability scholarship[17] and Terry Carney in social security law.[18] However, more theoretical work is needed to refine vulnerability theory as a tool for legal analysis. The distinction between scholarship that explicitly applies vulnerability theory and scholarship that discusses the relationship between the law and vulnerable populations without engaging vulnerability theory is instrumental. This is because the failure to engage (or not) explicitly with vulnerability theory may contribute to a perception that vulnerability theory, rather than the concept of vulnerability itself, is overly capacious. In this book, I have addressed this distinction in practice by distinguishing between the vulnerability of unaccompanied child asylum seekers, in the ordinary sense in the discussion in Chapters 2 and 3, and the application of vulnerability theory in this and the following chapters.

This book applies vulnerability theory in the context of asylum-seeker rights and border protection to flesh out what might constitute a necessary State response in practice. Despite its critics, vulnerability theorists argue that a rethinking of the traditional structure of legal regulation ought to logically follow from recognising all people's mutual vulnerability and reliance on State assistance.[19] Herring has argued that 'a legal response based on a norm of vulnerable people would be a more realistic and effective one'.[20] I agree. I argue that applying vulnerability theory in the particular context of State border regulation practices has two key instrumental values. First, comprehending the universal dependence of unaccompanied child asylum seekers on the State *and* the particularity of their vulnerability is necessary to determine a requisite holistic response to them as being/becoming children. Second, it clarifies how the law particularly privileges and provides for the normative liberal subject and fails those who are not[21] and identifies the sites where those failures manifest to address them better.

Unaccompanied child asylum seekers are vulnerable, like all humans, because childhood is a universal time of precariousness in which children are dependent on adults to meet their care, protection and development needs.[22] Vulnerability theory resists construing an individual or group as more or less vulnerable, uniquely vulnerable or specifically or especially vulnerable being premised, as it is, on vulnerability being both universal and constant. On a surface reading, this seems to resist acknowledging that layers of interwoven vulnerabilities may underpin the universal vulnerability of particular individuals or groups, such as unaccompanied child asylum seekers. Vulnerability theory is not blind to these. Instead of comparing individuals or groups as *prima facie* more or less vulnerable, it accommodates particular vulnerabilities at the point of an individual's or group's increased dependency or increased resilience, as amplified by State practice. In this way, vulnerability theory acknowledges their universal vulnerability as normatively dependent children[23] and their dependence on State practice as an area that can either increase their dependencies or build their resilience by addressing their complex triple burden of minority, alienage, and separation from their parents.[24]

The law commonly privileges and provides for the normative liberal subject and fails the vulnerable.[25] Here, vulnerability theory chimes most clearly for the need for disruption. Herring succinctly captures the argument:

> the role of the law can shift to restricting and reducing the power of the powerful, rather than seeking to protect the vulnerable from an exercise of power. Those labelled 'vulnerable' are not some pre-existing category but better seen as having been labelled as such in order to legitimate political ends and to justify current inequalities.[26]

In States such as Australia, disruption is especially necessary for unaccompanied child asylum seekers who are demonised to legitimate and justify border securitisation practices and rhetoric in defiance of the States' obligations as the paradigmatic duty-holder to respond to these children upon arrival.[27]

Vulnerability theory provides a new way of looking at the relationship between the State and the non-citizen child seeking asylum *and* States' accountability for the impact of State practice that arises from this special relationship. Recognising that unaccompanied children's experience of vulnerability, like all peoples, is shaped by their social, economic and political positioning in society allows vulnerability theory to interrogate government choices about the quantity and quality of assistance provided to these children through State programs, institutions, laws and policies and the way that this contributes to their accumulation or degradation of resilience. By illuminating their profound dependence on the State by virtue of their minority and by being unauthorised in a State and seeking asylum without parents to mediate, compensate and lessen their vulnerability and to support and develop their resilience, vulnerability theory emphasises the responsibility of the government to mediate, compensate and lessen their vulnerability. As discussed in Chapter 2, because the provision of legal guardians is the States' normal legal response to the arrival of unaccompanied children in their jurisdiction, vulnerability theory also exposes the imperative significance of their legal guardian as a gatekeeper of their access to State institutions that provide primary care, protection, development and legal services.

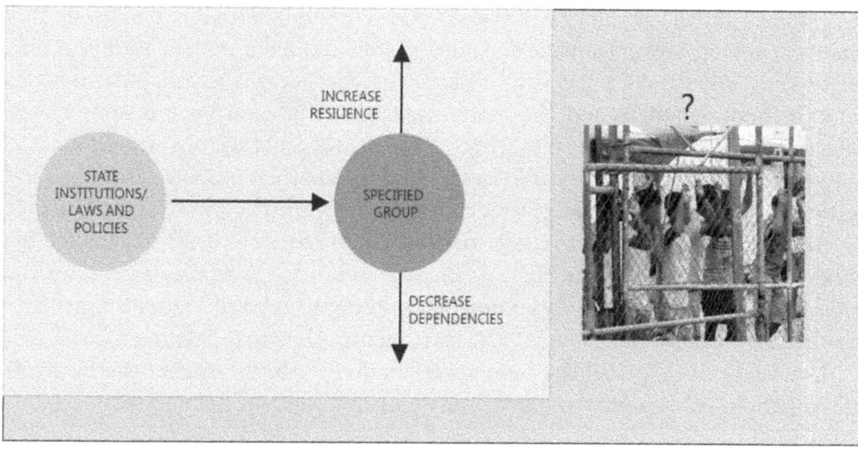

Figure 4.2 Vulnerability theory as a supplementary imperative for an urgent response to non-citizen children?

Vulnerability scholarship, thus, connects the relationship between these children's vulnerability and the impact of State practice and State responsibilities for its legitimised and empowered institutions that increase or undermine these children's resiliencies.[28] But, as noted in Section 4.1, vulnerability theory has traditionally been confined to citizens as liberal subjects and excludes these children, as depicted in Figure 4.2, 'Vulnerability theory as a supplementary imperative for an urgent response to non-citizen children?'

The following section argues that vulnerability theory should be expanded to apply to unaccompanied child asylum seekers because their vulnerability and the nature of their spatial, temporal and relational proximity to the territory of a State legitimately brings them within vulnerability theory's protective scope.

4.3 Expanding vulnerability theory beyond the citizen insider to encompass unaccompanied child asylum seekers: the proximate vulnerable child

Fineman has stated in passing that non-citizens 'should be afforded equality on the same terms as citizens if they are residents of the state or long term visitors or have some *other connection* that would make placing state responsibility for them and their situation appropriate' (emphasis added).[29] I argue that the highlighted reference to *other connections* is vital in expanding vulnerability theory to unaccompanied child asylum seekers. Specifically, their physical, temporal and *relational* proximity to the State provides the basis for this sufficient other connection that obliges the responsive State to take responsibility for them.

Proximity encapsulates an unaccompanied child asylum seeker's physical and temporal presence but also the relative closeness and distance in the relationship between them and the State. Unaccompanied child asylum seekers under Australia's control are directly physically and temporally proximate in a way that children seeking asylum outside Australia's jurisdiction are not. In addition, they are directly relationally proximate because the absence of their parents to act as a buffer between them and the State places them in a direct and unmediated relationship of dependence on the State. This convergence of their urgent need to have their acute triple vulnerability responded to *and* their physical, temporal and relational proximity to the State situates them in a heightened state of dependence on the State. This convergence, captured by the category of 'proximate vulnerable children', generates the sufficient *other connection* that warrants extending the protective scope of Fineman's vulnerability theory to expand State responsibility for them, as illustrated in Figure 4.3, 'Proximate vulnerable children'.

The category of 'proximate vulnerable children' brings together the elements of their triple vulnerability and proximity and captures three elements:

- unaccompanied child asylum seekers' inherent exposure to harm and dependency as being/becoming asylum-seeking children;
- their physical and temporal presence in the State where they are unauthorised non-citizens seeking asylum; and
- the unmediated relationship between the child and the border protection machinery of the State because they are without an adult caregiver or State of nationality willing or able to offer protection.

Without parents to care for and protect them and provide for their development during the processing of the claim for asylum or to stake their claim for non-refoulement or asylum due to the failure of their State of nationality to provide them with protection, their dependence on the proximate State to provide this care and these protections is absolute. This relationship of direct physical

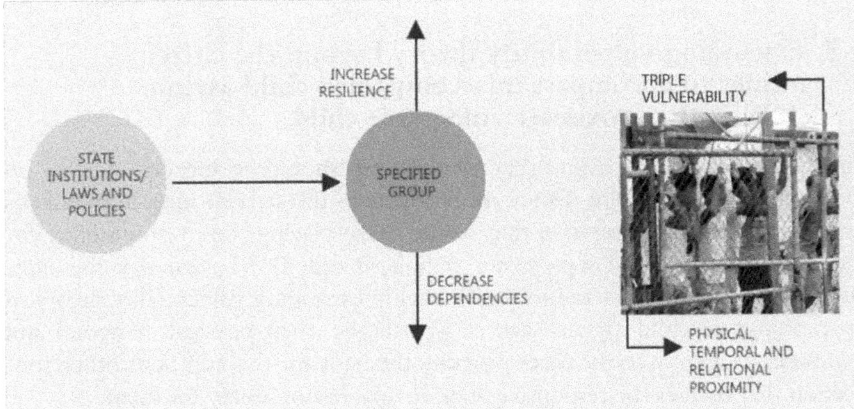

Figure 4.3 Proximate vulnerable children

proximity, along with the child's direct and unmediated dependence on the State, triggers specific State obligations to respond to them. The State is singularly positioned to exacerbate or ameliorate their vulnerabilities by permitting or restricting their access to assistance and resources.

Confining vulnerability theory to 'citizens' would discriminate against other categories of 'subject', the nature of whose 'connections' generate ethically compelling claims to a State response to their vulnerability. Unaccompanied child asylum seekers' acute burden of vulnerability constitutes such a connection. Reading vulnerability theory expansively to encompass these non-citizen children delineates the impact of State practice on them and its role in increasing their resiliencies and decreasing their dependencies, as well as enabling the prioritisation of law and policy reforms to redress vulnerability in a way that human rights law does not. As discussed in Chapter 3, human rights law lacks a compelling domestic accountability mechanism to ultimately 'close the case' for these children to have the State address their vulnerabilities. Yet, for vulnerability theory, the corollary of recognising the particular vulnerability of people is a requisite State response that eliminates and does not create sites of vulnerability. Vulnerability theory provides a supplementary normative framework for holding States to account for their role in ameliorating or exacerbating these children's vulnerabilities without displacing the broader framework of human rights.

The next section applies a mitigating vulnerability framework to a concrete analysis of the role of the 'responsive state' to these children in domestic law and policy.

4.4 Determining what constitutes a mitigating vulnerability framework

Applying vulnerability theory must do more than mark when legal measures or remedies for vulnerability are required because ordinary extant usage of the term vulnerability in the law and public policy already does that. Vulnerability theory has been justifiably criticised for its limited proscriptive value as a tool for defining the appropriate role of government.[30] Existing legal scholarship identifies both the difficulty in and the necessity for vulnerability theory to articulate the content of necessary interventions for its application in concrete situations.[31] Carney especially has isolated the undeveloped notion of the 'responsive state' as a critical gap in applying extant vulnerability theory in legal scholarship.[32]

Fineman's vulnerability theory stops short of the specificity required to determine the content of a mitigating vulnerability framework, how to assess the impact of State practice in increasing resiliencies and decreasing dependencies in a particular context or how to prioritise reforms to decrease dependencies.

What, then, is the State's required mitigating vulnerability framework to the proximate vulnerable child? Is their *other connection* sufficient to generate obligations identical to those that the State has to its citizens, or are the obligations different? What is the relevance, if any, of the fact that, unless they are granted residence as refugees, their connection is temporary?

This section argues that close analysis of the sites and sources of the vulnerability of proximate vulnerable children reveals that the requisite State response is necessarily context dependent. It contends that the gravity of the consequences of States' failure to respond to these children's acute and urgent vulnerabilities on arrival necessitates prioritising addressing new vulnerabilities generated by, and existing vulnerabilities that are exacerbated by, relevant laws and policies. It also argues that a universal three-stage process can be applied to determine the appropriate mitigating vulnerability framework in a particular context. Chapters 5, 6 and 7 then apply this process to examine the requisite mitigating vulnerability framework to the specific context of unaccompanied child asylum seekers in Australia following the suite of legislative and policy amendments between 2012 and 2014.

4.4.1 Distinguishing between multiple vulnerabilities

4.4.1.1 Embedding a taxonomy to distinguish between vulnerabilities

Fineman's vulnerability theory does not incorporate a taxonomy that distinguishes between types of vulnerabilities in practice. A taxonomy is necessary for three reasons. First, so that vulnerability theory can be utilised in practice in specific contexts to characterise interactions between an individual and the relevant social, political and legal structures as ameliorating or worsening vulnerability. Second, to delineate sources of vulnerabilities. Third, to inform and prioritise law and policy reforms.

To address this, the mitigating vulnerability framework that I propose embeds a vulnerability taxonomy developed in philosophy scholarship by Mackenzie, Rogers and Dodds[33] to distinguish between inherent, situational, occurrent and pathogenic vulnerabilities.[34] By distinguishing between sources and states of vulnerability generated by the operation of laws and policies in specific contexts, this response enables scrutiny of the causes and impact of intersecting sites of vulnerability and prioritisation of reforms, supplementing traditional human rights analysis.

Mackenzie, Rogers and Dodds distinguish two states of vulnerability: dispositional (individual attributes that render an individual at risk of sustaining a particular harm) and occurrent (circumstances in which individuals are acutely at risk of sustaining harm). Additionally, they characterise sources of vulnerability as inherent, situational and pathogenic. Inherent vulnerability arises from 'sources of vulnerability that are inherent to the human condition and that arise from our corporeality, our neediness, our dependence on others, and our affective and social natures'.[35] Situational vulnerability arises in a context that is 'caused or exacerbated by the personal, social, political, economic or environmental situations of a person or social group'.[36] In contrast, pathogenic vulnerability is a state of being at risk of having situational or inherent vulnerabilities increased or created as a result of ongoing relationships or socio-political situations that have negative or harmful effects.[37]

Occurrent and pathogenic vulnerabilities may arise inadvertently. For example, interventions designed to address inherent or situational vulnerabilities may have unforeseen new or aggravating consequences if they are based on, for example, incorrect assumptions about existing social relationships, structural injustices or socio-political situations. However, they can also arise, predictably, as a consequence of law and policy interventions that are blind to the inherent or situational vulnerability of given cohorts.

4.4.1.2 Applying the taxonomy in practice

To illustrate, applying the taxonomy to consider the sources and states of vulnerability of unaccompanied child asylum seekers, they arrive in a State with the inherent sources of vulnerability that they share with all children. They also share the situational vulnerabilities of being unauthorised child asylum seekers without parents. But the quality of law and policy responses determines whether the State further exposes them to circumstances in which they are acutely at risk of sustaining harm (occurrent vulnerability) or exposed to pathogenic sources of vulnerability by harmful relationships or socio-political situations that put them at risk of increasing their situational or inherent vulnerabilities or generating new ones. They are, thus, profoundly dependent on State law and policy responses to ameliorate their inherent, dispositional and situational vulnerabilities as far as possible and to not generate occurrent states, or pathogenic sources, of vulnerability.

Applying the types and sources of vulnerability taxonomy illuminates the context specificity of the vulnerabilities of unaccompanied children subject to laws and policies that implement offshore processing. Using the taxonomy to deconstruct the vulnerabilities of unaccompanied children transferred offshore, by Australia to Nauru for processing illustrates why a gravity of consequences approach that prioritises avoiding the creation of or repealing existing laws and policies that generate occurrent or pathogenic vulnerabilities is necessary. To do otherwise inflames the acute and avoidable vulnerabilities of these children.

Further, while all children are inherently predisposed to experiencing anxiety in inhospitable physical environments, placing unaccompanied child asylum seekers with pre-existing trauma in contexts that are trauma-inducing generates a further occurrent vulnerability when they are detained. The social and political structures that create or perpetuate inhospitable and trauma-inducing environments produce occurrent and pathogenic sources of vulnerability for these children because of the lack of access to appropriate trauma remediation or freedom from risk of new generators of trauma in their present environment. This overlays the situational vulnerability they experience living with pre-existing trauma in this context.

Similarly, all asylum seekers are dispositionally and inherently vulnerable to experiencing illnesses and infections in a new tropical climate because of their human embodiment. However, unaccompanied child asylum seekers who have arrived with illnesses or disabilities following their transit or who developed illnesses in Australian immigration detention centres prior to transfer are occurrently more vulnerable to risks of medical complications. While all asylum seekers living in shared facilities in the offshore processing centre on Nauru experience situational vulnerability to violence if they do not have adequate security, child asylum seekers also face specific occurrent vulnerabilities. These are related to their susceptibility to physical and sexual violence and abuse because of their age and lack of parental protection, especially if they are not placed in secure purpose-built environments.

Likewise, applying the taxonomy to the 2012–2014 changes to the *Migration Act*, which limited proximate vulnerable children's access to onshore RSD processes, illustrates the context dependency of the requisite State response. Unaccompanied children's situational vulnerability arising from seeking asylum was increased by effectively removing the possibility of being granted asylum from Australia if they arrived by boat and forcing them to seek asylum from a third country.[38] The legislative changes that reintroduced Boat Turnbacks in 2013 generated occurrent and pathogenic vulnerabilities by rendering them more vulnerable to the possibility of refoulement.[39] The impacts of law and policy were different in Australia during the New Directions period[40] and different still in other States that do not utilise offshore processing or Boat Turnbacks or that, unlike Australia, have independent statutory appointed guardians.

These examples illustrate how specific legal and policy responses that develop inadequate physical immigration infrastructures and environments of care potentially exacerbate these children's inherent and situational vulnerabilities. Conversely, if the legal and policy responses instead had addressed their inherent and situational vulnerabilities, occurrent and pathogenic vulnerabilities would not have been created.

Distinguishing between types and sources of vulnerability usefully discriminates between multiple vulnerabilities to facilitate analysis of the types of vulnerabilities that could and should be addressed by the State, and at what point, so that responses can be targeted and appropriate. By applying this taxonomy, vulnerability theory can be utilised in specific contexts to delineate sources of vulnerabilities and inform policy on operational priorities so that circumstances that negatively or harmfully increase individuals' inherent and situational vulnerabilities can be avoided.[41]

4.4.2 Prioritising redress

In a purist reading of vulnerability theory, the State's goal should be to ameliorate the inherent and situational vulnerability for all vulnerable subjects and avoid creating occurrent or pathogenic vulnerabilities by enacting laws and policies that produce specific instances, incidents or environments that are likely to induce harmful effects. Similarly, from the perspective of the being/becoming child, the amelioration of their vulnerabilities is the ideal. However, I argue that the acute vulnerability of unaccompanied children upon arrival, coupled with their potentially time-limited proximity, makes it appropriate to prioritise State responses to urgently address those vulnerabilities created or made worse by laws and policies, then those that are situational, and lastly, those that are inherent for the following reasons.

First, from the perspective of the being/becoming child, their vulnerability immediately upon and following arrival in a State is acute, distinct and urgent. As discussed in Chapter 2, this vulnerability arises from pre-existing traumas generated by the persecution or harm that led them to flee their country of origin, and their transit journey. The normative value placed on the well-being of the being/becoming child is the primary imperative for avoiding occurrent and pathogenic vulnerabilities that compound their existing inherent and situational vulnerabilities.

Second, from the State's perspective, the approach is pragmatic given the potentially temporal nature of the child's proximity to the State. Since, at the time of processing, it is unclear whether the child's claim will ultimately be settled in the processing State or in a third country or returned to their State of origin, that child's long-term care needs could, ultimately, become the responsibility of any of those States. For this reason, each State has an interest – while the child is physically or relationally proximate to the State or under its effective control for processing their asylum claim – in prioritising not compounding vulnerabilities that they may be responsible for remediating once the child's refugee status is determined. Moreover, given the potential sequential impacts of maltreatment by potentially successive receiving and asylum processing States on that child's well-being, each State benefits from not exacerbating existing harms or generating new ones because of even the possibility of an ongoing relationship of settlement between the State and the child.

Accordingly, it is in the States' interest to prioritise not exacerbating existing vulnerabilities and specifically avoid generating new vulnerabilities for the period that the child is physically or relationally proximate to the State.[42] Once States have avoided exacerbating existing or generating new vulnerabilities, the amelioration of the child's situational and inherent vulnerabilities can then be prioritised. This prioritisation also accords with the reality that if the child is granted asylum by the State, attending to these vulnerabilities will fall to it in due course. And if not, the responsibility for amelioration in the longer term will fall to their State of nationality or a third State in which they are ultimately settled.

States such as Australia that intend to sever the child's proximity and deny any reciprocal responsibility for them once they transfer them for offshore processing still have an interest in prioritising and not compounding these children's vulnerabilities while they are under its effective joint control. This is congruent with States' non-delegable duty of care in both domestic and international law to child asylum seekers sent offshore, where offshore authorities act as agents implementing the sending State's policy. Using Nauru to illustrate, Australia has 'seconded' Australian Government officials and contractors to exercise public powers over those transferred and contracted private organisations to provide health and education services to asylum seekers there. Australia and Nauru exercise joint effective control. Under domestic law, a series of cases since 2016 have held that the

Commonwealth Government owes a duty of care to refugees sent offshore to provide a reasonable and adequate standard of medical care in an appropriate environment that is suitable to meet their needs, including their mental health needs, particularly if the requisite care is not available offshore.[43] Australia has consequently found itself remediating and treating medically evacuated asylum seekers with serious medical complications resulting from their treatment in Nauru.

4.4.3 Determining the requisite mitigating vulnerability response of the State to these children

In this section and Section 4.3, I have contended that an expanded application of vulnerability theory underpins States' moral obligation to respond to these children in a particular way. I have identified a taxonomy to distinguish between and characterise harms. I have also provided a gravity of consequences rationale for redress that prioritises addressing occurrent and pathogenic vulnerabilities. Fineman's theory does not reach to developing a taxonomy of vulnerabilities or a method for prioritising redress, nor does it prescribe a model or process for determining appropriate responses in different contexts. To answer the question of how amendments to Australian law and policies in 2012, 2013 and 2014 responded to the complex vulnerabilities of these children and whether the response was adequate, it is necessary to identify the nature and operation of the amendments, their impact on the vulnerabilities of these children and any necessary reforms.

This section now advances a model to enable examination of these components that satisfies my criteria of gravity of consequences and that can be applied across different legal contexts to identify the content of the requisite response.

Prior to applying the vulnerability taxonomy to distinguish between and characterise harms in a given context, there must be an examination of the legal and policy context defining the relationship between the responsive State and the subject(s) of the inquiry. Once the operation of the laws and policies on the subject(s) of the inquiry is understood, the impact of those laws and policies can then be determined by applying the vulnerability taxonomy to distinguish between and characterise those impacts that have ameliorated inherent and situational vulnerabilities and decreased dependencies from those that have created or exacerbated pathogenic and occurrent harms. Finally, when this is understood, priorities for reform based on a gravity of consequences rationale can be identified. Accordingly, I propose the following three-stage process to determine an appropriate mitigating vulnerability response in specific legal contexts:

1. Examine the operation of the relevant laws and policies governing the relationship between the designated group and the State in a specified context and time period.
2. Discern the impact of the laws and policies on the designated group by applying a vulnerability taxonomy to identify which changes have ameliorated existing inherent or situational sources of vulnerability, generated new

pathogenic sources of vulnerability, or exacerbated an individual's dispositional vulnerability into an occurrent one.

3. Identify those impacts that can be addressed by legislative and policy change and propose the content of those changes and the priorities for reform to first address impacts that create occurrent states of vulnerability or new pathogenic sources of vulnerabilities.

This book will now apply this three-stage process to determine the impact of amendments to the *Migration Act* and the *IGOC Act* between 2012 and 2014 on the vulnerabilities of unaccompanied child asylum seekers in Australia generated by their minority (Chapter 5), alienage (Chapter 6), and separation from their parents (Chapter 7) and to propose priorities for law reform.

This analysis supplements a traditional human rights approach by correlating types and sources of vulnerabilities with specific laws and policies and determining priorities for reform that first alleviates the worst avoidable harms. This analysis will reveal that political and border securitisation imperatives have created acute occurrent vulnerabilities and generated new pathogenic vulnerabilities for these children in relation to their care, protection and development needs arising from their minority by subjecting them to physical and mental violence and foreseeable harm and neglect in the arrangements for their care. They have also created critical occurrent vulnerabilities and generated new pathogenic vulnerabilities for these children in relation to their legal precariousness and unauthorised presence by failing to ensure that they were not refouled or refused access to a RSD procedure. Lastly, the amendments will be shown to have created significant occurrent vulnerabilities and generated new pathogenic vulnerabilities for these children arising from their separation from their parents by failing to appoint them with an independent guardian with the legislative and functional responsibilities to prevent them from being harmed, refouled or refused access to RSD.

4.5 Conclusion

This chapter has argued that to engage in a constructive account of vulnerability and State responsiveness, vulnerability theory scholarship needs to articulate what a mitigating vulnerability response requires in particular contexts. It began by introducing the relevant conceptual foundations of vulnerability theory and arguing that this theory promises a compelling supplementary normative, ethical justification to hold States accountable domestically for how they respond to unaccompanied asylum-seeking children. This is because it facilitates a critical analysis of the role of government and the suitability of existing social and legal institutions to respond to individuals who are experiencing or are at risk of experiencing serious harm. It argued that although vulnerability theory, as traditionally conceived, does not explicitly include unaccompanied non-citizen children in its protective scope, it ought to encompass these proximate vulnerable children because of their triple vulnerability and the nature of their spatial, temporal and relational proximity to the territory of a State. So extended, vulnerability theory provides the necessary normative justification for a supplementary framework that grounds States' domestic obligation to respond to their vulnerability without displacing the broader framework of human rights. I argue that the requisite mitigating vulnerability response is necessarily context dependent but can be arrived at in different legal contexts by applying a three-stage process. It also argued that the gravity of consequences of States' failure to respond to the acute and urgent vulnerabilities of these children on arrival necessitates prioritising reforms that address occurrent and pathogenic vulnerabilities first.

Using Australian law and policy as a case study, the next three chapters apply the three-stage mitigating vulnerability framework analysis to assess the effects of the sweeping amendments to the *Migration Act* between 2012 and 2014 and to identify priorities for reform, with each chapter focusing on one of the three sites of vulnerability: minority, alienage, and separation from parents. Chapter 5 first examines the context for and historical treatment of unaccompanied child asylum seekers prior to the 2012 amendments. It then explores the operation and impact of the amendments to legislation and policy on unaccompanied children seeking asylum in Australia, to assess the extent to which they responded to the distinct vulnerabilities of these children generated by their minority.

Notes

1 Martha Albertson Fineman, 'The Vulnerable Subject and the Responsive State' (2010) 60 *Emory Law Journal* 251, 269 ('The responsive State').
2 See for example, Bryan Turner, *Vulnerability and Human Rights* (Pennsylvania State University Press, 2006), David Weissbrodt and Mary Rumsey (eds), *Vulnerable and Marginalised Groups and Human Rights* (Edward Elgar Publishing, 2011).
3 Anna Grear, 'Vulnerability, Advanced Global Capitalism and Co-Symptomatic Injustice: Locating the Vulnerable Subject' in Martha Fineman and Anna Grear (eds), *Vulnerability: Reflections on a New Ethical Foundation for Law and Politics* (Ashgate, 2013) 44–46.
4 Martha Albertson Fineman, 'The Vulnerable Subject: Anchoring Equality in the Human Condition', (2008) 20(1) *Yale Journal of Law and Feminism* 1 ('Anchoring equality'); Martha Albertson Fineman, 'The Responsive State' (n 1) 25.
5 Martha Albertson Fineman, 'Anchoring Equality' (n 4) 8.
6 Ibid.
7 Ibid.
8 See Judith Butler, *Frames of War: When Is Life Grievable?* (Verso, 2009) 14. Butler also argues that an inclusive and egalitarian recognition of the precariousness of all people 'should take the form of concrete social policy regarding issues such as shelter, work, food, medical care, and legal status' at 13.
9 Martha Albertson Fineman, 'Equality, Autonomy, and the Vulnerable Subject in Law and Politics' in Martha Albertson Fineman and others (eds), *Vulnerability: Reflections on a New Ethical Foundation for Law and Politics* (Ashgate, 2013) 17, 19 ('Equality, Autonomy, and the Vulnerable Subject').
10 Martha Albertson Fineman, 'The Responsive State' (n 1) 269.
11 Martha Albertson Fineman, 'Anchoring Equality' (n 4) 8–10.
12 Susan Dodds, 'Depending on Care: Recognition of Vulnerability and the Social Contribution of Care Provision' (2007) 21 *Bioethics* 500, 507:

> We are all vulnerable to the exigencies of our embodied, social and relational existence and, in recognising this inherent human vulnerability, we can see the ways in which a range of social institutions and structures protect us against some vulnerabilities, while others expose us to risk.

13 Shelley Bielefeld, 'Cashless Welfare Transfers for "Vulnerable" Welfare Recipients: Law, Ethics and Vulnerability' (2018) 26 *Feminist Legal Studies* 1, 1–2.

14 Terry Carney, 'Vulnerability: False Hope for Vulnerable Social Security Clients?' (2018) 41(3) *University of New South Wales Law Journal* 783, 786 ('Vulnerability'); Kate Brown, Kathryn Ecclestone and Nick Emmel, 'The Many Faces of Vulnerability' (2017) 16 *Social Policy and Society* 497, 498.

15 Terry Carney, 'Vulnerability' (n 14) 783. Carney also acknowledges criticisms of vulnerability theory by scholars for being 'susceptible to abuse by powerful interests intent on increasing coercive surveillance, discipline and disentitlement for those designated as "vulnerable"'.

16 Jonathan Herring, *Vulnerable Adults and the Law* (Oxford University Press, 2016).

17 Beverley Clough, 'Disability and Vulnerability: Challenging the Capacity/Incapacity Binary' (2017) 16 *Social Policy and Society* 469. See also Mikaela Heikkilä, Hisayo Katsui and Maija Mustaniemi-Laakso, 'Disability and Vulnerability: A Human Rights Reading of the Responsive State' (2020) 24(8) *The International Journal of Human Rights* 1180.

18 There is also Judith Butler's closely related scholarship of precariousness and Laurie Berg's scholarship on the precariousness of migrant workers. See Laurie Berg, *Migrant Rights at Work: Law's Precariousness at the Intersection of Immigration and Labour* (Routledge, 2016) 13.

19 Martha Albertson Fineman, 'Grappling with Equality: One Feminist Journey' in Martha Albertson Fineman (ed.), *Transcending the Boundaries of Law: Generations of Feminism and Legal Theory* (Routledge, 2011) 58 ('Grappling with Equality').

20 Jonathan Herring, 'Forward' (2018) 41(3) *University of New South Wales Law Journal* 626.

21 Ibid. Herring notes that Fineman spells out the significance of premising analysis of the law on the liberal subject 'marked by autonomy, self-sufficiency, and self-determinacy' quoting Fineman:

> When we only study the poor, the rich remain hidden and their advantages remain relatively unexamined, nestled in secure and private spaces, where there is no need for them or the state to justify or explain why they deserve the privilege of state protection … We need to excavate these privileged lives.

See Martha Albertson Fineman, 'Grappling with Equality' (n 19) 58.

22 Martha Albertson Fineman, 'Anchoring Equality' (n 4) 1, 8, 12.

23 See John Tobin, 'Understanding Children's Rights: A Vision Beyond Vulnerability' (2015) 84 (2) *Nordic Journal of International Law* 155.

24 Jacqueline Bhabha, 'Independent Children, Inconsistent Adults: International Child Migration and the Legal Framework' *Innocenti Discussion Paper* (UNICEF Innocenti Research Centre, 2008). Bhabha references the 'triple burden' as a statement of fact, but she does not theorise its content.

25 For example, by assuming that the person before the law is cis-gendered, able-bodied or neurotypical.

26 Jonathan Herring, 'Forward' (n 20).

27 In addition to being the human rights duty holder. See Bryan Turner, *Vulnerability and Human Rights* (Pennsylvania State University Press, 2006) 33.

28 Martha Albertson Fineman, 'Equality, Autonomy, and the Vulnerable Subject' (n 9) 13, 22.
29 Martha Albertson Fineman, 'The Responsive State' (n 1) 256.
30 Nina Kohn, 'Vulnerability Theory and the Role of Government' (2014) 26(1) *Yale Journal of Law & Feminism* 2014, 11–14.
31 Jonathan Herring, 'Forward' (n 20). Herring acknowledges that much work is needed to articulate how to implement the theoretical principles of vulnerability theory in concrete situations.
32 Terry Carney, 'Vulnerability' (n 14) 785. Carney's consideration of the utility of vulnerability theory in his analysis of recent reforms in Australian social security law acknowledges its value as a paradigm-shifting new lens for understanding the dimensions and character of social disadvantage, for analysing aspects of law and policy and as a possibly transformative idea for rethinking the nature and role of government. But he laments the undeveloped notion of the 'responsive state'. Carney concludes that there is little evidence that vulnerability has either any current doctrinal purchase or that it is a suitable criterion for incorporation into legislative reform in Australian welfare law.
33 Catriona Mackenzie, Wendy Rogers and Susan Dodds, 'Introduction: What is Vulnerability and Why Does it Matter for Moral Theory?' in Catriona Mackenzie, Wendy Rogers and Susan Dodds (eds), *Vulnerability: New Essays in Ethics and Feminist Philosophy*, (Oxford Publishing, 2014) 32 ('What is vulnerability').
34 Catriona Mackenzie, Wendy Rogers and Susan Dodds, 'Why Bioethics Needs a Concept of Vulnerability' (2012) 5(2) *International Journal of Feminist Approaches to Bioethics* 11, 24–25.
35 Ibid 24.
36 Ibid.
37 Ibid 25.
38 *Migration Legislation Amendment (Regional Processing and Other Measures) Act 2012* (Cth), the *Maritime Powers Act 2013* (Cth), the *Migration Amendment (Unauthorised Maritime Arrivals and Other Measures) Act 2013* (Cth) and the *Migration and Maritime Powers Legislation Amendment (Resolving the Asylum Legacy Caseload) Act 2014* (Cth).
39 Unaccompanied child asylum seekers who arrived prior to 13 July 2013 were eligible to have their claim for protection processed in Australia and were originally held in closed immigration detention but were subsequently released into community detention on the Australian mainland. Those children who arrived after 13 July 2013 were held in closed immigration detention prior to transfer to Nauru.
40 As examined in Section 1.2, in this period between 2008 and 2011, the Australian Government adopted a more humane approach, especially to children and families seeking asylum, and included requiring justification for detention based on risk, ending the detention of children and ensuring administrative review of the length and conditions of detention.
41 See, for example, Evelyne Durocher et al., 'Understanding and Addressing Vulnerability Following the 2010 Haiti Earthquake: Applying a Feminist Lens to Examine Perspectives of Haitian and Expatriate Health Care Providers and Decision-Makers' (2016) 8(2) *Journal of Human Rights Practice* 219. The authors illustrate how that taxonomy can, for example, inform operational priorities in the delivery of humanitarian assistance.
42 Here, I draw conceptually on Mackenzie, Rogers and Dodds's work, which identifies 'pathogenic vulnerability' as 'a state of being at risk of having situational or inherent vulnerabilities increased or created as a result of ongoing relationships or sociopolitical situations that have negative or harmful effects'. Catriona

Mackenzie, Wendy Rogers and Susan Dodds, 'Why bioethics needs a concept of vulnerability' (n 34) 24–25.

43 *Plaintiff S99/2016* v *Minister for Immigration and Border Protection* (2016) 243 FCR 17; *D7* v *Minister for Immigration and Border Protection* (2016) FCA 1331; *FRX 17 as litigation representative for FRM17* v *Minister for Immigration and Border Protection* (2018) FCA 63; *AYX18* v *Minister for Home Affairs* (2018) FCA 283. This duty of care persists despite the repeal of the *Legislation Amendment (Miscellaneous Measures) Act 2019* (Cth) that created a framework for transfer of persons in regional processing centres needing urgent medical or psychiatric assessment or treatment by the *Migration Amendment (Repairing Medical Transfers Act) 2019* (Cth).

5 Vulnerability analysis of provision of care to unaccompanied asylum-seeking children, using Australia as a case study

5.1 Introduction

This chapter applies the three-stage mitigating vulnerability framework articulated in Chapter 4 to assess the adequacy of the environment of care provided to unaccompanied child asylum seekers pursuant to amendments to Australian law and policy between 2012 and 2014 and then provides recommendations for reform. As examined in Chapter 2, unaccompanied asylum-seeking children arrive in States with a critical and urgent need for care and protection. They bear the vulnerabilities shared by all children. They are dependent on the State to simultaneously meet their current care and protection needs by providing food, shelter and adequate health care as well as their development needs while their claim for asylum is processed.[1] Applying vulnerability theory, these children also have additional situational vulnerabilities arising from their exposure to pre-flight traumatic events, their asylum journey and their separation from, or loss of, parents and other family members.[2] They present with this situational vulnerability when they arrive at the borders of destination countries,[3] and their development remains vulnerable to its impacts, which may persist for many years.[4] They are also occurrently vulnerable, depending on the nature of the State response to their care and protection needs, to neglect, abuse, trafficking and sex and labour exploitation while they are seeking to have their asylum claim determined.

The following three sections of this chapter align with the three stages of the mitigating vulnerability framework. Section 5.2 examines the effects of the changes to the *Migration Act* in 2012, 2013 and 2014 on Australia's provision of care and protection to unaccompanied child asylum seekers. It describes how the amendments resulted in a return to onshore mandatory immigration detention and then created two distinct environments of care based solely on the date of arrival in Australia: onshore community detention and offshore detention in a regional processing centre on Nauru. Section 5.3 then examines the impact of Australia's actual provision of care and protection to these children under onshore and offshore processing. It argues that mandatory immigration detention generated a new occurrent vulnerability that these children would not be adequately cared for and protected whilst in detention and that detention created a pathogenic vulnerability that persisted post-release as ongoing trauma. It then

DOI: 10.4324/9781003260134-6

argues that the inherent and situational vulnerabilities of children released into community detention on the Australian mainland, pursuant to a residence determination until their asylum claims were finalised, were largely not exacerbated by the care arrangements provided for them. As a general rule, these children were spared the very restricted access to support services that exacerbated the vulnerability of other adult and family group asylum seekers.[5] Finally, it contends that unaccompanied children subject to offshore processing were subjected to the occurrent vulnerabilities generated by their mandatory immigration detention on the mainland *compounded by* exposure to occurrent and pathogenic vulnerabilities on Nauru. These included occurrent vulnerabilities of medical complications and not having prior trauma remediated as well as pathogenic vulnerabilities of not having their basic needs for care and protection met, being exposed to new trauma and physical or sexual violence, and harm because of the inadequate custodial arrangements in Nauru. Section 5.4 then identifies the priorities for legislative and policy reform.

5.2 Operation of the 2012–2014 legislative amendments: environments of care based on the date of arrival, not on care and protection needs

This section examines the legal and policy context defining the relationship between Australia, as a responsive State in vulnerability theory, and unaccompanied child asylum seekers. In doing so, it sets out the operation of the amendments prior to examining the impact of those laws on their vulnerability in Section 5.3. In the years prior to the 2012 statutory amendments, the Rudd (Labor) and then Gillard (Labor) governments had generally adopted a relatively humane approach to child asylum seekers. With negligible new boat arrivals between 2002 and 2009, the detention centres on Nauru and Manus Island that housed asylum seekers after the first Pacific Solution were closed, and unaccompanied children that had been detained in locked immigration centres on the mainland were released into community detention while their claims were processed. But after 2009, the number of asylum seekers arriving in Australia by boat escalated,[6] and the mandatory immigration detention of asylum seekers, including unaccompanied children, resumed.

In 2012, the Gillard (Labor) government negotiated with Nauru and PNG to reopen their regional processing centres. The passage of the *Migration Legislation Amendment (Regional Processing and Other Measures) Act* 2012 (Cth) allowed offshore processing of the protection claims of boat arrival asylum seekers. In practice, the effect of this Act was that from 13 August 2012, asylum seekers who arrived in Australia by boat were subject to processing in Nauru and on Manus Island in PNG. However, they could still be settled in Australia if found to be refugees. The second Rudd (Labor) government announced on 19 July 2013 that, as discussed in Chapter 1, irregular boat arrivals who arrived from that date would be processed offshore and would *never* be resettled in

Australia.[7] From that date, only adult males were eligible for transfer to Manus Island, while all other males and all women and children, including unaccompanied children, would be sent to Nauru. The approximately 1,000 men, women and child maritime arrivals who entered Australia between 13 August 2012 and 18 July 2013 and had been taken to Nauru or Manus Island were then returned to Australia for processing to free up capacity for the offshore immigration detention of the post-19 July arrivals.[8]

Unaccompanied child asylum seekers were not accommodated differently under these policy changes. The arbitrariness of the dates effecting policy changes, the initial transfers to and fro, and the subsequent mandatory transfers all illustrate the blindness of Australian border control to the relative vulnerability of individual children or the legitimacy of their asylum claim.[9] This vulnerability blindness was compounded on 18 February 2014 by a guideline issued by the then minister for immigration, Scott Morrison. It stated that asylum seekers arriving after 19 July 2013 were generally 'not to be referred for my consideration [for a discretionary grant of a residence determination under s. 197AB *Migration Act*] … unless there are exceptional reasons or I have requested it'.[10] Being an unaccompanied child was not an exceptional reason.

While all unaccompanied child asylum seekers in the research period were initially detained in closed immigration detention centres, these amendments created two distinct arrangements for the subsequent provision of their care that flowed solely from their date of arrival in Australia. First, children who arrived before 13 August 2012, who had remained on the Australian mainland or who had arrived between 13 August 2012 and 18 July 2013 and either remained on the mainland or had been sent offshore initially but then returned were eligible for release into community detention on a residence determination while their claims were assessed. Second, unaccompanied children who arrived after 19 July 2013 were held in closed immigration detention facilities on Christmas Island pending transfer to the Nauru regional processing centre (RPC) under the effective joint control of the Australian and Nauruan Governments.[11]

Having examined the effect of the operation of the amendments on the environment of care provided by Australia in response to these children's minority, the next section applies stage two of the mitigating vulnerability framework. It uses the vulnerability taxonomy to distinguish between and characterise responses that ameliorated inherent and situational vulnerabilities and decreased dependencies from those that created or exacerbated pathogenic and occurrent harms in providing environments of care for unaccompanied child asylum seekers.

5.3 Impact of Australia's punitive environments of care

This section delineates and analyses evidence about the environments of care provided to unaccompanied child asylum seekers from material on the public record about asylum seekers generally. This includes the following: UNHCR monitoring reports of Nauru,[12] the 2014 AHRC *Forgotten Children Inquiry Report*,[13] the 2014 'Moss Review',[14] the 2015 Senate Select Committee inquiry on the *Recent*

Allegations Relating to Conditions and Circumstances at the Regional Processing Centre in Nauru (*Taking Responsibility Inquiry*),[15] the 2016 Senate Legal and Constitutional Affairs Committee inquiry,[16] reports by advocacy groups[17] and individuals regarding children in detention,[18] Department of Immigration procedure manuals,[19] annual reports and audits,[20] a community detention evaluation conducted in 2013[21] and a 2018 report by the AHRC of its inquiry into a human rights complaint by three families transferred to Nauru in 2013.[22]

This evidence informs the examination of the *impact* of Australian law and policy on unaccompanied child asylum seekers during this period that has been largely absent in existing studies, reports and evaluations that focus on child asylum seekers generally. This section will show that initial mandatory immigration detention exacerbated the situational vulnerability of these children. Yet, community care arrangements were not inherently exacerbating.[23] Rather, they went some way towards ameliorating existing vulnerabilities. In contrast, arrangements for the provision of care for unaccompanied children subject to onshore and offshore immigration detention both exacerbated existing inherent and situational vulnerabilities and generated occurrent and pathogenic vulnerabilities by providing inadequate care and protection and failing to protect children from physical or mental violence, neglect or foreseeable harm.[24]

5.3.1 *Impacts on the Legacy Caseload cohort (unaccompanied asylum seeker children on the Australian mainland)*

5.3.1.1 *Mandatory immigration detention*

The grave impacts of Australia's mandatory immigration detention system have been thoroughly documented (see Section 3.4). It exacerbates children's inherent and situational vulnerability in complex, unnecessary and preventable ways, and prolonged detention especially generates pathogenic vulnerabilities. An institutional, punitive detention environment cannot ameliorate the inherent vulnerabilities of unaccompanied child asylum seekers because it is inimical to providing the stimulation, care, protection and personal attention to meet their immediate development needs or to equip them with the skills and resiliencies that they need to reach future age-appropriate developmental benchmarks and psychological maturity milestones.[25] Instead, it exacerbates pre-existing situational vulnerabilities and generates new pathogenic psychological and physiological vulnerabilities, as evidenced by cases of insomnia, nightmares, mutism, bedwetting[26] and 'heightened rates of suicide, suicide attempts and self-harm, mental disorder, and developmental problems, including severe attachment disorder'.[27]

Medical research clearly establishes a causal relationship between the use of mandatory immigration detention and long-term damage to children's social and emotional functioning[28] and that the damage escalates the longer the detention is continued. Evidence to the AHRC *Forgotten Children Inquiry* about the impact of prolonged detention on rates of self-harming amongst detainees stated:

> what we know from the research in this area is that the rates of self-harming in detention are fairly low when the periods of detention are low and when the period in detention increases and particularly when it increases above 6 months the rates start to increase and then they increase at an exponential rate.[29]

For the being/becoming child, prolonged immigration detention threatens their present development and mental health.[30] It also exerts a long-term impact on their psychological well-being for a substantial period after they have left detention,[31] which affects their long-term social and emotional functioning into their adult life.

Additionally, the research establishes that the immigration detention environment exacerbates pre-existing trauma and inhibits recovery.[32] As discussed in Chapter 2, unaccompanied children on Nauru endured varying but universally harrowing journeys to arrive in Australia by boat. To illustrate, one unaccompanied child gave evidence to the *Forgotten Children Inquiry* about how they arrived in 2013:

> Actually the way to come here was not easy; first we came to Malaysia and then from Malaysia to Indonesia, we spent nights in the jungles there before coming to here. ... This way is very very dangerous. There was space for 150 people in the boat and the boat was packed by 250 people; we were all sitting on each other, but nobody was thinking about going back ... better to die. We had no food or water for five days, it was so horrible. In ... the Indian Ocean the boat sank down; 110 people were rescued and many people were drowned. ... Sixteen hours I swam in the water to survive when our boat sank.[33]

They also share experiences of past trauma, which are unique to their personal circumstances. For example, the submissions made by two unaccompanied children to the *Forgotten Children Inquiry* illustrate their common experience of past trauma and physical and mental insecurity, as well as their continuing distress and growing and pervasive anxiety:

> I miss freedom ... know I'm 17 years old. I don't have my famil in here...I miss my famill my famil is know in Afghanistan. Afganistan is no safe for living...I don't know what happen for my futur ... my famil alos have a lote of serious about me. I have a menta healt [sic].[34]
>
> I am tired of life. I cannot wait much longer. What will happen to us? What are we guilty of? What have we done to be imprisoned? .... I am alone here on Nauru. Neither my father nor my mother is with me. It is very difficult for me to live in this prison. In my country, there is war, murder and blood. I am Hazara and a Shiite Muslim. In my country, anyone who is a Hazara or a Shiite Muslim is killed and murdered. If I had stayed in my country, I would have been murdered by now.[35]

Unaccompanied child asylum seekers require specialist services and care environments to remediate the effects of past trauma. Conversely, they face an occurrent situational vulnerability when they are detained in trauma-inducing contexts. As discussed in Chapter 4, child asylum seekers with pre-existing trauma are occurrently vulnerable in environments that are unsuitable for recovery from trauma or that compound the effects of the traumatic experience by agitating intense 'feelings of [helplessness] and desperation'.[36] Put simply, immigration detention is inimical to the provision of conditions in which traumatised children can recover.

Further, while mandatory detention is deeply harmful to all asylum-seeking children, it is particularly unsuitable for unaccompanied children because they are without parents or guardians available to meet their emotional and support needs.[37] The AHRC *Forgotten Children* report found 'causal links between detention, mental health deterioration and self-harm in unaccompanied children'.[38] The vulnerability of all children recovering from past trauma in immigration detention is exacerbated for unaccompanied children because they:

> are deprived of the normal reference points for the development of identity during the crucial adolescent period, which includes interactions with a peer group of their choosing, family and cultural community. Detention also restricts the availability of normal coping strategies and options for adaptive control, and as a result these young people often develop behaviours such as passivity, submission, withdrawal, excessive help-seeking, self-harm and in some instances violent protests.[39]

5.3.1.2 *Community detention*[40]

After being released from mandatory immigration detention, unaccompanied child asylum seekers were transferred to several possible placements: alternative places of detention (APODs),[41] immigration residential housing,[42] immigration transit accommodation or community detention. While placement statistics are incomplete,[43] it is apparent that the vast majority of unaccompanied children in the Legacy Caseload cohort moved out of immigration detention centres from 2014 and were placed into community detention under residence determinations.[44] They generally resided in group homes with three or four other unaccompanied child asylum seekers. The Minister remained their exclusive statutory guardian and was ultimately responsible for decisions, such as those relating to residential placements, schooling and major health procedures. But the day-to-day responsibility for meeting the children's social, health, psychological, material and educational needs was delegated to full-time carers (custodians) contracted by State child welfare services.[45] The discussion in this section focuses on the extent to which this delegation of the Minister's custodianship, or day-to-day care, obligations created an environment of care that responded to their situational vulnerability as children in need of care and protection and provided development opportunities.

The children were subject to conditions, including where they lived, restrictions on their behaviour and school attendance and curfews.[46] But they attended schools with local children, had access to health care through a network of community-based providers and were supported to take part in after-school community activities, such as soccer clubs, art or music classes and other recreational or creative activities.[47] These custodial arrangements clearly went some way towards ameliorating the children's inherent and situational vulnerabilities as child asylum seekers by providing them with appropriate medical, psychological and emotional support and opportunities for development, including age-appropriate education and recreational activities.

State welfare agencies also had various criteria to ensure that custodial carers were appropriately skilled and qualified. These included that they were at least 21 years of age, willing to provide care for the unaccompanied minor, acceptable to the child, capable of providing care for the unaccompanied minor, of good character and willing to undergo a police check and assessed as being able to provide a sustainable placement and had with no conflict of interest.[48] Custodians in group home settings were able to respond to and ameliorate children's specific vulnerabilities by meeting their ongoing emotional and psychological needs as adolescents. As articulated by an unaccompanied child in a group home:

> [My carer] is really good because he is trying to be like kind of my family, he is always trying to make me happy and trying to forget all the worry I have about my family. Even if you can't go to sleep at 3am [he says] knock on my door and I come and sit with you and help.[49]

Although vastly preferable to mandatory immigration detention, it should not be forgotten that community detention remains a form of detention and, as such, has inevitable drawbacks. Three key concerns identified by unaccompanied children and their custodial carers about arrangements at the time included a lack of consistency in the Department's monitoring visits of group homes,[50] difficulties in obtaining timely approval for children to participate in age-appropriate activities (such as overnight stays) from Department delegates[51] and concerns about notifications regarding incidents of potential harm regarding children.[52] While the substance of these concerns could clearly induce suffering in already vulnerable children, they could each be addressed by administrative directions without displacing the broader framework of care that generally ameliorated their situational vulnerabilities. The content and frequency of reporting by Department service provider case managers on unaccompanied children in community detention group homes should be standardised, as should the framework for monitoring the implementation of recommendations for action by case managers when issues are reported. Instead of requiring custodians to obtain advance approval from the legal guardian or delegated guardian for overnight stays, this oversight should be delegated to the child's case manager. Lastly, concerns raised by unaccompanied children about incident reporting subjectivity[53] and the impact of service provider reports about them on their visa decision[54] should be addressed by using best practice methods of both explaining, and confirming that the child has understood, and reporting protocols and consequences during their induction into community detention.

Further, all the children in community detention had previously been in mandatory immigration detention. While the evidence is clear that prolonged immigration detention exacerbates existing pathogenic vulnerabilities and generates new ones, more research is needed to examine the extent to which care in a group home setting has an ameliorating effect on the long-term impacts of prior mandatory immigration detention. As articulated by one unaccompanied child:

> Those who been for long time in detention, they don't want to talk to anyone, even their family, because they are depressed, they only want to stay in the corner of the room because they are depressed. Before [I received a positive decision], I had the same feeling. I was not talking to people, and I was just in my home, and I wanted to do kind of harm myself, kill myself, by train or whatever.[55]

Anecdotal evidence from unaccompanied children and their carers suggests that their release into group homes with appropriate care structures provided a respite for this cohort. As explained by one unaccompanied child:

> In the last two and a half years I had really bad experience. There is 120% difference between detention centre and community detention because detention centre is like a jail, and community – it's like freedom, like relaxed.[56]
>
> It is always positive that people are moved into the community. For a lot of people there is visible improvement.[57]

However, anecdotally too, the respite was perhaps dependent on their status being resolved and community detention also not going on indefinitely:

> it is still a very, very vulnerable group, and if they are torture and trauma survivors they are still dealing with past torture and trauma experiences. [And] many people whilst in detention ... have witnessed a lot of self-harm, a lot of conflict – that does re-traumatise people. The longer people are in detention, [including] community detention, the more likely that their mental health is going to suffer.[58]

Future empirical research focusing on the impact of different types of custodial care through a vulnerability lens could identify whether removing unaccompanied children into a group home setting can partially or fully alleviate the exacerbating effects of prior immigration detention on their inherent and situational vulnerability.

5.3.2 *Impacts on the Offshore Transferee cohort (unaccompanied asylum seeker children 'cared for' on Nauru)*

In contrast to the care, protection and opportunities for development in community detention settings, the situational vulnerability of children subject to offshore processing was exacerbated into occurrent and pathogenic vulnerabilities because of failures in Australian policy to adequately provide care, protection and opportunities for development for unaccompanied children on Nauru. This section considers four key failures in turn: failing to provide an adequate care environment; failing to provide adequate trauma remediation and, instead, compounding existing traumas; failing to respond to their occurrent vulnerability to medical complications in offshore detention; and failing to protect them from violence.

5.3.2.1 Inhospitable care environment

Nauru is a 21-km phosphate rock island that is 53 km south of the equator and 4,494 km from Australia. Nauru was aggressively mined for phosphate until the 1990s, causing permanent damage to the island's environment. It has a hot climate year-round and monsoon rains between November and February. It has no natural rivers and limited natural freshwater resources. The external environment of the Nauru RPC is harsh and provides little natural shelter from the elements. Nauru imports nearly all processed and manufactured goods, including diesel fuel necessary for power. Locals regularly lack access to adequate potable drinking water or water for basic hygiene, relying on rooftop storage tanks and desalination plants fuelled by diesel for water. Nauru's 12,000 nationals have poor health outcomes, and Nauru lacks critical national infrastructure, including fully functioning hospitals.

On its face, the *Memoranda of Understanding* (MOU) entered into by the Rudd (Labor) government with Nauru and with PNG on 3 August 2013 noted, 'special arrangements will be developed and agreed to by the Participants for vulnerable cases, including unaccompanied minors'.[59] They also stated the respective States would 'conduct all activities in respect of this MOU in accordance with [their] Constitution[s] and all relevant domestic laws'.[60] The *Asylum Seekers (Regional Processing Centre) Act 2012* (Nauru) (*Asylum Seekers Act*) also acknowledged the specific needs of asylum-seeking children, including unaccompanied children, and was rights based. Section 6 imposed a general duty on the operational manager of the RPC 'to ensure that each protected person residing at the centre is treated in a fair and humane manner consistent with the law of Nauru'.[61] It also catalogued particular duties of the operational manager that apply to adults and children but that accord with many of the articles of the CRC. These included providing sufficient food to maintain health and well-being;[62] clean and sufficient clothing, adequate bedding and other essential items;[63] access to appropriate washing and toilet facilities;[64] access to counselling facilities;[65] and access to medical care and treatment to the standard that they might reasonably have access to if he or she were living in the general community in Nauru.[66] Section 6 also makes specific provisions for children by requiring the operational manager to give children access to facilities for obtaining an education to the standard that they might reasonably access if living in the general community in Nauru.[67] Significantly, Section 6(1)

(p) also provides specifically for unaccompanied children by imposing a duty on the operational manager to ensure that they are provided with 'anything else that the Secretary thinks ought to be provided … because he or she is … an unaccompanied child'.[68]

However, neither the memoranda nor the legislation delivered what was promised on a literal reading. Serious concerns regarding the provision of care for unaccompanied children on Nauru have been extensively documented.[69] There is an abundance of evidence in the *Forgotten Children Inquiry*,[70] reports by UNHCR,[71] the *Taking Responsibility Inquiry Report*[72] and submissions by offshore processing centre (OPC) contractors and from visiting Australian medical personnel and child asylum seekers detained in Nauru[73] about the failure to deliver on expectations. The evidence reveals a lack of consistently available adequate drinking and toileting water, inadequate nutrition and overcrowded shelter with inadequate privacy and security that was not appropriately adapted for the climate and landscape. Further, it shows insufficient access to timely and appropriate healthcare and educational facilities.

The Nauru RPC was a closed detention centre until October 2015, comprising three compounds, OPC 1, OPC 2 and OPC 3. The Director of Policy and Public Affairs at Save the Children told the AHRC *Forgotten Children Inquiry* that unaccompanied child asylum seekers, who were all transferred after October 2013, received 24-hour custodial care in a separate and secure air-conditioned compound within OPC 1.[74] Structured recreational activities occurred in one large open tent in OPC 3. The totality of the care arrangements – including the common areas (eating, ablution and laundry facilities) and recreation, healthcare and education facilities – must be adequate to meet their care and development needs to prevent their vulnerabilities from being exacerbated or pathogenised. As one of the unaccompanied children told the *Forgotten Children Inquiry* in 2014:

> Here on Nauru have nothing. The camp is too small 4 tents for 27 UAMs boys and all we can do is eating and drinking in one spot. no facilities. no internet, no mobile with other groups and I am very isolated. I have insomnia. I can't sleep.[75]

In October 2015, the government announced that the remaining 650 asylum seekers in detention would have 'complete freedom of movement'[76] and that the RPC would move to an 'open centre' arrangement. However, as will be discussed below, the opening of the centre occurred without sufficient consideration of unaccompanied children's lack of physical security.

5.3.2.2 Lack of adequate trauma remediation and compounding of existing traumas

Unaccompanied child asylum seekers require specialist services and care environments to remediate the effects of past trauma. Detaining them in trauma-inducing contexts makes them occurrently vulnerable to not recovering from past trauma and pathogenically vulnerable to experiencing new traumas.

Since the first Pacific Solution, medical research has confirmed the long-term and destructive mental and physical effects of indefinite offshore detention, particularly for children with pre-existing trauma arising from their and their family members' treatment in their home country and from the transit journey.[77] It is also clear that asylum seekers with past trauma are psychologically vulnerable and at greater risk of post-traumatic stress disorder if exposed to further trauma or adverse conditions.[78]

The evidence in the research period confirms that unaccompanied children on Nauru were occurrently vulnerable to a lack of access to trauma remediation services. The Republic of Nauru lacked a multidisciplinary mental health team to provide the necessary trauma remediation inpatient care for unaccompanied children. The Department gave evidence to the *Taking Responsibility Inquiry* that all transferees were supported under the psychological support program policy, 'based on the psychological support programme in use at Australian immigration detention centres which in turn has been developed and refined over time using extensive input from clinicians'.[79] However, this evidence was countered by clinicians working on Nauru. Dr Peter Young, former director of the provider of mental health services to Nauru, gave evidence to the *Forgotten Children Inquiry* that the Nauru RPC lacked the specialised staff to help children who had experienced torture and trauma and adequate mental health facilities to respond to the complex and specific needs of unaccompanied children. This was especially so because there was no full-time child psychiatrist or psychologist in Nauru, and the rotation of staff to make up a full-time equivalent left gaps in coverage.[80] Staff from the Royal Children's Hospital Melbourne, who had treated children detained on Nauru, testified that:

> We have seen evidence of mental health pathology in all of our patients who have been on Nauru. Symptoms include features of post-traumatic stress disorder (PTSD), depression, anxiety, learning difficulties, bedwetting in previously continent children, nightmares, behavioural regression, memory loss, separation issues, and/or somatization in the form of stomach aches and/or headaches. … Nauru RPC is an environment characterised by insecurity and fear. These children are the most traumatised cohort of patients with whom we have worked.[81]

Following its October 2013 visit to Nauru, the UNHCR reported that detainees were concerned about the deteriorating mental health of children and the trauma associated with their detention.[82] United Nations agencies, not-for-profits and reporters who visited the Nauru detention centre and staff who worked there all provided extensive reports about the extent of persistent self-harm of child asylum seekers on Nauru, including attempting suicide. Save the Children employees reported having observed self-harming behaviours and an increasing preoccupation with thoughts of self-harm amongst children on Nauru.[83] Further, a Nauru detention centre staff report, leaked in 2014, detailed evidence of two suicide attempts by 17-year-old unaccompanied asylum seekers.[84] In October 2014, after the government announced its proposal to transfer detainees from Nauru to Cambodia, the media reported that ten asylum seekers, including six boys who had already been detained on Nauru for more than 12 months, sewed their lips shut and were refusing food and water[85] as an act of protest and self-harm.

The Department conceded to the *Forgotten Children Inquiry*, 'it is clear … from well-established medical evidence, that mental illness and mental health does suffer through extended periods of time in detention'.[86] The failure to respond to the specific known vulnerabilities of these children in a way that ameliorated this suffering exacerbated existing and generated new and preventable pathogenic vulnerabilities. Unlike children who were released from mandatory immigration detention on the mainland into group homes with qualified custodial carers and access to trauma remediation services, unaccompanied children transferred to Nauru experienced both *de novo* psychological distress and re-traumatisation. For them, the process of being transferred to Nauru and the inadequate environment of care there exacerbated the inherent and situational vulnerability they experienced by living with pre-existing trauma in this context. The Nauru RPC was, thus, an occurrent and pathogenic source of vulnerability because the environment and the lack of access to appropriate trauma remediation generated new trauma.

5.3.2.3 Failure to respond to children's occurrent vulnerability to medical complications in transfer arrangements and in offshore detention

Unaccompanied children transferred to Nauru were also exposed to an occurrent vulnerability to medical complications evidenced by outbreaks of lice, gastroenteritis and hand, foot and mouth disease. These diseases were common on Nauru and difficult to contain due to the inadequate hygiene in the centre and detainees sharing close living quarters, common toilets, showers and eating areas.[87] The Royal Australasian College of Physicians expressed its concern in 2013 that the 48-hour transfer procedures to Nauru meant that asylum seekers would be unlikely to receive an adequate medical assessment prior to being transferred. Additionally, they were likely to face 'significant health issues' post-transfer, given the difficulty in appropriately assessing and caring for asylum seekers with acute or chronic illnesses in this timeframe.[88] All child asylum seekers are inherently vulnerable to experiencing illnesses and infections in a new tropical climate. Unaccompanied child asylum seekers who arrived with pre-existing disabilities, who had developed illnesses during their transit or who had developed illnesses or disabilities in Australian immigration detention centres were occurrently more vulnerable to risks of medical complications.

Substantial evidence establishes that the physical and psychological environment of the Nauru RPC exacerbated unaccompanied children's existing health problems. It is clear that primary, allied and hospital health facilities were inadequate in terms of the breadth and depth of provision. In 2013, International Health and Medical Services (IHMS) delivered general practitioner, nursing and mental health care clinics seven days per week for transferees and refugees settled in Nauru.[89] It supplemented these services by providing visiting health practitioners and a telehealth service. IHMS gave evidence to the *Taking Responsibility Inquiry* that transferees could access a review by a nurse and then a referral to a doctor or other healthcare professional during clinic hours. But initial medical care provision on Nauru was 'often slow to be provided', 'could involve asylum seekers queueing for long periods' and 'was often inadequate'.[90] For unaccompanied children with existing disabilities, there was no access to certain allied health or medical specialists. These included speech therapists, optometrists, orthodontists or educational psychologists who could diagnose learning difficulties.[91] Unaccompanied children with disabilities, in particular, are almost invisible in the research literature[92] and should be the subject of further research, particularly regarding their relative susceptibility to the generation of new pathogenic vulnerabilities in this context.

Between 2012 and 2015, the Nauru hospital lacked the facilities needed to provide appropriate health care to its citizens, let alone unaccompanied child asylum seekers. The Department gave evidence to the *Taking Responsibility Inquiry* that it was upgrading a ward and dental area of the Nauru hospital. The works included painting, insect screen replacement, refurbishment of the toilet and shower area, replacing mouldy ceilings and broken ceiling fans and doing gutter repairs. The Department also stated that it would conduct further upgrades to equipment and supplies at the hospital, including to the blood bank and neonatal equipment, in July 2015.[93] The failure to make these upgrades prior to arrangements for the transfer of asylum-seeking children with acute needs recklessly exposed them to the risk of avoidable harms.

The evidence also clearly establishes that, from 2013, asylum seekers on Nauru developed acute or chronic illnesses, including potentially life-threatening illnesses, such as dengue fever, tuberculosis and the Zika virus.[94] The Department's Chief Medical Officer gave evidence to the AHRC's investigation into a complaint of human rights abuses on Nauru, stating that asylum seekers were diagnosed with tuberculosis in 2014 but that, despite recommendations from visiting paediatricians, testing of all children for latent tuberculosis did not commence until January 2015.[95] The Chief Medical Officer gave further evidence that there had been '40 positive symptomatic cases' of dengue fever as at May 2014, that cases were under-reported and that a number of them required blood transfusions.[96] Lastly, in 2016, the Department confirmed that it was 'aware that cases of Zika virus have been confirmed in Nauru' but did not provide details about the numbers of asylum seekers at the Nauru RPC who had contracted the Zika virus during the outbreak in the Pacific between 2013 and 2015.[97]

The lack of appropriate essential primary, allied or hospital health care, combined with the risk of serious disease transmission, subjected these children to serious occurrent vulnerabilities that children released into community detention on the mainland avoided.

5.3.2.4 Failure to protect children from physical and sexual violence

All asylum seekers living in shared facilities in the Nauru RPC experienced inherent vulnerability to violence without adequate security. Child asylum seekers also faced situational vulnerabilities related to their susceptibility to physical and sexual violence and abuse because of their age and lack of parental protection that they would not encounter in a secure purpose-built environment. Unaccompanied children on Nauru were occurrently vulnerable to violence both within the centre and in the community after the centre moved to an open arrangement in 2015.

While detained in the closed centre environment before 2015, the *Taking Responsibility Inquiry* heard evidence that there was 'a high level of risk in the design and provision of accommodation'.[98] Transfield Services, a company contracted by the Australian Government to provide services at the Nauru RPC, gave evidence that they were working with the Department to 'enhance personal safety and privacy', including adding lighting in walkways, open areas, toilets, ablution areas and laundries.[99] The failure to make the necessary upgrades *prior to their transfer* from Australia to Nauru exposed these children to an avoidable occurrent vulnerability to physical and sexual violence.

The *Forgotten Children Inquiry*, UNHCR, the 'Moss Review' and the *Taking Responsibility Inquiry* all heard consistent evidence from multiple sources about children's susceptibility at the Nauru RPC to physical and sexual assault by other detainees or contracted staff. This appeared to be caused both by the detention conditions and by the quality of legal protection and law enforcement on Nauru. The *Forgotten Children Inquiry* received a submission about unaccompanied children's 'fears for their safety while being held in the family compound within the RPC'.[100] The *Taking Responsibility Inquiry* reported that, since 2012, Transfield Services recorded 45 allegations of child abuse and sexual assault[101] and that, in December 2013, child protection workers with Save the Children had reported to then Minister for Immigration Scott Morrison an incident of an alleged indecent assault of a child asylum seeker by a cleaner engaged by Transfield Services at the OPC.[102] The *Taking Responsibility Inquiry* also heard allegations of sexual harassment of minors by staff at the RPC reported in April 2014.[103]

Additionally, the *Taking Responsibility Inquiry* heard evidence of the lack of an existing child protection framework or functioning social services in Nauru to deal appropriately with allegations or incidents of child abuse or the complex protection and support needs of unaccompanied children.[104] There was no statutory authority to intervene or remove a child where abuse has been substantiated.[105] Nor, apparently, did the Nauru Police Force have the capacity to properly investigate and charge perpetrators of physical and sexual assaults reported at the RPC.[106] These failures, combined with that of the Department to take the security needs of children seriously, left them extremely vulnerable to an ongoing risk of assault and harassment at the RPC. Nauru lacked the mandatory reporting requirements that provide some protection for children in Australia from sexual and other physical assault. Much like unaccompanied children's exposure to avoidable occurrent vulnerabilities of re-traumatisation and medical illness, this failure to implement fundamental protection frameworks prior to the centre being opened exposed unaccompanied child asylum seekers to an avoidable occurrent vulnerability to violence.

The Minister instigated the 'Moss Review' in September 2014 after extensive media reporting about sexual abuse of asylum seekers in Nauru. The 'Moss Review's' recommendations included that the Department review relevant policies and guidelines for reporting and responding to allegations of abuse, provide support to the Nauruan Government to enhance its legal and policy framework and the capability of relevant authorities to investigate and respond to cases of sexual and other physical assault and for child protection.[107] The Abbott (Coalition) government publicly accepted all of the recommendations.[108] The Department announced that it would develop a 'comprehensive action plan', including 'developing a child protection framework to accompany existing policies, and the provision of specialised child protection training to all staff and service providers who interact with children'.[109] It is unclear whether any of these recommendations or objectives were ever implemented. The failure to have these fundamental child protection frameworks in place prior to the decision to transfer unaccompanied children to the RPC generated an avoidable occurrent vulnerability to abuse or assault.

Rather than responding to these serious public reports by implementing proper environments of care, the Australian Government responded to this documented vulnerability with further punitive measures to silence vulnerable subjects and those advocating for them. The *Border Forces Act 2015* (Cth) prohibited anyone working with or for the Department, including workers in OPCs, from disclosing information obtained by them during the course of their work,[110] with offences punishable by up to two years' imprisonment.[111] Although exceptions were made for disclosures made to prevent or lessen a serious threat to the life or health of an individual,[112] the onus was on the person making the disclosure to establish that the disclosure was required for this purpose.[113]

Then, on 1 October 2014, authorities released the remaining 29 unaccompanied children into the Nauruan community. In the following weeks, a group of locals physically and verbally attacked a 17-year-old Iranian boy and a 16-year-old boy from Myanmar. Both required hospitalisation as a result of their injuries.[114] The *Taking Responsibility Inquiry* found that 'this was a serious assault yet no action was taken in prevention or education in the community'.[115] The Department continued moving such children into the community without adequate protection, knowing that there was a culture of hostility toward them, and without taking appropriate measures to ensure their security. The *Taking Responsibility Inquiry* received evidence that:

> the Nauruan community is not a safe place for resettlement to occur, in addition to the allegation made that minors have been assaulted, it was also argued that there is a culture of resentment towards asylum seekers and refugees in the community: Children were attacked by local citizens at an alarming rate.[116]

The *Senate Select Committee Inquiry* reported growing community resentment and threats of violence against asylum seekers and refugees 'as refugees were released and transitioned into the community' without any appropriate action by either the Department or the government of Nauru for the transition to succeed.[117] It recommended that the Australian Government clarify incident reporting guidelines with all contracted service providers 'to ensure that the safety of all asylum seekers, including children, is protected and all incidents are appropriately reported whether or not they occur within the physical boundaries of the RPC'.[118] Ultimately, it concluded that:

> children are not only denied a reasonable approximation of childhood in the [RPC], but often do not feel safe, and in fact often are not safe. Their extreme vulnerability is further exacerbated by their location in a country which lacks an adequate legal or policy framework for their protection.[119]

They noted 'children who have been assaulted and mentally harmed from detention in Nauru remain with no remedy or relief?[120] and concluded that 'the RPC Nauru is neither a safe nor an appropriate environment for children and that they should no longer be held there'.[121]

5.4 Priorities for reform

This chapter has examined the effect of the operation of the *Migration Act* amendments on the environment of care provided by Australia in response to these children's minority. It has also applied the vulnerability taxonomy to distinguish between and characterise those impacts that have ameliorated inherent and situational vulnerabilities and decreased dependencies from those that have created or exacerbated pathogenic and occurrent harms. This section now applies stage three of the mitigating vulnerability framework and proposes priorities for reform based on a gravity of consequences rationale.

The needs of these being/becoming children for targeted care and protection immediately upon and following arrival in a State were acute, distinct and urgent. Their vulnerabilities, as discussed in Chapter 2, arose from pre-existing traumas generated by the persecution or harm that led them to flee their country of origin and that were compounded by their journey, usually on overcrowded and unseaworthy fishing boats for many days with limited access to food and water. In this context, the mitigating vulnerability framework model identifies the well-being of the being/becoming child as the primary imperative for prioritising amendments to laws and policies that create new pathogenic sources of vulnerability and new occurrent harms first.

The evidence clearly establishes that immigration detention itself is the key exacerbator of these children's situational vulnerability, as captured neatly by the *Forgotten Children Inquiry*:

> Despite the best efforts of the Department and its contractors to provide services and support to children in detention, it is the fact of detention itself that is causing harm. In particular the deprivation of liberty and the exposure to high numbers of mentally unwell adults are causing emotional and developmental disorders amongst children.[122]

Urgent policy changes are critical to ensure the devastating impacts of mandatory immigration detention in Australia and the inadequate environment of care in Nauru that generate occurrent and pathogenic harms cannot recur. Mandatory immigration detention of all unaccompanied children should be limited to no longer than 72 hours in purpose-built child-friendly reception centres before transferring them into foster care, a sponsorship arrangement, or, as a last resort, community detention on the Australian mainland while their asylum claim is processed. These changes would also respond to unaccompanied children's occurrent vulnerability to medical complications and violence in offshore detention. Urgent policy changes should also address these children's existing trauma by providing them with access to trauma remediation services while their asylum claim is processed. Neither of these proposed reforms requires legislative changes. The Minister can achieve the first by revoking their guideline directing that residence applications for asylum seekers arriving after 19 July 2013 not be referred for consideration unless there are exceptional reasons or the Minister has requested it. The second requires funding for these children to be able to access existing specialist services.

Once these occur, practice improvements in arrangements for the provision of care of unaccompanied children in community detention on the mainland should be implemented. These should include enabling custodians to permit overnight stays,[123] regularising Department case manager visits, monitoring and feedback requirements and fully informing unaccompanied children about incident reporting protocols and consequences. These can all be achieved by administrative directions. Systematic, consistent and transparent monitoring of the quality of care provided to unaccompanied children by service provider case managers is essential to ensure that they receive appropriate levels of support from their allocated service provider and are provided with fully functional accommodation, attending school, given access to health services, having their religious needs supported and building confidence to live independently.

The reforms also require consistent monitoring and reporting on the frequency of visits and follow-up action taken on issues reported by unaccompanied children or their case manager. In addition, the Department should ensure that, during their induction into community detention, unaccompanied children demonstrate a clear understanding of incident reporting protocols and potential consequences for non-compliance. Lastly, appropriate arrangements are critical for unaccompanied young people leaving group living arrangements to ensure that they have the necessary support and skills to transition safely and effectively to living independently. Unaccompanied children should continue to receive appropriate care and protection, opportunities for development and full social services until they turn 21.

Finally, if governments persist with offshore processing at Nauru RPC in the future, no unaccompanied child should be transferred there or to any other RPC until a mitigating vulnerability assessment has been conducted and facilities and services are in place to effectively respond to their complex care needs.[124]

This chapter has examined the utility of a vulnerability analysis of the impact of the changes to the *Migration Act* in 2012, 2013 and 2014 on the environments of care provided to unaccompanied children seeking asylum in Australia. It illustrated how legal and policy responses that do not respond to the complex and specific vulnerability of these being/becoming children generate avoidable occurrent and pathogenic harms. The vulnerability analysis also clarified the Australian Government's responsibility for the avoidable acute occurrent and pathogenic impacts of mandatory immigration detention and the exposure of unaccompanied children to disease, violence and traumatisation from the inadequate care arrangements in Nauru. Lastly, the vulnerability analysis clarified the sites and sources generating the most acute harms to these children and informed concrete measures and priorities for reform.

The next chapter explores Australia's response to vulnerabilities generated by the alienage of unaccompanied children. I examine the operation and impact of Australian laws and policies between 2012 and 2014 on their situational vulnerability as asylum seekers. I will argue that those changes progressively restricted access to RSD using pre-transfer assessments, enhanced screening and mandatory offshore processing and wound back Australia's non-refoulement obligation and, ultimately, restricted entry completely. In outlining this argument, I will establish that a mitigating vulnerability framework requires the overhaul of laws that denied these children access to RSD and entry to the State, subjecting them to a grave risk of refoulement.

Notes

1 For example, by ensuring they have access to age-appropriate education, training and opportunities to foster their expanding abilities.

2 Tine Jensen et al., 'Long-Term Mental Health in Unaccompanied Refugee Minors: Pre- and Post-Flight Predictors' (2019) 28(12) *European Child & Adolescent Psychiatry* 1671.

3 Ilse Derluyn and Eric Broekaert, 'Different Perspectives on Emotional and Behavioural Problems in Unaccompanied Refugee Children and Adolescents' (2007) 12(2) *Ethnicity and Health* 141.

4 See, for example, Serap Keles et al., 'Resilience and Acculturation among Unaccompanied Refugee Minors' (2016) 42(1) *International Journal of Behavioural Development* 52; Tine Jensen et al., 'Development of Mental Health Problems – A Follow-Up Study of Unaccompanied Refugee Minors' (2014) 8 *Child Adolescent Psychiatry and Mental Health* 29.

5 See, for example, the discussion in Australian Human Rights Commission, *Lives on Hold: Refugees and Asylum Seekers in the 'Legacy Caseload'* (Commonwealth Government, 2019).

6 Janet Phillips and Harriet Spinks, 'Boat Arrivals in Australia since 1976', *Parliamentary Library Research Paper* (Commonwealth Parliamentary Library, 2017) 22.

7 'Asylum Seekers Arriving in Australia by Boat to be Resettled in Papua New Guinea', *ABC News* (online at 20 July 2013) <http://www.abc.net.au/news/2013-07-19/manus-island-detention-centre-to-beexpanded-under-rudd27s-asy/4830778>.

8 Elibritt Karlsen, 'Australia's Offshore Processing of Asylum Seekers in Nauru and PNG: A Quick Guide to Statistics and Resources', *Research Paper Series 2016–17* (Commonwealth Parliamentary Library, 2016) 3–4.

9 These policy changes were implemented by the *Migration Amendment (Unauthorised Maritime Arrivals and Other Measures) Act 2013* (Cth). The effect of the Act was that all 'unauthorised maritime arrivals' – families, adult females, adult males and unaccompanied minors – who arrived after 19 July 2013 simply 'transited' in Australia, prior to being sent offshore to Nauru or Manus Island, and asylum claims were processed under the respective laws of Nauru or PNG. The impact of these laws on the vulnerabilities of unaccompanied children generated by their alienage will be interrogated in Chapter 6.

10 For discussion of these guidelines, see *Mr BF on behalf of Master BG v Cth of Australia (DIBP)* (2017) Aus HRC 114.

11 Unless the Minister exercised his non-compellable, non-delegable intervention power under section 197AB of the *Migration Act 1958* (Cth) (*Migration Act*) to grant the child a residence determination enabling them to live in community detention if still under 18 pending resolution of their protection claim.

12 UNHCR, *Mission to the Republic of Nauru, 3 to 5 December 2012: Report* (UNHCR, 2012) and UNHCR, *Monitoring Visit to the Republic of Nauru 7 to 9 October 2013* (UNHCR, 2013) <https://www.refworld.org/docid/5294a6534.html> (*Monitoring Visit to the Republic of Nauru*).

13 Australian Human Rights Commission, *The Forgotten Children: National Inquiry into Children in Immigration Detention* (Commonwealth Government, 2014) 1 (*The Forgotten Children Inquiry*).

On 3 February 2014, the President of the AHRC launched an inquiry into children in enclosed immigration detention. The inquiry received 239 submissions, conducted five public hearings and 13 visits to 11 immigration detention centres and conducted interviews with 1,233 current and former detainees. Its report, *The Forgotten Children Inquiry*, was provided to the government in November 2014 and tabled in the Senate on 11 February 2015.

14 Philip Moss, *Review into Recent Allegations Relating to Conditions and Circumstances at the Regional Processing Centre in Nauru* (Final report, Department of Immigration and Border Protection, 2015) ('Moss Review'). The 'Moss Review' was announced by the then Minister for Immigration on 3 October 2014 to identify and report on claims of sexual and other physical assault of asylum seekers as well as on the conduct and behavior of staff members employed by contracted service providers between July 2013 and October 2014. The report was provided to the Department on 9 February 2015, and a redacted version of the report was published on the Department's website on 20 March 2015.

15 On 26 March 2015, the Senate established the *Select Committee on the Recent Allegations Relating to Conditions and Circumstances at the Regional Processing Centre in Nauru* to inquire into the responsibilities of the Commonwealth

Government in connection with the management and operation of the Nauru RPC. The inquiry received 101 submissions, held public hearings in Canberra on 19 May, 9 June, 20 July and 20 August 2015, and tabled its final report on 31 August 2015: *Taking Responsibility: Conditions and Circumstances at Australia's Regional Processing Centre in Nauru* (Commonwealth Government, 2015) (*Taking Responsibility Report*).

16 Senate Legal and Constitutional Affairs Committee, *Conditions and Treatment of Asylum Seekers and Refugees at the Regional Processing Centres in the Republic of Nauru and Papua New Guinea* (Interim report, Commonwealth Government, 2016).

17 Amnesty International, *Nauru Offshore Processing Facility Review 2012* (Amnesty, 2012); Amnesty International, *Island of Despair: Australia's 'Processing' of Refugees on Nauru*, (Amnesty, 2016); Human Rights Watch and Amnesty International, *Australia: Appalling Abuse, Neglect of Refugees on Nauru* (Human Rights Watch and Amnesty, 2016).

18 See for example, Keith Hamburger, *Nauru Review 2013: Executive Report of the Review into the 19 July 2013 Incident at the Nauru Regional Processing Centre* (Knowledge Consulting, 2014); Wendy Bacon et al., *Protection Denied, Abuse Condoned: Women on Nauru at Risk* (Australian Women in Support of Women on Nauru, 2016); Paul Farrell et al., 'The Nauru Files: Cache of 2,000 Leaked Reports Reveal Scale of Abuse of Children in Offshore Detention', *The Guardian (Australia)* (online at 10 August 2016) <https://www.theguardian.com/australia-news/2016/aug/10/the-nauru-files-2000-leaked-reports-reveal-scale-of-abuse-of-children-in-australian-offshore-detention>.

19 Department of Immigration and Border Protection, *Status Resolution Support Services Policy Advice Manual* (DIBP, 2016) (online at 18 November 2018) <https://www.border.gov.au/AccessandAccountability/Documents/20161006_FA160700108_documents_released.pdf>.

20 Department of Immigration and Border Protection, *Annual Report 2014–2015* (Commonwealth Government, 2015), Department of Immigration and Border Protection, *Annual Report 2015–2016* (Commonwealth Government, 2016) (*Annual Report 2015–2016*).

21 Ilan Katz, Geraldine Doney and Effie Mitchell, *Evaluation of the Expansion of the Community Detention Program: Final Report SPRC 12/13 to the Department of Immigration and Citizenship* (DIAS, 2013) (*Community Detention Evaluation*).

22 *Ms BK, Ms CO and Mr DE on Behalf of Themselves and Their Families v Commonwealth Department of Home Affairs)* (2018) AusHRC 128 (*(2018) AusHRC 128*). This was a report into the practice of the Australian Government of sending to Nauru families with young children who arrived in Australia seeking asylum.

23 Although individual children could certainly still have had exacerbating experiences while in community care, the nature of the care arrangements, unlike immigration detention in closed centres, was not inherently exacerbating.

24 The impacts flowing from the limitations associated with transfer process itself will be considered in Chapters 6 (from the perspective of the exacerbation of their vulnerabilities generated by their alienage) and 7 (from the perspective of the exacerbation of their vulnerabilities generated by their separation from their parents).

25 Michael Dudley et al., 'Children and Young People in Immigration Detention' (2012) 25(4) *Current Opinion in Psychiatry* 285.

26 Carolyn Hamilton et al., *Administrative Detention of Children: A Global Report* (UNICEF, 2011) 95–96.

27 Ibid 96.

28 See, for example, Louise Newman et al., 'Seeking Asylum in Australia: Immigration Detention, Human Rights and Mental Health Care' (2013) 21(4) *Australasian Psychiatry* 316; Nicholas Proctor et al., 'Suicide and Self-Harm in Immigration Detention' (2013) 199(11) *The Medical Journal of Australia* 730.

29 Dr Peter Young, 'Transcript of Sydney Public Hearing to Australian Human Rights Commission', *National Inquiry into Children in Immigration Detention* (31 July 2014) 13. <https://www.humanrights.gov.au/sites/default/files/Dr%20Young.pdf>.

Dr Young was, relevantly, the psychiatrist and former director of mental health for the company contracted to provide medical care in detention centres in Australia and in offshore detention centres on Nauru and Manus Island.

30 See Michael Dudley et al. (n 25) 285–292 and Karen Zwi and Sarah Mares, 'Stories from Unaccompanied Children in Immigration Detention: A Composite Account' (2015) 51(7) *Journal of Paediatrics and Child Health* 659.

31 Zachary Steel et al., 'Impact of Immigration Detention and Temporary Protection on the Mental Health of Refugees' (2006) 188(1) *The British Journal of Psychiatry* 58.

32 See 'Transcript of Sydney Public Hearing to Australian Human Rights Commission', *National Inquiry into Children in Immigration Detention* (4 April 2014) 11:

> You can make the services as world class as they can be but at the end of the day they are still in detention and that is the environment really that is creating the problem in the first place.

33 Ilan Katz, Geraldine Doney and Effie Mitchell (n 21) 43.

34 'Unaccompanied Child, Handwritten Submission No. 145, Australian Human Rights Commission', *The Forgotten Children Inquiry* (undated) 1–2.

35 'Unaccompanied Child, Submission No. 147, Australian Human Rights Commission'. *The Forgotten Children Inquiry* (25/5/2014) 1.

36 Dr Peter Young (n 29) 13.

37 I acknowledge that it is also difficult for adults detained with their children to meet these needs in a detention environment. There are sound reasons for not detaining families in immigration detention centres, but that discussion is beyond the scope of this book.

38 Australian Human Rights Commission, *The Forgotten Children Inquiry* (n 13) 169–170.

39 The Forum of Australian Services for Survivors of Torture and Trauma, Submission No. 210, Australian Human Rights Commission, *The Forgotten Children Inquiry* (13 June 2014) 15.

40 The Department describes community detention as:

> An alternative term for 'residence determination', which allows a person, who is required or permitted to be taken into immigration detention or who is in immigration detention, to reside in the community at a specified address and in accordance with certain conditions, instead of being detained at a place of immigration detention. Under the *Migration Act*, the Minister has a non-compellable, non-delegable power to make, vary or revoke a residence determination if it is thought to be in the public interest to do so.

See *Annual Report 2015–2016* (n 20) 303.

41 APODs are low security detention facilities for families and children, such as places where medical treatment is provided; hotels, motels and apartments; home-based care using private accommodation owned or leased by relatives or persons with established close relationships with the person in detention;

and community-based care provided through non-governmental organisations (NGOs) using accommodation provided by the NGO or a community group.

42 The most flexible housing environment for persons in immigration detention.

43 Inconsistencies in reporting methodologies by the Department make it difficult to identify how many unaccompanied children were cared for in each custodial arrangement in the research period. *The Forgotten Children Inquiry* (n 13) provides a 'point in time statistic' reporting that, as of 31 March 2014, Australian detention centres held 56 children between the ages of 13 and 17 who had travelled to Australia without parents or a legal guardian. In contrast, the 2014 DIBP Annual Report stated that, as of 30 June 2014, there were 331 unaccompanied children living in community detention and an undisclosed number in APODs, immigration residential housing or immigration transit accommodation. Subsequent DIBP Annual Reports do not distinguish between accompanied and unaccompanied children in placement statistics. For example, the DIBP 2014–2015 Annual Report notes only that, as at 30 April 2015, there were 1,092 children living in community detention under a residence determination, 69 children in APODs on the Australian mainland, 16 children in immigration residential housing in Sydney and 42 children in immigration transit accommodation in Adelaide, Brisbane and Melbourne.

44 The impacts of the legislative changes on the vulnerabilities of children detained in immigration residential housing, immigration transit accommodation and APODs would all have been different. The impacts of those alternate sites could be the subject of future research.

45 See Department of Immigration and Border Protection, *Annual Report 2013–2014* (Commonwealth Government, 2014) 197.

46 *Migration Act* s 197AB(2)(b).

47 Ilan Katz, Geraldine Doney and Effie Mitchell (n 21) 40.

48 Ibid 19, 40. Some concerns have been raised about the variable standard of care provided across Australia in light of the lack of consistent or compulsory qualification and training requirements of custodians employed by NGOs and agencies at the time.

49 Ibid 66.

50 Ibid 113. Unaccompanied children expressed a concern about inadequate oversight of the different service providers, with a consequent lack of transparency and accountability for some households/providers.

51 Ibid 73. Requiring the permission of the delegated guardian for decisions, such as overnight stays, means that, in practice, the child often misses the opportunity:

> If at night-time we want to go to somewhere – our friends or relatives home, the carer also are not given permission [to authorise the visit]; they are not responsible. If we want to go we have to get permission from DIAC. We should fill a form and give to carer. The carer will pass it to company. Company will pass it to case manager. Case manager will pass it to DIAC. Sometimes they say yes, sometimes they say no.

52 Service providers are required to notify the DIBP of all reportable incidents. These include perceived flight risks, fights/assaults, threatened/actual/or attempted self-harm, voluntary starvation, client not residing at/returning to approved address, all medical incidents requiring transport by ambulance or other relevant emergencies, emergency incidents, protest action or group disturbances and charging of a client in breach of the law. See *Department of Immigration and Border Protection, Procedure Advice Manual, PAM3 – Client Placement* [A 165.4] 5.3.1.

53 Ilan Katz, Geraldine Doney and Effie Mitchell (n 21) 51.

54 Ibid.
55 Ibid.
56 Ibid 59.
57 Ibid.
58 Ibid.
59 *Memorandum of Understanding between the Government of the Independent State of Papua New Guinea and the Government of Australia, Relating to the Transfer to, and Assessment and Settlement in, Papua New Guinea of Certain persons, and Related Issues*, signed 3 August 2013.

Memorandum of Understanding between the Republic of Nauru and the Commonwealth of Australia, Relating to the Transfer to and Assessment of Persons in Nauru, and Related Issues, signed 3 August 2013.

60 Ibid.
61 *Asylum Seekers (Regional Processing Centre) Act 2012* (Nauru) s 5.
62 Ibid s 6(1)(c).
63 Ibid s 6(1)(d).
64 Ibid s 6(1)(e).
65 Ibid s 6(1)(i).
66 Ibid s 6(1)(f).
67 Ibid s 6(1)(g). The Act requires that asylum seekers be provided with medical care and treatment and educational services 'to the standard that he or she might reasonably have access to if he or she were living in the general community in Nauru'. Legitimate concerns have been raised about the impact of Australia's offshore processing policy on asylum seekers, particularly children, because of the disparity between the quality of medical care and treatment and educational services on Nauru and that provided on the Australian mainland.
68 Ibid s 6(1)(p).
69 UNHCR, *Monitoring Visit to the Republic of Nauru* (n 12) 1–3.
70 Mat Tinkler, 'Transcript of Evidence to Australian Human Rights Commission', *The Forgotten Children Inquiry*, Sydney Public Hearing (4 April 2014) 6. <https://www.humanrights.gov.au/sites/default/files/Mr%20Tinkler_0.pdf>.

Mat Tinkler, Director of Policy and Public Affairs at Save the Children, described the physical conditions of the Nauru RPC to the *Forgotten Children Inquiry* as follows:

> … the environment is hot, it's humid, it's dusty, living conditions are very cramped. The island is very isolated the detention centres within the island are isolated. There is no shade, it's a difficult place to live …
>
> The centre of the island is full of fossilised coral pinnacles, they are called, with jungle and growth over them. It's not a hospitable environment and they've literally been bulldozed and had gravel poured on top and on top of that is the tents that people are living in.

71 UNHCR, *Monitoring Visit to the Republic of Nauru* (n 12) 16 [89]. The UNHCR noted the harsh conditions of the RPC with little natural shelter from the heat during the day, which is exacerbated by all the challenges arising from residing in a construction zone, including significant noise and dust, as well as the proximity to phosphate mining, which causes a high level of dust.
72 The 2015 *Taking Responsibility Report* (n 15) at [5.64] expressed its deep concern that 'standards of living for asylum seekers in the Regional Processing Centre are unacceptably low in a range of areas, including exposure to the elements, lack of privacy, poor hygiene and insufficient access to water and sanitation'.

73 Unaccompanied child asylum seekers on Nauru gave evidence to the AHRC *Forgotten Children Inquiry* about the 'very dirty tents', which often 'become flooded when the rain begins [and afterwards] have leaks and holes'. See, for example, 'Name Withheld (Child Detained in Nauru OPC), Submission No. 95, Australian Human Rights Commission', *The Forgotten Children Inquiry* (26 May 2014) <https://humanrights.gov.au/sites/default/files/Submission%20No%2095%20-Name%20withheld%20-%20Child%20detained%20in%20Nauru%20OPC.pdf?_ga=2.24710387.878436188.1589764716-644388670.1588671908>; 'Name Withheld (16-Year Old Detained in Nauru OPC), submission No. 91, Australian Human Rights Commission', *The Forgotten Children Inquiry* (27 May 2014) <https://humanrights.gov.au/sites/default/files/Submission%20No%2091%20-%20Name%20withheld%20-%2016%20year%20old%20detained%20in%20Nauru%20OPC.pdf?_ga=2.216574687.878436188.1589764716-644388670.1588671908>.

74 Mat Tinkler, 'Transcript of Evidence to Australian Human Rights Commission', *The Forgotten Children Inquiry* (n 70) 1.

75 'Name Withheld (Unaccompanied Child Detained in Nauru OPC), Submission No. 143 to Australian Human Rights Commission', *The Forgotten Children Inquiry* (undated) 1.
<https://humanrights.gov.au/sites/default/files/Submission%20No%20143%20-%20Name%20withheld%20-%20Unaccompanied%20child%20detained%20in%20Nauru%20OPC.pdf?_ga=2.44082797.878436188.1589764716-644388670.1588671908>.

76 Tom Allard, 'Nauru's Move to Open its Detention Centre Makes it 'More Dangerous' for Asylum Seekers' *Sydney Morning Herald* (online at 9 October 2015) <http://www.smh.com.au/federal-politics/political-news/naurus-move-to-open-its-detention-centre-makes-it-more-dangerous-for-asylum-seekers-20151008-gk4kbt.html>.

77 Derrick Silove, Philippa McIntosh and Rise Becker, 'Risk of Retraumatisation of Asylum-Seekers in Australia' (1993) 27 *Australian and New Zealand Journal of Psychiatry* 606; Rise Becker and Derrick Silove 'Psychiatric and Psychosocial Effects of Prolonged Detention on Asylum-Seekers' in Mary Crock (ed), *Protection or Punishment: The Detention of Asylum Seekers in Australia* (Federation Press, 1993).

78 Zachary Steel and Derrick Silove, 'The Mental Health Implications of Detaining Asylum Seekers' (2001) 175 *Medical Journal of Australia* 596.

79 *Taking Responsibility Report* (n 15) [3.119].

80 Dr Peter Young (n 29) 14.

81 Royal Children's Hospital Melbourne, Submission to the *Taking Responsibility Inquiry* (2 April 2016) 2–3.

82 UNHCR, *Monitoring Visit to the Republic of Nauru* (n 12) 21 [115].

83 Employees of Save the Children Australia in Nauru (names withheld), 'Submission No. 183, Australian Human Rights Commission', *Forgotten Children Inquiry* (undated) 9, 41, 42.
<https://humanrights.gov.au/sites/default/files/Submission%20No%20183%20-%20Names%20withheld%20-%20Employees%20of%20Save%20the%20Children%20Australia%20in%20Nauru_0.pdf?_ga=2.77504988.878436188.1589764716-644388670.1588671908>.

84 Oliver Laughland and Ben Doherty, 'Nauru Staff Report Persistent Child Abuse and Self-Harm, Leaked Documents Show', *The Guardian* (online at 4 October 2014)
<http://www.theguardian.com/australia-news/2014/oct/04/nauru-detention-centre-staff-persistent-child-abuse-self-harm>.

85 Ben Doherty, 'Nauru Asylum Seekers Sew Lips Shut in Protest over Cambodia Transfer', *The Guardian* (online at 2 October 2014) <http://www.theguardian.com/world/2014/oct/02/nauru-asylum-seekers-sew-lips-shut-protest-cambodia-transfer>.

86 Department of Immigration and Border Protection, Second Public Hearing of the *National Inquiry into Children in Immigration Detention* 2014, Melbourne (2 July 2014) 6. <http://www.humanrights.gov.au/our-work/asylum-seekers-and-refugees/national-inquiry-children-immigration-detention-2014-1>.

87 See Employees of Save the Children Australia in Nauru (names withheld) (n 83) 4–5. See also [2018] AusHRC 128 (n 22) 39–40.

88 Oliver Laughland, 'Doctors Concerned by 48-hour Turnaround Target for Asylum Seekers' *The Guardian* (online at 25 September 2013) <http://www.theguardian.com/world/2013/sep/25/doctors-concerned-asylum-seeker-health>.

89 Senate Select Committee, *Taking Responsibility Report* (n 15) [3.99].

90 Ibid [3.108].

91 Mat Tinkler, 'Transcript of Evidence to Australian Human Rights Commission', *The Forgotten Children Inquiry* (n 70) 3.

92 The exceptions are research by Mary Crock et al., *Protection of Refugees with Disabilities: Forgotten and Invisible?* (Edward Elgar Publishing, 2017) and Karen Soldatic et al., '"Nowhere to be Found": Disabled Refugees and Asylum Seekers within the Australian Resettlement Landscape' (2015) 2(1) *Disability and the Global South* 501.

93 Senate Select Committee, *Taking Responsibility Report* (n 15) [3.121].

94 [2018] AusHRC 128 (n 22) 37–41.

95 Ibid 39.

96 Ibid 40–41.

97 Department of Immigration and Border Protection, 'Submission No. 18', *Senate Legal and Constitutional Affairs Committee Inquiry into the Conditions of Treatment of Asylum Seekers and Refugees at the Regional Processing Centres in the Republic of Nauru and Papua New Guinea* (March 2016) 22. <https://www.aph.gov.au/DocumentStore.ashx?id=fabbe9e5-2ed3-47cd-86c2-f313a6f1b7e8&subId=411483>.

98 Senate Select Committee, *Taking Responsibility Report* (n 15) [4.59].

99 Ibid [3.43].

100 ChilOut, 'Submission No. 168, Australian Human Rights Commission', *The Forgotten Children Inquiry* (May 2014) 6. <https://humanrights.gov.au/sites/default/files/Submission%20No%20168%20-%20ChilOut.pdf?_ga=2.120120769.878436188.1589764716-644388670.1588671908>.

101 Senate Select Committee, *Taking Responsibility Report* (n 15) [5.29]. The figures do not differentiate between accompanied and unaccompanied children.

102 Ibid [4.35].

103 Ibid [4.37].

104 Ibid [4.87].

105 Ibid [4.88].

106 Ibid [4.89].

107 Ibid Recommendation 11 [5.76].

108 Tony Abbott MP, 'Joint Press Conference, Hamilton Island' (Media Release, 21 March 2015) <http://pmtranscripts.pmc.gov.au/release/transcript-24309>.

109 Senate Select Committee, *Taking Responsibility Report* (n 15) [4.42].

110 *Australian Border Force Act 2015* (Cth) s 42(1).

111 Ibid s 42(1).

112 Ibid s 42(2)(a), s 48.

113 Ibid s 42(2).

114 Ibid.
115 Senate Select Committee, *Taking Responsibility Report* (n 15) [2.163].
116 Ibid [2.163].
117 Ibid.
118 Ibid Recommendation 12 [5.79].
119 Ibid [5.74].
120 Ibid [4.64].
121 Ibid [5.75].
122 Australian Human Rights Commission, *The Forgotten Children Inquiry* (n 13) 30.
123 Being able to organise spontaneous overnight stays with friends enables unaccompanied children to develop regular age-appropriate friendships. Custodians should still be required to obtain consent from the legal guardian or delegated guardian in relation to health care and residency decisions, travel plans, placing an unaccompanied minor in the care of another person or allowing them to leave the State in which they reside.
124 Although, as will be discussed in Chapter 6, even if the government could ensure that expert wrap-around allied healthcare services and specialist custodians were provided, the legitimacy of offshore processing as an Australian, but not a regional solution, will still need to be justified.

6 Vulnerability analysis of Australia's processing of asylum claims of unaccompanied children

6.1 Introduction

This chapter applies the mitigating vulnerability framework to assess the operation and impact of amendments to Australian law and policy in 2012, 2013 and 2014 on the acute vulnerabilities generated by the alienage of unaccompanied asylum-seeking children and makes recommendations for reform. As examined in Chapter 2, these children bear the vulnerabilities shared by all children and, additionally, three vulnerabilities arising from their alienage: their non-citizenship, their unauthorised presence, and their seeking asylum after fleeing persecution in their homelands. Through applying vulnerability theory, these vulnerabilities can be understood as situational, overlaying their shared inherent vulnerabilities. Depending on States' responses, these inherent and situational vulnerabilities can either be ameliorated or exacerbated into occurrent or pathogenic vulnerabilities.

Applying the first stage of the mitigating vulnerability framework, Section 6.2 examines how changes to the *Migration Act* in 2012, 2013 and 2014 operated to affect the inherent and situational vulnerability of unaccompanied children seeking asylum in Australia. The amendments effectively created three cohorts of unaccompanied children in Australia: a 'Legacy Caseload' of unaccompanied children eligible to have their claim processed on the mainland, those whose claim for asylum from Australia was deflected and relegated to the Nauruan Government to determine, and those whose claim was deflected outright by the reintroduction of Boat Turnbacks and Takebacks.

Section 6.3 then applies the second stage, examining the impact of these changes on the relative vulnerabilities of unaccompanied child asylum seekers in each cohort. For those in the 'Legacy Caseload', definitional and procedural changes to the RSD process rendered them occurrently vulnerable to incorrect determinations through the introduction of restricted 'fast-track' merits review and limiting access to judicial review. The amendments also made them pathogenically vulnerable to lethal hopelessness caused by delays in processing RSDs. Further, these changes, in principle, exposed unaccompanied children to an occurrent risk of refoulement by altering the criteria for refugee status and winding back recognition of Australia's non-refoulement obligations in the *Migration Act*. However, the risk of refoulement was largely ameliorated in practice by the

DOI: 10.4324/9781003260134-7

provision of free specialist legal assistance. For the children transferred to Nauru, the legislative changes generated a number of occurrent vulnerabilities. These included the risk of inaccurate age determinations leading to their detention in adult male compounds, the risk of not being able to prosecute their claim for asylum and the risk of being transferred offshore without a proper pre-transfer best interest assessment. These children were also pathogenically vulnerable to cruel, inhuman and degrading treatment on Nauru such as to constitute refoulement. Finally, for the children subjected to Boat Turnbacks and Takebacks, critical pathogenic vulnerabilities arose through the introduction of 'on-sea' screening and refusing entry to the State, which both directly subjected them to an unmediated risk of refoulement. Section 6.4 attends to the third stage of the mitigating vulnerability framework by identifying the priorities for legislative and policy reform.

Framing their experiences under these amendments in terms of vulnerabilities supplements traditional human rights analysis that this State practice breached these children's rights to non-refoulement and access to special assistance with their claim for asylum. It does so by distilling with specificity the sites where the amendments progressively exacerbated these children's inherent and situational vulnerability arising from their alienage and the exact sources of devastating occurrent and pathogenic harms. So doing, it both illuminates the imperative for States to avoid these harms by providing unaccompanied children with special assistance in processing their claim for asylum, notwithstanding their unauthorised presence, and demonstrates where priorities for legislative and policy reform should be directed.

6.2 Operation of the 2012–2014 legislative amendments: downgrading unaccompanied children's ability to seek asylum in Australia

This section applies Stage 1 of the mitigating vulnerability framework to examine how changes to the *Migration Act* between 2012 and 2014 operated to affect the inherent and situational vulnerability of unaccompanied children generated by seeking asylum. This examination and setting out of the legal and policy context, defining the relationship between Australia, as the responsive State, and these children, is required before we can assess the impact of the amendments in Stage 2, or the priorities for reform in Stage 3. Prior to 2012, the RSD process for assessing the protection claims of unaccompanied children who arrived by boat was essentially robust. It evaluated their claim for protection against the Refugee Convention's definition of refugees,[1] entitled asylum seekers to permanent protection and acknowledged Australia's non-refoulement obligations in accordance with international law. Primary decisions were subject to merits and judicial review. These children also had access to government-funded legal assistance, and the processing of their claims was not unreasonably prolonged.

However, the passage of four key pieces of legislation between 2012 and 2014 diminished access to a robust RSD for all maritime asylum seekers *and* failed to make any special provision for unaccompanied children. These changes progressively restricted the eligibility of asylum seekers (including unaccompanied child asylum seekers) who arrive by boat in Australia to claim asylum.

The *Migration Legislation Amendment (Regional Processing and Other Measures) Act 2012* authorised the removal of unauthorised maritime arrivals from Australia and the offshore processing of their protection claims.[2] As examined in Chapter 5, unaccompanied children who arrived by boat after 13 August 2012 were subject to processing in Nauru or Manus Island, although they could still be settled in Australia if found to be a refugee.[3]

The *Migration Amendment (Unauthorised Maritime Arrivals and Other Measures) Act* 2013, implemented by the Rudd (Labor) government, announced on 19 July 2013 that irregular boat arrivals who arrived from that date would be processed offshore and would never be resettled in Australia.[4] The Act enabled all 'unauthorised maritime arrivals' – families, adult females, adult males and unaccompanied minors – who arrived after 19 July 2013 to be 'transited' in Australia, prior to being sent offshore to Nauru or Manus Island, and required their asylum claims to be processed under the respective laws of Nauru or PNG. These asylum seekers could not make a valid application for a visa in Australia while in transit unless the Minister personally declared it was in the public interest to do so. The Act did not make provision for adequate pre-transfer assessments or Best Interest Determinations for unaccompanied children. Nor was there any provision for them to receive independent legal advice from the time they arrived in Australia up until the time they were removed.

Prior to 19 July 2013, Australia's non-refoulement obligations under international human rights law had been partly incorporated into domestic law in Sections 5(1) and 36 of the *Migration Act*. These provisions enabled unaccompanied child asylum seekers who arrived in Australia to apply for a protection visa on the basis that they were owed protection obligations under the Refugee Convention or would face a real risk of significant harm if removed from Australia. However, amendments to the *Migration Act* in 2013 precluded asylum seekers who arrived by boat after 19 July 2013 from accessing those protections against refoulement.[5] These amendments precluded all 'unauthorised maritime arrivals' and 'transitory persons' from applying for a visa, including a protection visa, unless the Minister deemed it was in the 'public interest' through the exercise of a non-compellable discretion.[6] The amendments effectively prevented asylum seekers who arrived by boat from accessing the visas that gave effect to Australia's non-refoulement obligations.

The *Maritime Powers Act 2013* set up the statutory framework to implement *Operation Sovereign Borders*, the Abbott (Coalition) government's policy of intercepting boats carrying asylum seekers before they reached Australian waters. It authorised Australian maritime officers to tow any person on a vessel in or outside Australian waters back to their original destination or, if their boat was unsafe, place them in lifeboats and direct them back to Indonesia.[7]

Then, the *Migration and Maritime Powers Legislation Amendment (Resolving the Asylum Legacy Caseload) Act* passed in December 2014, implemented a further suite of measures that signalled Australia's explicit retreat from its international obligations. The Abbott (Coalition) government argued these were necessary to reinforce 'the government's powers to undertake maritime turnbacks and to introduce rapid processing and streamlined review arrangements'[8] to 'stop the boats' and resolve 'Labor's legacy caseload of around 30,000 cases'.[9] This Act dramatically affected the claim to protection of both unaccompanied children already in Australia and those still at sea or yet to arrive. It made extensive changes to Australia's RSD framework for unaccompanied children seeking asylum in Australia. These included reintroducing temporary protection visas without family reunion rights or a right to re-enter Australia[10] and a new fast-track merits review process for boat arrivals between 13 August 2012 and 1 January 2014.[11] In addition, express references to the Refugee Convention in the *Migration Act* were replaced with vaguer language, which reduced protection obligations[12] and deemed Australia's non-refoulement obligations as 'irrelevant' to removals carried out under Section 198 of the *Migration Act*.[13]

For unaccompanied children still at sea or yet to arrive, the *Migration Act* expressly authorised the transfer of asylum seekers intercepted at sea, even if this would amount to the return of people to persecution or other forms of significant harm.[14] It provided that the rules of natural justice do not apply to the exercise of these powers.[15] It also provided that exercises of power under these provisions are not invalidated even if there has been a failure to consider Australia's international obligations, there has been a 'defective consideration' of those obligations or the taking of a person to that place is inconsistent with these obligations.[16]

The effect of these legislative changes on unaccompanied children's eligibility to have their claim for asylum processed and their eligibility for resettlement is captured in Table 6.1, 'Eligibility to apply for asylum by date of arrival'.

As Table 6.1 illustrates, Australia's response to the alienage-generated vulnerabilities of unaccompanied child asylum seekers constricted steadily between 2012 and 2013. From being eligible to have their claim for asylum processed in Australia and be resettled in Australia if found to be a refugee in 2012, unaccompanied children, since 2013, have been variously subjected to Boat Turnbacks, Takebacks or transfers to a regional processing country and prevented from making a claim at all. Moreover, the recognition of unaccompanied children as 'special cases', notwithstanding their unauthorised presence, has not so much been reduced as dispensed with altogether, as the trajectory of Australia's legislative reforms in this period foreground the principle of deterrence rather than human rights protection.

6.3 Impact of denying access to RSD and protections against refoulement: augmenting the protection gap for unaccompanied child asylum seekers

As discussed in Chapter 2, unaccompanied children's vulnerability arising from their alienage is multifaceted, with indeterminate beginnings and ends. These vulnerabilities are situated in multiple and potentially overlapping sites: from the

Table 6.1 Eligibility to apply for asylum by date of arrival

Date of arrival	*Processing of asylum claim*	*Eligibility to settle in Australia if found to be a refugee*
Before 13 August 2012	Asylum claim processed in Australia	Can be resettled in Australia if found to be a refugee
After 13 August 2012 and before19 July 2013	Transferred initially to a third country (Nauru or Papua New Guinea) for asylum claim processing after 'transiting' in Australia (on Christmas Island); subsequently transferred back to Australia for processing of their claim (Legacy Caseload)	Can be resettled in Australia if found to be a refugee
After 19 July 2013	Transferred to a third country (Nauru or Papua New Guinea) to have their asylum claim processed after 'transiting' in Australia (on Christmas Island)	Cannot be resettled in Australia if found to be a refugee
After September 2013	Ineligible to make a claim for asylum in Australia; asylum seekers are subject to Turnbacks, Takebacks or transfers to a regional processing country	No opportunity to settle in Australia

persecution experienced in their home country, mistreatment or exploitation on their journey or at the border control, resistance to their claim for protection or all the above. Also, unaccompanied children's vulnerability on account of their seeking asylum is acute and heightened compared to other unaccompanied children who have been authorised entry as refugees,[17] and their vulnerability on account of their unauthorised presence is particularly dependent on the character of the State's political response to them. This section examines the impact of the legislative amendments as the second stage of the mitigating vulnerability framework. Their inherent and situational vulnerability arising from their dependence on the State to process their asylum claim becomes an occurrent (and potentially pathogenic) vulnerability when States do not provide them with special assistance in prosecuting their refugee claim, do not process their claims in a timely fashion and do not adhere to rules of natural justice. Further, their dependence on the State to not refoul them is absolute, and States' failure to ameliorate this vulnerability aggravates their situational vulnerability into a potentially pathogenic one.

6.3.1 Impacts on the Legacy Caseload cohort eligible for processing of their asylum claim on the Australian mainland

The definitional and procedural changes to the RSD process rendered unaccompanied children in the Legacy Caseload cohort occurrently vulnerable to incorrect determinations arising from the restricted fast-track merits review and limited access to judicial review. They also became pathogenically vulnerable to lethal hopelessness caused by RSD processing delays and to a risk of refoulement by winding back recognition of Australia's non-refoulement obligations in the *Migration Act*.

Prior to the introduction of the fast-track merits review process, asylum seekers who received a negative primary decision on their visa application could apply to the Administrative Appeals Tribunal (AAT) for a merits review of protection visa applications. This review considered the facts, law and policy aspects of the original decision; could take into account new information that was not available to the original decision-maker; and could conduct hearings to test and take new evidence. However, the new fast-track merits review referred unsuccessful applicants to review before an Immigration Assessment Authority (IAA).[18]

In contrast to the AAT, the IAA could not interview asylum seekers[19] nor accept or request information that was not available to the primary decision-maker to determine whether the original decision was correct except in exceptional circumstances.[20] Here, their situational vulnerability as asylum seekers became an occurrent vulnerability because they were denied an opportunity for a procedurally fair merits review of the primary decision. Moreover, it became a potentially pathogenic vulnerability if that denial heightened their risk of being incorrectly denied protection and returned or removed to situations in breach of Australia's non-refoulement obligations.[21] Although asylum seekers who received a negative decision on their visa application at the IAA could still apply for judicial review, this could only correct legal errors in the making of the decision (such as whether a decision-maker was biased, applied the wrong criteria in coming to their decision or failed to take relevant information into account). Since judicial review does not assess whether the decision-maker was correct in determining whether a person is or is not entitled to protection as a refugee, it does not alleviate the occurrent vulnerability of unaccompanied child asylum seekers generated by the fast-track merits review process.

The amendments also made these children pathogenically vulnerable to lethal hopelessness caused by prolonged delays in processing RSDs. After third country processing was reintroduced in 2012, the processing of visa applications for people in the Legacy Caseload cohort was paused.[22] The Department's Protection Visa Processing Guidelines specify that applications from unaccompanied children should be accorded higher priority than others.[23] Nevertheless, the reintroduction of temporary protection visas and suspension of visa processing until May 2015 caused such substantial delays that the Department estimated that the primary assessments for this cohort will not be completed before December 2021.[24] Since the Legacy Caseload cohort comprises asylum seekers who arrived in Australia and had not had their application determined before 1 January 2014, some in this cohort had their claims pending for at least seven years.

These children's situational vulnerability can be exacerbated into an occurrent vulnerability in which the prolonged delay in finalising RSD becomes a stressor in and of itself.[25] This is evidenced by a growing body of research establishing that these children were subjected to a pathogenic vulnerability of 'lethal hopelessness'. For example, prolonged delays in the processing of the claims of the Legacy Caseload cohort generated 'increasing reports of many people within the asylum seeker community being at advanced stages of feeling mentally trapped, figuratively boxed in and especially hopeless and helpless'.[26] While the available research does not address unaccompanied child asylum seekers specifically, it is clear that children as young as ten were expressing suicidal ideation.[27] Therefore, the impact of this aspect of the amendments on the vulnerabilities of unaccompanied child asylum seekers is likely to have undermined Australia's otherwise largely adequate care arrangements in community detention, as examined in Chapter 5.

A further key impact of these legislative changes for this cohort was to potentially exacerbate their situational vulnerability as an unauthorised entrant by exposing them to the pathogenic vulnerability inherent in refoulement. The criteria for refugee status introduced by the *Legacy Caseload Act* essentially maintained the criteria in the Refugee Convention.[28] However, by replacing most express references to the Refugee Convention in the *Migration Act* with a new statutory RSD framework[29] and by including additional criteria beyond the Refugee Convention, its overall impact was to reduce Australia's compliance with its protection obligations. Specifically, the additional criteria required asylum seekers to establish that they had a 'well-founded fear of persecution' in 'all areas' of their country of origin,[30] not just in their home city or the place they fled from; that no 'effective protection measures' were available in their country of origin from their government, non-State parties, or organisations;[31] and that there were no 'reasonable steps' that they could take to modify their behaviour to avoid persecution.[32] For unaccompanied children, in particular, the amendment requiring that their fear of persecution extend to all areas might require them to return to their country and relocate to an area where they have no family or support network. These amendments, coupled with the express stipulation that Australia's non-refoulement obligations are 'irrelevant' to removals carried out under Section 198 of the *Migration Act*,[33] exacerbate these children's situational vulnerability to a pathogenic vulnerability to being denied refugee status, removed from Australia and refoulement even if they have a well-founded fear of persecution within the meaning of the Refugee Convention.

It must be noted that unaccompanied children on the mainland were eligible to receive assistance with visa processing and merits review of decisions under either the government-funded Immigration Advice and Application Assistance Scheme[34] or the Primary Application Information Scheme (PAIS) (after 31 March 2014). Although their access to legal representation was ad hoc and not automatic, PAIS funded the provision of assistance by a not-for-profit, the Refugee Advice and Casework Service (RACS), which ran a Legal Help for Unaccompanied Children service. Based in Sydney, RACS sub-contracted registered migration agents in Tasmania, Victoria and the Northern Territory to assist these children with their visa applications.[35] As of 30 June 2014, RACS reported it was assisting more than 30 unaccompanied children at imminent risk of removal to Nauru, but because of the 'lack of funding and capacity of staff, RACS cannot presently provide comprehensive legal assistance for all children in immigration detention'.[36] As a result, access was dependent on the ability of the child to obtain the necessary information and assistance to contact the service and RACS' capacity to cope with demand. Nevertheless, these children's occurrent vulnerability to having incorrect determinations made, or pathogenic vulnerability to a risk of refoulement, was lessened when they accessed this free specialist legal assistance.

6.3.2 Impacts on the Offshore Transferee cohort

Applying the Stage 2 vulnerability taxonomy to distinguish between and characterise impacts of the legislative amendments on unaccompanied children in the Offshore Transferee cohort reveals four acute impacts. First, they were occurrently vulnerable to not being provided with adequate pre-transfer assessments for eligibility for offshore processing. Second, they were given inadequate representation in the age determination processes. Third, they received no special assistance to prosecute their claim for asylum. And finally, these failures exposed them to such a risk of significant or irreparable harm (including cruel, inhuman or degrading treatment) on Nauru as to constitute a pathogenic vulnerability to refoulement.

6.3.2.1 Pre-transfer assessments for offshore processing

The government conducted pre-transfer Best Interest Assessments of unaccompanied children subject to offshore processing. This purported to assess the possible exercise of the Minister's discretion under Section 198AE (1) of the *Migration Act* to declare that the requisite Section 198AD transfer to a regional processing country did not apply to that child. The applicable pre-transfer policy differed depending on whether an unaccompanied child arrived in the period between 13 August 2012 to 19 July 2013 or after 19 July 2013.[37] However, the government mandated that 'in making the transfer decision, the best interests of such children are outweighed by other primary considerations, including the need to preserve the integrity of Australia's migration system and the need to discourage children taking, or being taken on, dangerous illegal boat journeys to Australia'.[38] The government explicitly conceded that 'while this assessment considers a range of factors to ensure that care, services and support arrangements are available to meet the needs of the individual child, it *does not consider whether the best interests of the child would be served by the individual child being transferred to an RPC*' (emphasis added).[39]

This was in breach of both Australian domestic and international law. Australian courts have confirmed that, although decision-makers must not treat any other considerations as inherently more significant than the child's best interests, other considerations (or their cumulative effect) may sometimes outweigh them.[40] But Australian law requires that the child's best interests must be identified first before they can be weighed against other considerations, which does not occur with the pre-transfer best interest assessment. Under international law (as discussed previously in Section 3.3.1), best interest assessments must involve a clear and comprehensive assessment of an individual child's specific circumstances.[41] They must be done in a friendly and safe atmosphere by qualified professionals trained in age and gender sensitive interviewing techniques.[42] They must be determined individually, on a case-by-case basis, before competing interests are taken into account[43] and provide reasons stating the child's factual circumstances, the relevant considerations, how they have been weighted to determine the child's best interests and whether the decision differs from the child's views.[44] If, exceptionally, the solution chosen is not, ultimately, in the best interests of the child, the decision must set out grounds to show that the child's best interests were, nevertheless, a *primary* consideration. The assessment should also provide formal mechanisms to appeal and revise decisions to address procedural or substantive decision-making errors,[45] including when best interest assessment requirements have not been complied with.[46]

An examination of the assessments conducted by the Department between 1 January 2014 and 1 March 2014 for children detained on Christmas Island revealed that they all failed to meet the minimum requirements for a best interests determination. All 27 unaccompanied children in immigration detention on Christmas Island were assessed for eligibility for transfer to Nauru, and all were recommended for transfer. The recommendations all adopted a set of highly generalised and almost identical reasons, stating: 'Appropriate arrangements are in place in Nauru, therefore the child's transfer is appropriate'. They also did not assess the strength of the child's claim for protection. Given that, as of 31 October 2016, of the 1,195 people who had their claims for asylum assessed by the Nauruan Government, 941 (79%) had been found to be refugees, it is probable that at least this percentage of unaccompanied children transferred would be found to be owed protection obligations as refugees.[47] Neither did any of the assessments include any individualised consideration of the children's educational, care, welfare and service-related needs. In certain cases, in which children aged 16 or 17 had no schooling, the officers declared that the educational services were appropriate without providing any information about what services were actually available. In relation to family support, there was no indication as to whether the child had adult relatives residing in Australia who may have been able to provide support to the child. Although the form provided space for the assessing officer to record specific considerations concerning the individual child,[48] this space was left blank on every single form. In practice, then, for unaccompanied child boat arrivals after 19 July 2013 who were subject to transfer to Nauru, there were only two possible outcomes to an assessment: officers approved the transfer or postponed it until such a time as it was reasonably practicable.

The UN High Commissioner for Refugees expressed concern in 2012 and again in 2013 about the ineffectiveness of the assessments as a mechanism for ensuring that especially vulnerable asylum seekers, such as children, were not transferred to Nauru.[49] These inadequate assessments exacerbated the situational vulnerability of these children as unauthorised arrivals to an occurrent vulnerability to being transferred offshore, where their acute needs as being/becoming children could not be met, as already examined in Chapter 5.

6.3.2.2 *Inadequate representation in age determination*

Unaccompanied child asylum seekers without legitimate identity documentation with a clear date of birth underwent an age determination interview conducted by two Department age determination officers and an interpreter.[50] The age determination officers explored multiple lines of inquiry, including the child's physical appearance, behaviour and demeanour, family composition and history, education and employment, and social history and independence.[51] The Department did not follow a set questionnaire during the interview process but, instead, reached a decision as to whether the person was likely to be a minor or an adult on the balance of probabilities.[52] Department policy stated that officers should err on the side of caution when making an assessment that the person is an adult. Also, when there was disagreement between officers, the person would be assessed as a minor.[53] The Department did not provide legal representation during age assessment interviews unless the child had already requested or retained a lawyer.[54] As a result, children without legal representation were incorrectly assessed as adults.[55] The process exacerbated the situational vulnerabilities of these children into an occurrent vulnerability of being detained in single male adult compounds.

6.3.2.3 *Prosecuting their claim for asylum*

Unaccompanied children subject to offshore processing were occurrently vulnerable to having an incorrect determination of their asylum claim because of the failure to automatically provide them with consistent State-sponsored legal representation to prosecute their claim for asylum from reception until their transfer.

In the research period, the Department required independent observers to be present whenever the Department or other government agency interviewed an unaccompanied minor.[56] But because independent observers were precluded from advocating on the child's behalf or advising them, the requirement did not compensate for the absence of a legal representative to assist and represent the child during these processes, as evidenced by the following statement from a former unaccompanied child:

> People interviewing us they harass us very much; instead of listening to [us] they harass us; they take our documents and say they're fake. They ask us the same questions from different angles, so we try our best to provide documents or evidence if we can, but sometime we don't have any.[57]

Unlike unaccompanied children in the Legacy Cohort, who commonly received government-funded legal assistance from RACS, the cohort in the Christmas Island immigration detention centre (IDC) rarely received legal representation. Access was dependent on RACS's available resources and funding and the ability of unaccompanied children to obtain the necessary information and assistance to access the service. Unaccompanied children detained on Christmas Island only received pre-transfer legal representation in their age assessment or pre-transfer assessment interviews if the designated solicitors were already present or were able to fly there to meet with them prior to their transfer. The AHRC found that most unaccompanied children in the Christmas Island IDC, as of March 2014, who had been detained for six to eight months had not 'spoken to a lawyer or were aware they might have a right to do so'.[58]

The lack of automatic provision of a legal representative to request that the Minister exercise his discretion to grant the child a residence determination compounded the inadequacy of the de-individualised pre-transfer assessment. It further exacerbated their situational vulnerability of being unauthorised arrivals into an occurrent vulnerability of being transferred offshore where their acute needs could not be met.

6.3.2.4 *Cruel, inhuman and degrading treatment on Nauru constituting refoulement*

As examined in detail in Chapter 5, independent expert reports have found that the conditions of Nauru RPC exposed unaccompanied children to acute and significant harm,[59] and the Australian Government was clearly aware of these acute risks. The inadequate pre-transfer assessment and age determination process and the lack of specialist assistance to these children to prosecute their claim for asylum were pathogenic sources of vulnerability that made these children occurrently vulnerable to refoulement by Australia by exposing them to a real risk of significant or irreparable harm (including cruel, inhuman or degrading treatment) on Nauru.

6.3.3 *Impacts on the Boat Turnbacks and Takebacks cohort (unaccompanied asylum seeker children subject to Boat Turnbacks and Takebacks)*

This section applies the Stage 2 vulnerability taxonomy to distinguish between and characterise the impacts of the legislative amendments on unaccompanied children in the Boat Turnbacks and Takebacks cohort. As discussed in Section 6.2, from 2014, the Minister was expressly empowered to detain asylum-seeking children on the high seas, immediately remove them from Australian territory and transfer them to third countries, notwithstanding Australia's non-refoulement obligations.[60] The legality of the detention of 157 Sri Lankan Tamil asylum seekers on an Australian customs boat for 29 days after their boat was intercepted from India was upheld by the High Court in *CPCF v Minister for Immigration and*

Border Protection,[61] and the legality of boat interdictions generally has not been challenged in Australian courts.[62] Statistics identifying the number of unaccompanied children involved in Boat Turnbacks, Takebacks and enhanced screening in the research period are unavailable.[63] The Abbott (Coalition) government and subsequent governments have refused to release 'details of "on-water" matters' conducted by Operation Sovereign Borders.[64] However, information is available on the frequency and outcome of Turnbacks and Takebacks from press releases, government speeches and government answers in parliamentary scrutiny processes, such as Budget Estimates Committees. These make clear that, from the commencement of Boat Turnbacks on 19 December 2013 until 5 February 2016, at least 23 vessels carrying more than 633 asylum seekers have been turned back. [65]

6.3.3.1 Enhanced screening

Unaccompanied child asylum seekers who arrived after 13 July 2013 from Sri Lanka and Vietnam were subject to an 'enhanced screening process' when Australian authorities first made contact with them, including on the seas, to decide whether to immediately remove them from Australian territory under Section 198(2) of the *Migration Act*.[66] Unaccompanied children were subject to the same enhanced screening process as adults, being interviewed by two Department officers who make a determination of whether a protection claim was raised or not.[67] If not, they were 'screened out' of the protection assessment process and removed from Australian territory in accordance with Section 198 of the *Migration Act*.[68] If they were assessed as potentially raising a protection claim, they were 'screened in' and sent to Christmas Island IDC to await transit to Nauru for their asylum claim to be processed under Nauru's RSD procedure.

The situational vulnerability of unaccompanied children subject to on-water enhanced screening and Boat Turnbacks and Takebacks is acute. Subjecting children to an identical screening process as adults and failing to provide them with any adult or legal representation exacerbates their situational vulnerability into an occurrent vulnerability to being turned back to an unsafe situation at sea or in the next transit country where they arrive and to a potentially pathogenic vulnerability to refoulement.

6.3.3.2 Risk of refoulement

In aid of the interception and removal powers introduced for Boat Turnbacks and Takebacks in 2014, Section 197C of the *Migration Act* was introduced to make clear that, for the purposes of removing unlawful non-citizens, 'it is irrelevant whether Australia has non-refoulement obligations' to them. As a result, the duty to remove them as soon as practicable 'arises irrespective of whether there has been an assessment, according to law, of Australia's non-refoulement obligations'. The failure to require this assessment exposes these children to a potentially pathogenic vulnerability to refoulement.

6.4 Priorities for reform

This chapter has examined the effect of the operation of the amendments on the children's ability to have their claim for asylum responded to by Australia. It has also applied the vulnerability taxonomy to distinguish between and characterise those impacts that ameliorated inherent and situational vulnerabilities from those that created or exacerbated pathogenic and occurrent harms. This section now applies Stage 3 of the mitigating vulnerability framework and proposes priorities for reform based on a gravity of consequences rationale.

Australia should also look overseas for models that comprehensively respond to these children's vulnerability and consider how these might translate in the Australian context. For example, Italy's *Law 47/2017* illuminates a mitigating vulnerability framework to unaccompanied children's alienage. *Law 47/2017* codified the prohibition on forced returns of unaccompanied children and introduced a procedure requiring an interview between the child, qualified staff at the first reception facility and an intercultural mediator to identify the child and the essential elements of their protection claim within ten days. Besides regulating the appointment of the child's legal guardian, which will be discussed further in Chapter 7, *Law 47/2017* also enabled an unaccompanied and/or separated child to be automatically granted a temporary residence permit upon their application for international protection. This protection application also entailed rights to be heard, to legal assistance and to a prioritised examination of their application. It permitted them to convert that permit to an adult temporary residence permit for study, work or job-seeking when they turn 18. It also provided transitional arrangements for their continued care and protection, irrespective of legal status, and access to social services until the age of 21.[69]

From the perspective of ameliorating the situational vulnerabilities of unaccompanied children arising from their alienage, Italy's *Law 47/2017* is an excellent starting point. It resolves their vulnerability as unauthorised entrants by granting them a residence permit and facilitates representation in and expedited access to the resolution of their protection claim.

Australia should progressively work towards responding proportionately to these children's temporal and physical presence and their relationship of acute need in a genuine regional processing system that ensures all asylum seekers have access to a consistent and timely RSD process, merits review and durable solutions. Exposure to refoulement (by both Boat Turnbacks and Takebacks and by transfer to Nauru RPC) and failure to provide special assistance in the prosecution of the child's protection claim can both be addressed by legislative and policy change. This section outlines five priorities for reform to avoid exacerbating existing vulnerabilities or generating new vulnerabilities. First, on-sea enhanced screening and Boat Turnbacks and Takebacks of unaccompanied children should cease, and they should be transferred to the mainland for assessment of their claim. Second, the Minister should make a Section 198AE (1) *Migration Act* declaration that the Section 198AD transfer to a regional processing country requirement does not apply to unaccompanied child asylum seekers.[70] The Minister should make such a declaration, preferably permanently, but at least until there is evidence that transferring children to Nauru does not constitute refoulement. Third, parliament should re-invoke Australia's non-refoulement obligations in full by making the necessary amendments to the *Maritime Powers Act 2013* and the *Migration Act*. Fourth, all unaccompanied children should be provided with specialist legal assistance from reception until the finalisation of their protection claim by expanding funding of existing service providers. Fifth, to avoid pathogenising their vulnerability, processing protection claims of unaccompanied children should be expedited, and custodial carers of the Legacy Caseload cohort in community detention group homes should urgently be trained to identify cases of 'lethal hopelessness' and provided with appropriate referral points.

In the longer term, other legislative reforms should be implemented. First, the full merits review of primary protection decisions by the AAT should be reintroduced, ensuring that status determinations for unaccompanied child asylum seekers comply with international norms. Second, if transfers to offshore processing are resumed, the pre-transfer best interest assessment should be a genuine and individualised assessment with a real possibility that the child not be transferred. Third, to build a sustainable regional response, there should be continued cooperation to build a regional processing system in Bali Process countries with consistent and timely access to the RSD process, merits review and durable solutions. This will facilitate realistic 'third country' settlement options if bipartisan government policy continues to refuse the prospect of settlement in Australia.

While Australia has not 'welcomed' asylum seeker boat arrivals since the 1980s, amendments to Australian migration law and policy between 2012 and 2014 effectively removed the possibility of people, including unaccompanied children, seeking asylum in Australia if they arrive by boat. The vulnerability analysis in this chapter has zeroed in on the sites in which the legislative amendments progressively exacerbated these children's inherent and situational vulnerability arising from their alienage and where devastating occurrent and pathogenic harms to these children were generated. This chapter has illustrated how a vulnerability analysis of the specific legislative amendments illuminates that Australian migration law has not properly construed or adequately responded to the actuality, complexity and specific vulnerability of unaccompanied child asylum seekers. The focus on sites of vulnerability, rather than human rights breaches, highlights the direct correlation between States' implementation of restrictive asylum practices and these harms and supplements a human rights imperative of recognising State responsibilities to provide unaccompanied children with special assistance in processing their claims for asylum as 'special cases' notwithstanding their unauthorised presence. The vulnerability analysis elucidated States' accountability for legal and policy choices that disavowed these children's absolute dependence on the State – because of their temporal, relational, and physical proximity – to implement robust processes for responding to their claims for asylum. Also, the vulnerability analysis, unlike human rights law, clarified the sites and sources of the most devastating impacts on being/becoming unaccompanied children's ability to seek asylum and informed concrete measures and priorities for reform. It illuminated where priorities for legislative and policy reform should be directed to reduce occurrent harms and pathogenic sources of vulnerability first, facilitating distinction between urgent and longer term priorities.

The next chapter examines Australia's response to vulnerabilities generated by unaccompanied children seeking asylum without an adult caregiver. I examine the operation and impact of amendments between 2012 and 2014 to the *IGOC Act* that designates the Minister responsible for the immigration portfolio as their exclusive legal guardian on unaccompanied child asylum seekers' situational vulnerability generated by their separation from their parents.

Notes

1 I note that the definition itself has been criticised as being too narrow, especially to capture refugees from climate change events.

2 The *Migration Legislation Amendment (Regional Processing and Other Measures) Act 2012* (Cth) received Royal assent on 18 August 2012. It inserted Sections 198AB and 198AD into the *Migration Act 1958* (Cth) (*Migration Act*). In *Plaintiff S156/2013 v Minister of Immigration and Border Protection* (2014) 254 CLR 28, the High Court unanimously upheld the constitutionality of the amendments. The Court held that Sections 198AB and 198AD, operating to affect the removal of a class of aliens from Australia (unauthorised maritime arrivals), were a valid exercise of the aliens' power. The plaintiff argued that the sections exceeded the scope of the aliens' power because they were a disproportionate response to the object of regulating the entry of aliens to, or their removal from, Australia (for reasons including they potentially exposed asylum seekers to refoulement and indefinite detention in a regional processing country). However, the Court rejected this finding that sections 198AB and 198AD merely operated to affect the removal of aliens; they did not regulate what happened post-removal.

3 The *Migration Legislation Amendment (Regional Processing and Other Measures) Act 2012* (Cth) amendments allowed for offshore processing of the protection claims of boat arrival asylum seekers and gave the government sufficient power to implement offshore processing arrangements.

4 'Asylum Seekers Arriving in Australia by Boat to be Resettled in Papua New Guinea', *ABC News* (online at 20 July 2013) <http://www.abc.net.au/news/2013-07-19/manus-island-detention-centre-to-beexpanded-under-rudd27s-asy/4830778>.

5 *Migration Amendment (Unauthorised Maritime Arrivals and Other Measures) Act 2013* (Cth).

6 *Migration Act* ss 46A, 46B. The Minister may 'lift the bar' if they think it is in the public interest to do so.

7 *Maritime Powers Act 2013* (Cth) s 72. See Patrick Emerton and Maria O'Sullivan, 'Rethinking Asylum Seeker Detention at Sea: The Power to Detain Asylum Seekers at Sea under *The Maritime Powers Act* 2013 (Cth)' (2015) 38(2) *UNSW Law Journal* 695, 709–712.

8 Commonwealth, *Parliamentary Debates*, House of Representatives, 25 September 2014, 10546 (Scott Morrison, Minister for Immigration and Border Protection).

9 Ibid 10545.

10 It also introduced a new form of TPV – the Safe Haven Enterprise Visa.

11 *Migration and Maritime Powers Legislation Amendment (Resolving the Asylum Legacy Caseload) Act 2014* (Cth) sch 4.

12 Ibid sch 5.
13 Ibid sch 5, item 2.
14 *Maritime Powers Act 2013* (Cth) s 69.
15 Ibid s 75B.
16 Ibid s 75A.
17 As noted in Chapter 1, my book is focused on unaccompanied child asylum seekers because Australia's current boat turnback laws – by intercepting vessels and returning them to sea and potentially refouling unaccompanied children – exacerbate their vulnerability in breach of Australia's most basic international human rights obligation. However, I do not assert that *only* unaccompanied child asylum seekers are so vulnerable as to enliven the mitigating vulnerability framework contended for in Chapter 4. Instead, provided the requisite 'sufficient connection' can be established, a mitigating vulnerability framework ought to be able to be made for different cohorts.
18 *Migration Act* s 473CA.

Unless they were an 'excluded fast-track review applicant' – people who, in the opinion of the Minister, have previously had their protection claims rejected in Australia, by another country, or by UNHCR; have provided a 'bogus document' in support of their application without a reasonable explanation; or make a 'manifestly unfounded' claim. See *Migration Act* s 5(1).
19 *Migration Act* s 473DB.
20 Ibid ss 473DC, 473DD.
21 In *Plaintiff M147/2016 v Minister for Immigration and Border Protection* (2018) HCA 18, [95], the High Court held that the IAA engages in de novo merits review despite these limits. Notwithstanding this, the risk of refoulement increases when applications for merits review are unsuccessful because of procedural factors.
22 Tony Burke, 'Split in the Opposition's Asylum Seeker Policy; Asylum Seeker Policy' (Transcript of press conference, 7 July 2013) <http://parlinfo.aph.gov.au/parlInfo/search/display/display.w3p;query=Id%3A%22media%2Fpressrel%2F3063861%22>.
23 Department's Protection Visa Processing Guidelines 3.6.1.
24 'Evidence to Senate Standing Committee on Legal and Constitutional Affairs Committee, Senate Estimates', Parliament of Australia, Canberra, 25 May 2015, 66 (Michael Manthorpe, Deputy Secretary, Visa and Citizenship Management, Department of Immigration and Border Protection).
25 Suresh Sundram and Samantha Loi, 'Long Waits for Refugee Status Lead to New Mental Health Syndrome', *The Conversation* (online at 23 May 2012) <https://theconversation.com/long-waits-for-refugee-status-lead-to-new-mental-health-syndrome-7165>.
26 Nicolas Procter et al., 'Lethal Hopelessness: Understanding and Responding to Asylum Seeker Distress and Mental Deterioration' (2018) 27 *International Journal of Mental Health Nursing* 448, 451.
27 Australian Human Rights Commission, *Lives on Hold: Refugees and Asylum Seekers in the 'Legacy Caseload'* (AHRC, 2019) 41.
28 For example, compare *Migration Act* s 5H with the Refugee Convention, opened for signature 28 July 1951, 189 UNTS 137 (entered into force 22 April 1954) arts 1(A), 1(F).
29 *Migration and Maritime Powers Legislation Amendment (Resolving the Asylum Legacy Caseload) Act 2014* (Cth) sch 5.
30 *Migration Act* s 5J(1)(c).
31 Ibid ss 5J(2), 5LA.
32 Ibid s 5J(3).

33 *Migration and Maritime Powers Legislation Amendment (Resolving the Asylum Legacy Caseload) Act 2014* (Cth) sch 5 item 2.
34 Department of Immigration and Border Protection, *Fact Sheet 63 – Immigration Advice and Application Assistance Scheme* <https://www.immi.gov.au/media/fact-sheets/63advice.htm>.
35 RACS, 'Submission No 217, Australian Human Rights Commission', *The Forgotten Children Inquiry* (30 June 2014) <https://humanrights.gov.au/sites/default/files/Submission%20No%20217-%20Refugee%20Advice%20%26%20Casework%20Service.pdf?_ga=2.210690128.456257149.1589840532-1976784639.1520134709>.
36 Ibid 34 [11.10].
37 See Department of Immigration and Border Protection (Cth), *Procedure Advice Manual 3: Refugee and Humanitarian – Regional Processing – Minister's s198AE Guidelines – Refugee and Humanitarian – Regional Processing – Pretransfer assessment* (*Procedure Advice Manual 3*).
38 Department of Immigration and Border Protection (Cth), *Notice to Produce: Best Interests Assessment for Transferring Minors to an RPC* (forming part of pre-transfer assessment), Schedule 3, first notice to produce; Australian Human Rights Commission, *The Forgotten Children: National Inquiry into Children in Immigration Detention* (Commonwealth Government, 2014) (*The Forgotten Children Inquiry*) Document 1.2.
39 Ibid.
40 See *Wan v Minister for Immigration and Multicultural Affairs* (2001) 107 FCR 133 [32].
41 UN Committee on the Rights of the Child, *General Comment No. 14 The Right of the Child to Have His or Her Best Interests Taken as a Primary Consideration*, UN Doc CRC/C/GC/14 (29 May 2013) (*General Comment No. 14*) [49].
42 Ibid [20].
43 Ibid [1].
44 Ibid [97].
45 Ibid [98].
46 Ibid.
47 Elibritt Karlsen, 'Australia's Offshore Processing of Asylum Seekers in Nauru and PNG: A Quick Guide to Statistics and Resources' *Research Paper Series 2016–17* (Commonwealth Parliamentary Library, 2016) 10.
48 Department of Immigration and Border Protection, 'Best Interests Assessment for Transferring Minors to an RPC: Guidance for Completing the Best Interests Assessment for Transferring Minors to an RPC', Version 1.4 ('Best Interests Assessment for Transferring Minors to an RPC') (13 February 2014) 1 <https://www.border.gov.au/AccessandAccountability/Documents/FOI/FA140201097.pdf>; *The Forgotten Children Inquiry* (n 38) 193.
49 Pressure from the Department of Immigration and Border Protection to complete PTAs within 48 hours reportedly affected their quality. See UNHCR, *Monitoring Visit to the Republic of Nauru 7 to 9 October 2013* (UNHCR, 2013) <https://www.refworld.org/docid/5294a6534.html> (*Monitoring Visit to the Republic of Nauru*) 25–26.
50 Department of Immigration and Border Protection (Cth), *Procedure Advice Manual 3* (n 37) [P A345.10].
51 Ibid [P A345.13].
52 Ibid [P A345.10].
53 Ibid.
54 Section 256 of the *Migration Act* provided that reasonable facilities for obtaining legal advice should be afforded to a detained asylum seeker if they request legal

assistance. However, there was no positive obligation on the Minister or the Department to provide representation or legal assistance otherwise.

55 Lenore Taylor, 'Boys Kept in Isolation at Manus Island Detention Centre', *The Guardian* (online at 4 November 2013) <http://www.theguardian.com/world/2013/nov/03/boys-kept-in-isolation-at-manus-island-detention-centre>. See also Australian Human Rights Commission, *The Forgotten Children* (n 38) 169, which reported that an unaccompanied boy from Afghanistan, who was incorrectly assessed as being over 18 was transferred to the single adult male compound (North West Point Detention Centre) on Christmas Island after his age determination interview.

56 Department of Immigration and Border Protection (Cth), *Procedure Advice Manual 3* (n 37) ch 2, para 22.

57 Ilan Katz, Geraldine Doney and Effie Mitchell, *Evaluation of the Expansion of the Community Detention Program: Final Report SPRC 12/13 to the Department of Immigration and Citizenship (DIAC)* (2013) 49.

58 Australian Human Rights Commission, *The Forgotten Children Inquiry* (n 38) 155.

59 See UNHCR, *Mission to the Republic of Nauru, 3 to 5 December 2012: Report* (UNHCR, 2012) and UNHCR, *Monitoring Visit to the Republic of Nauru* (n 49).

60 *Migration and Maritime Powers Legislation Amendment (Resolving the Asylum Legacy Caseload) Act 2014* (Cth) sch 5 item 2.

61 (2015) ALJR 207, 243. The Commonwealth argued that the detention was authorised by Section 72(4) of the *Maritime Powers Act 2013* (Cth) and/or the executive power under Section 61 of the *Constitution.* The High Court held by a 4:3 majority in its decision, handed down on 28 January 2015, that the detention was authorised by the *Maritime Powers Act 2013.* The case attracted domestic controversy because proceedings were initiated, but before the High Court handed down its decision, Parliament passed the *Migration and Maritime Powers Legislation Amendment (Resolving the Asylum Legacy Caseload) Act 2014* (Cth), which significantly amended the *Maritime Powers Act 2013*, including provisions that were being contested in the High Court proceedings.

62 Unfortunately, the Court decision did not address submissions about the extraterritorial application of Australia's non-refoulement obligations and the plaintiff's risk of refoulement by India to Sri Lanka, although French CJ and Crennan J acknowledged in obiter that they may exist. There has also been a significant volume of academic commentary, in particular, on the conditions, duration and legality of the detention of asylum seekers interdicted at sea pursuant to Operation Sovereign Borders. See, for example, Patrick Emerton and Maria O'Sullivan, 'Rethinking Asylum Seeker Detention at Sea' (2015) 38(2) *UNSW Law Journal* 695, 697.

63 Australian immigration officials had also been accused of paying people smugglers to reroute vessels back to Indonesia in May 2015. See Shalailah Medhora, 'Asylum Seekers: 23 Vessels Turned Back but Coalition Stays Silent on Payments' *The Guardian* (online at 5 February 2016) <https://www.theguardian.com/australia-news/2016/feb/05/asylum-seekers-23-vessels-turned-back-but-coalition-stays-silent-on-payments>.

64 Scott Morrison, 'Operation Sovereign Borders Update' (Transcript of press conference, 8 November 2013) <https://newsroom.abf.gov.au/releases/transcript-press-conference-operation-sovereign-borders-update-8>.

65 Senate Legal and Constitutional Affairs Legislation Committee, Immigration Portfolio, Supplementary Budget Estimates 2014–15, *Suspected Illegal Entry Ventures Removed from Australian Waters* (20 October 2014) Tabled document 6; Harriet Spinks, 'Boat arrivals in Australia: a quick guide to the statistics since 2001' (Commonwealth Parliamentary Library, 2018) <https://www.aph.gov.au

/About_Parliament/Parliamentary_Departments/Parliamentary_Library/pubs/rp/rp1819/Quick_Guides/BoatTurnbacksSince2001>.

66 Section 198(2) of the *Migration Act* imposes a duty on the Department to remove a non-citizen who is not the holder of a valid visa and has not made an application for a substantive visa, has not been cleared for immigration, and is detained under Section 189 of the Act, as soon as reasonably practicable.

67 Australian Human Rights Commission, 'Tell Me About: The "Enhanced Screening Process"' (*AHRC*, 2013) <https://www.humanrights.gov.au/our-work/asylum-seekers-and-refugees/publications/tell-me-about-enhanced-screening-process>.

68 Department of Immigration and Border Protection, Supplementary Budget Estimates Hearing, Legal and Constitutional Affairs Committee, 19 November 2013, answer to question on notice SE13/0115 <http://www.aph.gov.au/~/media/Estimates/Live/legcon_ctte/estimates/sup_1314/DEPARTMENT/SE13-0115.ashx>.

69 As discussed in Chapter 5, appropriate arrangements are critical for unaccompanied young people leaving group community detention living arrangements to ensure that they have the necessary support and skills to transition safely and effectively to living independently.

70 This complements the recommendation in Chapter 5 that the Minister utilise their existing discretionary power to release unaccompanied children from mandatory immigration detention for processing under a residence determination. The Minister should revoke their guideline directing residence applications for asylum seekers arriving after 19 July 2013 to not be referred for consideration unless there are exceptional reasons, or the Minister has requested it, as it has exposed those cohorts to an unnecessary occurrent risk of continued mandatory immigration detention and offshore transfer.

7 Vulnerability analysis of Australia's provision of guardianship to unaccompanied asylum-seeking children

7.1 Introduction

This chapter applies the mitigating vulnerability framework to assess the operation and impact of Australian law and policy on the provision of guardianship to unaccompanied child asylum seekers and makes recommendations for reform. Globally, States respond to the acute vulnerability of unaccompanied children by appointing a legal guardian. The guardian's role is complex but pivotal in responding to the being/becoming child. It involves overseeing both the protection of the child from present harm and the provision of opportunities to recover from past trauma and continue development. The guardian should also provide access to and assistance with the State's asylum procedure. Seeking asylum without parental assistance is an additional situational vulnerability overlaying the universal inherent vulnerabilities of all children. The quality of guardianship provided determines whether that inherent and situational vulnerability is ameliorated or exacerbated, such as by exposure to the acute risk of harm (occurrent vulnerabilities) or the addition of State-created vulnerabilities (pathogenic vulnerabilities).

Section 7.2 attends to the first stage of the mitigating vulnerability framework. It examines the origins and subsequent transformation of the operation of the *IGOC Act* to explain the legal context of Australia's unique arrangement in which the Minister responsible for immigration (the Minister) also became the legal guardian of unaccompanied children arriving in the country. It argues that this dual responsibility was allowed to arise without regard to the distinct situational vulnerability of unaccompanied child asylum seekers. The changes to the *IGOC Act* between 2012 and 2014 cemented existing failures to safeguard their best interests or secure their proper representation by explicitly subjugating the Minister's responsibilities as guardian to their border control powers under the *Migration Act*, thus giving rise to a pathogenic vulnerability to a lack of protective guardianship.

Section 7.3 then focuses on the second stage of the mitigating vulnerability framework by examining the impact of these changes on the vulnerabilities of unaccompanied child asylum seekers generated by their separation from their parents. It argues that the continuation of the Minister as their exclusive statutory

DOI: 10.4324/9781003260134-8

guardian, particularly while they were in mandatory immigration detention, perpetuated the situational vulnerabilities of unaccompanied children in the Legacy Caseload cohort. By maintaining the Minister's dual role and failing to provide this cohort with an independent guardian, these children became occurrently vulnerable[1] to remaining in mandatory immigration detention and to a lack of representation of their best interests while detained. Further, once released into community detention, although their custodial care was mostly adequate (as discussed in Chapter 5), they remained occurrently vulnerable to receiving no independent representation. This section also argues that these amendments created further occurrent vulnerabilities for the cohort subject to transfer to Nauru. These children experienced the same occurrent vulnerabilities as the Legacy Caseload cohort while in mandatory immigration detention prior to transfer. However, the subordination of the Minister's duty to consider their best interests to border protection priorities generated an additional pathogenic vulnerability that their individual best interests would not genuinely be considered, or advocated for, in the crucial pre-transfer assessment period. Finally, this section argues that the impact of the amendments was to generate a pathogenic vulnerability to refoulement and neglect for unaccompanied children subject to on-sea enhanced screening under the Boat Turnbacks policy by effectively excising them from Australia's guardianship regime.

Lastly, Section 7.4 discharges the third stage of the mitigating vulnerability framework by identifying the priorities for legislative and policy reform.

7.2 Operation of the 2012–2014 legislative amendments: cementing the Minister responsible for border protection as the inherently conflicted guardian

This section examines the legal and policy context defining the relationship between Australia, as a responsive State in vulnerability theory, and children seeking asylum while separated from their parents, to clarify the operation of the amendments before examining the impact of those laws on their vulnerability in Section 7.3.

Globally, different guardianship models exist along the migration response continuum. Yet, a common factor is that guardianship is the key legal mechanism for prescribing legislative and functional responsibility to provide unaccompanied children with care and protection from harm in the present, circumstances that enable their development, and access to assistance to process their asylum claim. Guardianship is key to satisfying unaccompanied children's human rights, and it is also required to address two core sites of situational vulnerability generated by their separation from their parents. First, there is the absence of an adult whose primary concern is caring for and protecting them and assisting them in transitioning to adulthood. Second, there is the absence of an adult to advocate for their claim for asylum. In Australia, even prior to the 2012–2014 legislative amendments, the appointment of the Minister as their statutory legal guardian disregarded this distinct situational vulnerability.

Recalling the historical background examination in Chapter 1, the *IGOC Act* was introduced in 1946 to provide for the reception of predominantly British immigrant children whose arrival was authorised post-World War II.[2] Although in Australia's federal system, statutory child protection is the responsibility of state and territory governments, the Act was enacted under the Commonwealth's power to legislate on immigration[3] to formalise existing Commonwealth and state agreements that vested legal guardianship of every non-citizen arrival with the Commonwealth Minister for Immigration.[4] Following state child welfare models, Section 6 of the Act vested the Minister with the same rights, powers, duties, obligations and liabilities as a natural guardian. But the Minister's powers and duties as guardian were never the subject of focused consideration because, shortly after the proclamation of the Act, the Minister delegated powers to state child welfare departments to oversee the custody and estate of the minors, to make home visits and to consent to marriages.[5] The Minister retained the limited power to allow their departure overseas, consistently with the separation of powers between the states and the Commonwealth. The Act's key provisions continue into the present, although the Minister's present-day obligations now cease when the ward turns 18 or leaves Australia's jurisdiction.[6]

As examined in Chapter 1, when the Australian parliament enacted the *Migration Act* in 1958 to regulate 'in the national interest, the coming into, and presence in, Australia of non-citizens',[7] neither the *Migration Act* nor the *IGOC Act* contained a provision expressly providing how the Acts should be read in relation to each other.[8] Parliamentary recognition that the *IGOC Act* applied to unaccompanied refugee minors first occurred in 1994,[9] and the scope of the Minister's duties as guardian to children claiming asylum without pre-authorised entry was first tested in litigation in the 1990s.

It is unnecessary to repeat here the detailed analysis by Crock, and Crock and Kenny of Australian Immigration Ministers' failure to properly discharge their guardianship obligations to unaccompanied children on account of the inherent conflict of interest.[10] It suffices here to make two necessary observations for the discussion that follows. Australian courts have acknowledged that Section 6 of the *IGOC Act* confers on the Minister all the usual responsibilities of guardianship. In common law and equity, a guardian stands in *loco parentis* to the child, provides for their maintenance and education, is empowered to make decisions for their welfare[11] and retains a fiduciary relationship towards them,[12] including the duty to protect the child from harm. Regarding unaccompanied children, the courts have confirmed that this extends to the provision of the child's basic needs, which may include legal advice and assistance,[13] and the obligation to ensure the protection of the fundamental human rights set out in the CRC, including the best interests principle.[14] As examined in Section 3.3, State obligations towards these children are extensive. However, the provisions of the *Migration Act* prevail in the event of inconsistency with obligations assumed under international human rights law, including those under the CRC.[15] Second, lawyers for unaccompanied child asylum seekers have had little success in persuading the courts to definitively outline the scope of the Minister's guardianship duty or to require the Minister to discharge the duty in conformity with established expectations of the diligent discharge of guardianship of minors at common law. The courts have held, for example, that tribunal review hearings can occur in the absence of a guardian actively representing the child's interests.[16] The Federal Court has determined that unaccompanied children bear a basic onus of proof in proving that they are minors. The Minister has no legal obligation to make inquiries about the age of asylum seekers or to adopt certain procedures to determine their age.[17] The High Court has found that a failure to transfer children from IDCs into the community does not breach the Minister's duty of care pursuant to Section 6 of the *IGOC Act*, even when the Court accepts that the detention is physically and psychologically harmful to the child.[18] This demonstrates the primacy of the legislative approach taken by the government of the day and the lack of any human rights or common law-based guardianship standards.

Unaccompanied child asylum seekers were spectacularly unsuccessful in any litigation against the Minister, alleging a failure to diligently or fully discharge their guardianship obligations, up until 2011. In that year, in *Plaintiff M70/2011*,[19] solicitors for a 16-year-old Afghan unaccompanied child sought an injunction restraining the Minister from removing the child to Malaysia. The High Court granted an injunction restraining the Minister from removing the child without exercising a separate statutory power as guardian and giving written consent to the removal after being satisfied that the granting of the consent would not be prejudicial to the child's interests.[20] Although the injunction was granted, consistent with previous decisions, the Court failed to give an expansive reading to the Minister's 'same rights, powers, duties, obligations and liabilities as a natural guardian' to the child under Section 6. Instead, the Court applied a technical statutory construction argument that the specific provision of the *IGOC Act* (requiring the Minister's written consent for the removal of the child) prevailed over the general unfettered provision in the *Migration Act* (enabling the removal of the child). Although the case resulted in an injunction, it still demonstrated unaccompanied child asylum seekers' vulnerability when the Minister is both the child's guardian and the enforcer of children's removals under migration laws.

The government responded to the decision with amendments to the *Migration Act* designed to undo its effects. In the 'Explanatory Memorandum' to the first suite of amendments, the government noted that:

> The High Court's decision does not align with the Government's policy intention which is that the Minister's consent under section 6A of the IGOC Act is not required for a non-citizen child to be removed, taken or deported from Australia under the Migration Act.[21]

The explicit intent and effect of the *Migration Legislation Amendment (Regional Processing and Other Measures) Act* 2012 (Cth) amendments, besides allowing for offshore processing (as discussed in Chapters 5 and 6), was to eliminate the requirement for the Minister's written consent upon being satisfied that removal was not prejudicial to the interests of the child.[22] Although yet to be tested by the courts, the unambiguously stated purpose of amending the Act was to clarify in Section 8 that the *Migration Act* 'is not subject to' the *IGOC Act*[23] when the Minister exercises powers to remove non-citizens under the *Migration Act*.[24] The *Migration and Maritime Powers Legislation Amendment (Resolving the Asylum Legacy Caseload) Act 2014* expanded the conflict inherent in the Minister's roles. It amended the *IGOC Act* to expressly state that it did not affect the performance of any function, duty or power relating to taking a non-citizen child to a place outside Australia under the *Migration Act* or the *Maritime Powers Act*. Lastly, the amendments effectively removed children subject to offshore processing and interception on the sea from Australia's guardianship regime and abdicated Australia's obligations to them in international human rights law in circumstances in which they were under Australia's joint effective control. In tandem with the amendments to the *Migration Act*, these extensive amendments to the *IGOC Act* between 2012 and 2014 progressively exacerbated the historic conflict inherent in the Minister being the statutory guardian of unaccompanied children to the exclusion of all others. Although the provision of guardianship to unaccompanied asylum-seeking children has always been problematic under the *IGOC Act*, the 2012, 2013 and 2014 amendments effectively eliminated any meaningful response to their separation from their parents through the provision of guardianship and explicitly avoided the care and protection obligations owed to them.

The effect of the amendments is captured in Table 7.1 'Eligibility for guardianship by date of arrival'.

Since the amendments, the Minister has been the exclusive statutory guardian of all unaccompanied child asylum seekers in the Legacy Caseload cohort and those awaiting transfer for offshore processing (as Table 7.1 illustrates). Unaccompanied children sent to Australia's OPC on Nauru are legally designated to have '[left] Australia permanently'. Consequently, the Minister ceases to be their legal guardian, and they become subject to the guardianship laws and policies of Nauru.[25] There is no provision for guardianship for unaccompanied child asylum seekers intercepted at sea who are subject to Australia's current Boat Turnback and Takeback policy.

The *IGOC Act* arguably has ameliorated the vulnerability of some children, such as those being adopted from overseas and unaccompanied refugee minors, but the *IGOC Act* was not subsequently adapted to take into account the guardianship needs of these proximate vulnerable child asylum seekers and has failed to similarly ameliorate their vulnerability.

Both unaccompanied refugee and asylum-seeking children share the triple vulnerability of being children who have experienced trauma, being unaccompanied by an adult or guardian, and being aliens by virtue of their non-citizenship. Unaccompanied child asylum seekers have the additional burdens of an unauthorised presence and a yet-to-be-determined asylum claim. Historically, Australian guardianship law and policy has failed to comprehend and respond to this unique

Table 7.1 Eligibility for guardianship by date of arrival

Date of arrival	*Processing of asylum claim*	*Eligibility to settle in Australia if found to be a refugee*	*Provision of guardianship*
Before 13 August 2012	Asylum claim processed in Australia	Can be resettled in Australia if found to be a refugee	Minister of Immigration and Border Protection
After 13 August 2012 and before 19 July 2013	They were transferred initially to a third country (Nauru or PNG) to have their asylum claim processed after 'transiting' in Australia (on Christmas Island) but have since been resettled in Australia and are awaiting finalisation of their claim as part of the Legacy Caseload cohort	Can be resettled in Australia if found to be a refugee	Minister of Immigration and Border Protection while in Australia pre- and post-transfer Subject to guardianship regimes of Manus Island or Nauru while offshore
After 19 July 2013	Transferred to a regional processing country (Nauru or PNG) to have their asylum claim processed after 'transiting' in Australia (on Christmas Island)	Cannot be resettled in Australia if found to be a refugee	Minister of Immigration and Border Protection while transiting in Australia Subject to guardianship regimes of Manus Island or Nauru post-transfer offshore
After September 2013	No access to processing of claims for asylum by Australia	No opportunity to arrive in Australia, subject to Boat Turnbacks and Takebacks	No provision of guardianship

situational vulnerability. *IGOC Act* guardianship, however attenuated compared to common law expectations, was sufficient for unaccompanied refugee children in relation to migration issues because they were not vulnerable to deportation or to conflict with migration policy considerations. Yet, for unaccompanied asylum seeker children, that conflict is at the very core of the matter. Appointing as statutory guardian the Minister, who has obligations to prosecute the provisions of the *Migration Act* and to mandatorily detain these children, exposed them to new acute vulnerabilities. This is evidenced by the rift between core expectations of guardianship of minors at common law and guardianship of these minors in the immigration context. Crock captured the problem neatly in 2005, observing that 'the simple and devastating problem for the young asylum seekers is that the Minister is both legal guardian, by virtue of Section 6 of the *IGOC Act*, and their prosecutor, judge and gaoler within the complicated matrix of the *Migration Act*'.[26] The 2012–2014 statutory amendments to the *IGOC Act* that occurred in tandem with the hardening of Australian migration laws and policy rendered guardianship nugatory in practice for all unaccompanied child asylum seekers other than the Legacy Caseload cohort. Crock's 2005 observation is even more pertinent after the 2012 and 2014 amendments. The following section examines the impact of these legislative changes on the inherent and situational vulnerability of asylum-seeking children separated from their parents.

7.3 Impact of the changes: the guardian gatekeeper vacated the space

Having examined the effect of the operation of the amendments on the provision of guardianship by Australia in response to these children's separation from their parents, this section applies Stage 2 of the mitigating vulnerability framework to the different contexts of children in the 'Legacy Caseload', 'Offshore Transferee' and 'Boat Turnbacks and Takebacks' cohorts. It utilises the vulnerability taxonomy to distinguish between and characterise responses that ameliorated inherent and situational vulnerabilities and decreased dependencies from those that created or exacerbated pathogenic and occurrent harms in the provision of guardianship.

Asylum-seeking children without parents are especially dependent on the receiving State to appoint them a legal guardian to oversee their protection from harm. The Legacy Caseload cohort experienced an occurrent vulnerability of being without an independent guardian to advocate for their release from mandatory immigration detention or to provide them with independent representation of their interests while they were in immigration detention. Further, once released into community detention, although their custodial care was mostly adequate (as discussed in Chapter 5), their occurrent vulnerability was not ameliorated because the amendments maintained the Minister's dual role. The amendments generated an additional occurrent vulnerability for the cohort subject to transfer to Nauru that no guardian would advocate for their individual best interests in the crucial pre-transfer assessment period.

7.3.1 *Guardianship of unaccompanied asylum seeker children in the Legacy Caseload cohort on the Australian mainland*

As discussed in Chapter 5, unaccompanied asylum-seeking children in the Legacy Caseload cohort were all subject to mandatory immigration detention. The failure to provide them with an independent and appropriately qualified guardian to represent their interests while in mandatory immigration detention exposed them to occurrent vulnerabilities of not having their best interests considered or met or of ensuring the provision of access to legal representation in processes for prosecuting their claims for asylum. These occurrent vulnerabilities persisted after their release into community detention.

The failure to provide unaccompanied children with an independent and appropriately qualified guardian whilst in mandatory immigration detention compounded their exposure to the occurrent and pathogenic vulnerabilities generated by the detention centre environment examined in Section 5.3.1. In 2013, the Commonwealth and Immigration Ombudsman highlighted children's 'particular vulnerability' in immigration detention. This was 'their dependence on the department and its service providers to supply an environment and care conducive to their developmental, health, educational and welfare needs' and the corresponding responsibility on the Department to 'avoid acting in ways that directly cause harm to children, but to also take action to prevent harm from occurring'.[27]

In fact, these matters continued to be the responsibility of the Minister as their legal guardian. In the research period, the Minister delegated his guardianship responsibilities to unaccompanied children in IDCs to nominated Department officers. These delegates were either detention centre or regional managers or held executive level 2 or higher positions within the Department.[28] The delegates were not required to have specific child-centred qualifications or experience related to childcare.[29]

The Department sought to justify guardianship delegations to detention centre or regional detention managers and department executive level 2 personnel, based on their seniority rather than expertise with young people and on the basis that 'the delegated guardian is required to make important decisions that relate to the care and welfare of children, such as decisions about medical treatment or education'.[30] However, unaccompanied children in IDCs have undergone separation from their family members and also have, to varying degrees, experienced loss, trauma, disruption and violence. The very gravity of the decisions being made necessitates that the decision-maker has expertise in assessing the impact of that decision on the needs of the child and expertise in ascertaining the unaccompanied child's own assessment of what they need. In *The Forgotten Children Inquiry Report*, the AHRC found that:

> the Minister for Immigration and Border Protection does not meet the criteria set out by the Committee on the Rights of the Child (in para 33 of General Comment No 6) to effectively perform the role of guardian for

> unaccompanied children.... the lack of expertise in the field of childcare on the part of the Minister or those within the Department to whom he delegates his guardianship responsibilities, render the Minister an inappropriate and ineffective guardian. [31]

I agree with that observation. But the failure to provide an independent and appropriately qualified guardian charged with acting solely in their best interests also spawned an occurrent vulnerability; namely, that no adult would advocate for their prompt release as soon as their health and identity checks were completed. Instead, they would remain in an environment inhibiting recovery from past trauma and exposing them to the risk of physical or psychological harm impacting their ongoing development.[32]

As discussed below, the failure to provide meaningful guardianship for children in immigration detention on Christmas Island who were subject to transfer to Nauru generated occurrent and pathogenic vulnerabilities for that cohort. However, both cohorts share a common key shortcoming in their failure to create a guardianship framework to secure their proper representation and safeguard their best interests through two primary means: first, by ensuring that agencies or individuals were ineligible for guardianship if their interests could potentially be in conflict with those of the child's; and second, by providing a legal representative in addition to the guardian.

7.3.2 Guardianship of unaccompanied asylum seekers in the Offshore Transferee cohort

Unaccompanied children subject to transfer to Nauru experienced the same occurrent vulnerabilities as the Legacy Caseload cohort of not having their best interests represented by an independent and appropriately qualified guardian.[33] Yet, the impact of the subordination of the Minister's duty to consider their best interests as their guardian to border protection priorities, combined with the failure to provide them with independent legal representation in the pre-transfer period, generated a new pathogenic vulnerability to their being transferred offshore with no guardian advocating for a genuine assessment of their individual best interests. These failures further exposed them to pathogenic vulnerability of refoulement, including, as noted in Section 6.3.2.4, exposure to cruel, inhuman or degrading treatment on Nauru.

The examination of the inadequacies of the pre-transfer Best Interest Determinations for unaccompanied children in Section 6.3.2.1 evidences the patent conflict generated by the Minister being both guardian and enforcer of Department law and policy. The pre-transfer best interests assessment acknowledged the child's best interests as a primary consideration but not the only primary consideration. It explicitly mandated that the individual child's best interests 'are outweighed by other primary considerations', which include the need to preserve the integrity of Australia's migration system and discourage children taking, or being taken on, dangerous illegal boat journeys to Australia. As noted in Chapter 3, this is a permissible application of the best interest principle under international law, so far as it relates to the State's general obligation to consider a child's best interests. However, it is not a permissible application of the principle so far as a guardian is concerned: the best interest of the unaccompanied child is to be their basic concern.[34] Yet, the insertion of Section 8 into the *IGOC Act*, discussed in Section 7.2, has effectively removed any best interests consideration that conflicts with the exercise of the Minister's powers under the *Migration Act* – the Minister's obligations under migration law and policies outweigh their obligations to give primacy to the unaccompanied child's best interests. The amendments made the Minister responsible for overseeing the conduct of these pre-transfer Best Interest Determinations in accordance with Australian migration policy. The impossibility of the Minister discharging this obligation *and* advocating for these children's individual best interests as their sole guardian clearly exposed them to an occurrent risk of not having their best interests properly contended for. This, in turn, exposed them to the pathogenic risks arising from transfer to Nauru RPC, as examined in Chapter 5.

Providing legal representation is a core duty of guardians of unaccompanied children.[35] As examined in Section 6.3.2.3, the Minister as guardian did not appoint a legal representative for unaccompanied children either on arrival or before their transfer offshore, and whether they received legal assistance depended on the resources and funding of the RACS and the child's ability to access the service. The Minister's failure as guardian to provide them with a legal representative generated an occurrent vulnerability that any claim they had to remain in Australia would not be prosecuted.

7.3.3 Guardianship of unaccompanied asylum seeker children in the Boat Turnbacks and Takebacks cohort

The *Migration and Maritime Powers Legislation Amendment (Resolving the Asylum Legacy Caseload) Act 2014* amendments essentially refused entry to unaccompanied child asylum seekers when intercepted at sea under the Boat Turnbacks and Takebacks policy, voiding their entitlement to the appointment of a guardian or someone charged with ensuring they have legal representation at the point of interception. This generated a pathogenic vulnerability to refoulement and exposed these children to the risk of new human rights abuses perpetrated by Australia that were utterly avoidable. Regard to these children's acute and specific vulnerability renders these legislative and policy changes that generate new human rights abuses unconscionable.

7.4 Priorities for reform

The vulnerability analysis in this chapter has foregrounded where the legislative amendments to the *IGOC Act* failed to ameliorate these children's existing situational vulnerability arising from their separation from their parents and the sites where they generated new and acute harm to them. The focus on the impact of the amendments as generators of avoidable situational and pathogenic sources of vulnerabilities and occurrent harms, rather than on human rights breaches, highlights the direct correlation between Australia's deliberate winding back of the provision of guardianship to these children and the inevitable harms. The vulnerability analysis also resounds the imperative of recognising State responsibilities to provide unaccompanied children with an independent and effective guardian, notwithstanding their unauthorised presence, because of their unmediated dependence on the State to provide them with an adult charged with protecting their interests. Unlike human rights law, it also illuminates where priorities for legislative and policy reform should be directed to reduce occurrent harms and pathogenic sources of vulnerability first, facilitating distinction between urgent and longer term priorities.

Having identified the impact of the relevant laws and policies that exacerbated or generated new vulnerabilities, two issues remain. First, which of these vulnerabilities can be addressed by legislative and policy change, and what should those changes entail? Second, what should the priorities for reform be?

The vulnerabilities identified in Section 7.3 are all attributable to the absence of an independent and appropriately qualified legal guardian who can advocate for the best interests of unaccompanied child asylum seekers in Australia. Australia should establish an independent statutory guardian for these children to cease the pathogenisation of their vulnerability under existing arrangements. An independent guardian is necessary to oversee the key reform priorities identified in Chapters 5 and 6. In fulfilling the guardian's ordinary core functions, for example, they would be responsible for ensuring that children are not detained for longer than 72 hours in child-friendly reception centres prior to transfer to foster care, a sponsorship arrangement or community detention, as a last resort. They would also ensure access to trauma remediation services while the asylum claim is processed. Similarly, they would ensure they have access to automatic legal representation from reception to finalisation of their claim or transfer from the jurisdiction and advocate for genuine and individualised best interests assessments for the child. Crucially, the guardian would have the legislative function of protecting unaccompanied children from torture or inhumane treatment and refoulement. The interplay between all of these priorities reinforces the critical role of the guardian as the 'rights gatekeeper' between the child and the border control machinery of the State.

Since the reintroduction of offshore processing, Australia's legal framework has failed to provide unaccompanied child asylum seekers with an adult to respond to their vulnerability caused by separation from their parents. As a result, they lack someone to care for them, provide them with opportunities to grow into adulthood or help them claim asylum. The Minister as their 'guardian' has not advocated on their behalf for an appropriate environment of care, has not provided them with automatic and free legal representation or advocated on their behalf for the proper conduct of best interests assessments. Instead, their guardian has enforced the full force of the border control machinery of the State against them, *knowingly* exposing them to occurrent and pathogenic vulnerabilities.

Repeated calls for legislative change to address the failures in Australia's current law to appoint an independent guardian for unaccompanied children and concerns about the unsuitability of the Minister as their guardian have been raised since the AHRC *National Inquiry into Children in Detention* in 2004 by not-for-profits, academics and parliamentary inquiries.[36] In February 2015, in *The Forgotten Children Inquiry Report*, the AHRC again recommended that an independent guardian be appointed for child asylum seekers who arrive in Australia without a parent or guardian.[37] The current law breaches Australia's international obligations, particularly under the CRC, ICCPR and ICESCR.[38]

In the past decade, proposed laws have been tabled calling for the creation of an independent statutory guardian of unaccompanied children.[39] The last of these was Senator Hanson-Young's introduction of a *Bill for the Guardian for Unaccompanied Children Act 2014* (The Greens' Bill). It attracted submissions from multiple stakeholders, most of whom agreed with the Bill and a small number proposing amendments. The Greens' Bill proposed establishing a new office of the guardian for unaccompanied non-citizen children as the guardian of every unaccompanied non-citizen child who arrives in Australia or who is in Australia at the time of the commencement of the Act. The Bill incorporated Australia's key obligations under the CRC and is compliant with the best practice requirements for guardianship in *General Comment 6* of the UN Committee on the Rights of the Child. However, in using the terminology 'unaccompanied non-citizen child', the Bill did not sufficiently acknowledge that unaccompanied child asylum seekers have an additional and separate vulnerability to unaccompanied humanitarian minors because their claim for asylum is not resolved.

The appointment of an independent guardian is necessary if Australia is to even minimally discharge its guardianship obligations to unaccompanied child asylum seekers. As illustrated throughout this chapter, the current conflict is actually not perceived, and the ramifications for children whose interests are not represented or protected are grievous. I propose the development of a Guardianship Act that complies with Australia's core obligations to respond to the complex vulnerabilities of these children through the provision of an effective guardianship framework.[40]

Recalling the six requirements for States to discharge their guardianship duties to unaccompanied children, I propose that the Bill create the legal framework to secure the proper representation and safeguard the child's best interests. It would ensure the guardian has the necessary childcare expertise to ensure their legal, social, health, psychological, material and educational needs are met in a continuum of care. The Bill could achieve both objectives by requiring a court[41] or independent body[42] to oversee the appointment process. The Bill would also preclude agencies or individuals whose interests could potentially conflict with those of the child's. Other jurisdictions maintain a clear distinction between the immigration and guardianship authorities by utilising child protection or youth services government agencies,[43] non-government bodies,[44] hybrid models[45] or appointing citizens of good standing, such as in Sweden.[46] The Bill would also provide unaccompanied children involved in asylum procedures or administrative or judicial proceedings with legal representation in addition to the appointment of a guardian. It could do this in Australia by comprehensively funding the provision of existing legal services to these children. The Bill would also make provision to monitor the quality of the exercise of guardianship to ensure the child's best interests are represented and to prevent abuse. This could utilise the state and territory Offices of the Children's Guardian in monitoring functions or establish a bespoke official community visitors program. Finally, it would establish mechanisms to ensure unaccompanied children are informed of arrangements with respect to guardianship and legal representation and that their opinions are taken into consideration.[47]

To ameliorate the situational vulnerability generated by these children's separation from their parents, the Bill would acknowledge the critical importance of the guardian's dual role as gatekeeper mediating the child's relationship of proximity with the State *and* as an individual in relationship with the child. As discussed in Chapter 6, Italy's *Law 47/2017* illuminates a mitigating vulnerability framework to these children's alienage. Italy also presents as a lighthouse model for Australia to develop a human rights compliant and vulnerability informed Guardianship Bill.[48]

Law 47/2017,[49] which came into force in May 2017, regulates the appointment of the child's legal guardian, the scope of their legal responsibilities (including safeguarding their best interests and ensuring legal representation) and the permissible ratio of three wards per guardian. The law provides a genuine assessment of the child's best interests by requiring qualified staff at the first reception facility to compile a *cartella sociale* (social file) for the child. It provides for three types of normative guardianship models: public-institutional, voluntary, and pro tempore with volunteer guardians (being the preferred appointment in practice). Volunteer guardians' selection and training are overseen by the children's ombudsman and/or the Italian Independent Authority for Children and Adolescents. The volunteer guardian model, appointed by youth courts from lists of approved guardians, has been particularly lauded because it enables the timely appointment of an appropriately qualified guardian in the immediate term. In the medium and longer term, the Italian volunteer guardian model discharges each of the six best practice requirements in international law. It also ensures the child is interconnected with all relevant actors, including social services, reception centres and regional education offices, and plays a fundamental role in supporting the integration and forging of positive relationships between the child and their surrounding social context in Italy.[50]

This chapter has illustrated how a vulnerability analysis of the specific legislative amendments to the *IGOC Act* in 2012, 2013 and 2014 illuminates that the amendments directed at this group of children explicitly avoided, rather than enhanced, the care and protection obligations owed by the Minister as their statutory guardian. It has argued that guardians have a critical role in achieving a mitigating vulnerability framework that addresses the exacerbation of existing vulnerabilities at the sites where these children's minority, alienage, and separation from their parents intersect. It has also shown that Australian law has failed to properly construe or adequately respond to their specific vulnerability because of their separation from their parents.

The vulnerability analysis exposed how all cohorts of children were occurrently vulnerable to not having their best interests represented because of the pre-existing conflict of interest inherent in the Minister being both their sole legal statutory guardian and responsible for enforcing Australia's migration laws. The *IGOC Act* was not originally designed to apply to asylum-seeking children at all, as Australian laws and policies regulating the guardianship of unaccompanied children were developed to respond to authorised immigrant children. Subsequent amendments failed to make special provisions to accommodate their different needs, vulnerabilities and arrival circumstances or even simply acknowledge that they are differently vulnerable to all other categories of ward under the Act because their legal status to remain in Australia is yet to be determined.

The 2012, 2013 and 2014 amendments directed at this group of children explicitly avoided, rather than enhanced, the care and protection obligations owed by the Minister as their statutory guardian by constraining guardianship obligations to the increasingly vanishing space not occupied by the Minister's border protection powers under the *Migration Act* or *Maritime Powers Act*. The impact of failing to provide the Legacy Caseload cohort with a guardian independent from the Minister responsible for border protection perpetuated the situational vulnerabilities of unaccompanied children in mandatory immigration detention by making them occurrently vulnerable to remaining in detention and to a lack of independent representation of their interests while detained. The impact of maintaining the Minister's dual role for children released into community detention failed to ameliorate their situational vulnerability as wards.

The impact of the amendments also significantly exacerbated the situational vulnerability for the cohort subject to transfer to Nauru. These children experienced the same exacerbating factors as the Legacy Caseload cohort whilst in mandatory immigration detention. However, the subordination of the Minister's duty to consider their best interests to border protection priorities generated two pathogenic vulnerabilities. First, that no adult would consider or represent their individual best interests in the crucial pre-transfer assessment period. Second, that they could potentially be refouled by being subjected to cruel and inhumane treatment on Nauru.

The impact of the amendments rendered unaccompanied children subject to Boat Turnbacks and Takebacks occurrently vulnerable to neglect and inhumane treatment and pathogenically vulnerable to refoulement by denying them access to any of the core protections guardians are mandated to extend to them or legal advice at the point of interception and prior to removal back into international waters.

The vulnerability analysis has exposed guardians' critical role in acting as a gatekeeper between the child and the State at the sites where these children's minority, alienage, and separation from their parents intersect. It has also clarified the sites and sources of the most devastating impacts on being/becoming unaccompanied children's separation from their parents and informed the concrete measures and priorities for reform that were proposed.

The next chapter concludes this book.

Notes

1 Recalling that Section 4.4.1.1 identifies and distinguishes inherent, situational, pathogenic and occurrent vulnerabilities.

2 Significant research has been conducted on the history and impact on the lives of former unaccompanied child migrants, including Barry Coldrey, *Good British Stock: Child and Youth Migration to Australia* (National Archives, 1999); Philip Bean and Joy Melville, *Lost Children of the Empire* (Unwin Hyman, 1989); Margaret Humphreys, *Empty Cradles* (Transworld, 2009); and Alan Gill, *Orphans of the Empire: The Shocking Story of Child Migration to Australia* (Random House, 1998). Several state government inquiries and reports have added significantly to this scholarship, and the inquiry by the Senate Community Affairs References Committee, *Lost Innocents: Righting the Record* (Commonwealth Government, 2001) comprehensively investigated unaccompanied child migration to Australia under approved schemes during the twentieth century. Additionally, Julie Taylor and Jordana Silverstein provide targeted Australian scholarship regarding the history of the *Immigration (Guardianship of Children) Act 1946* (Cth) (*IGOC Act*) and the guardianship of unaccompanied children. See Julie Taylor, 'Guardianship of Child Asylum-Seekers' (2006) 34(1) *Federal Law Review* 204 and Jordana Silverstein, 'I am responsible: histories of the intersection of the guardianship of unaccompanied child refugees and the Australian border' (2016) 22(2) *Cultural Studies Review* 65 for analysis of the history of the *IGOC Act*.

3 The Act was enacted under the Commonwealth's power to legislate on immigration in s 51(xxvii) of the *Commonwealth Constitution*.

4 Or was exempted from the provisions of the *IGOC Act* under a discretionary right of the Minister or delegate. As initially enacted, s 6 stated that:

The Minister shall be the guardian of the person in Australia, of –

> (a) every evacuee child (b) every immigrant child who arrives in Australia after the commencement of this Act, to the exclusion of the father or mother and every other guardian of the child, and shall have as guardian, the same rights, powers, duties, obligations and liabilities as the natural guardian of the child would have, until the child reaches the age of twenty-one years, or leaves Australia permanently, or until the provisions of this Act cease to apply to and in relation to the child, whichever happens first.

5 The state premiers' conference on 20 August 1946 resolved that the Commonwealth should continue to be the sole authority for migration activities overseas and that the states and territories would carry out the function of reception on arrival in Australia. See Community Affairs References Committee, Parliament of Australia Senate, *Lost Innocents: Righting the Record* (n 2) 26 [2.64] and Taylor (n 2) 185.

6 The purpose of this provision was to protect children 'from any person who would wish to entice him away from Australia for any purpose other than the good of the child'. See Commonwealth, *Parliamentary Debates*, House of Representatives, 18 November 1948, 3203 (Dame Edith Lyons).

7 *Migration Act 1958* (Cth) (*Migration Act*) s 4.

8 The Courts subsequently acknowledged that the Minister's statutory obligations as the legal guardian of a non-citizen child may give rise to a potential 'conflict of roles' in respect of the performance of functions under the *Migration Act*; see *Odhiambo v Minister for Immigration and Multicultural Affairs* (2002) 122 FCR 29 at 47–48 [90] (*Odhiambo*).

9 Commonwealth, *Parliamentary Debates*, House of Representatives, 3 March 1994, 1694 (Phillip Ruddock, Minister for Immigration and Ethnic Affairs).

10 Mary Crock, 'Lonely Refuge: Judicial Responses to Separated Children Seeking Refugee Protection in Australia' (2005) 22(2) *Law in Context* 128; Mary Crock, *Seeking Asylum Alone, Australia: A Study of Australian Law, Policy and Practice Regarding Unaccompanied and Separated Children* (Themis Press, 2006); Mary Crock, 'Of Relative Rights and Putative Children: Rethinking the Critical Framework for the Protection of Refugee Children and Youth' (2013) 20 *Australian International Law Journal* 33; Mary Crock and Mary Anne Kenny, 'Rethinking the Guardianship of Refugee Children after the Malaysian Solution' (2012) 34(3) *Sydney Law Review* 437.

11 Provided that the child does not have the competence to make the decision: *Secretary, Department of Health and Community Services v JWB and SMB* (1992) 175 CLR 218, 235–6 (Mason CJ, Dawson, Toohey and Gaudron JJ), 278 (Brennan J), 289, 293–4 (Deane J), 315 (McHugh J).

12 *Clay v Clay* (2001) 202 CLR 410, 430; John Eekelaar, 'What are Parental Rights?' (1973) 89 *Law Quarterly Review* 201, 230.

13 *X v Minister for Immigration and Multicultural Affairs* (1999) 92 FCR 524 [41] and [43] (*X v Minister for Immigration and Multicultural Affairs*); cited with approval in *Odhiambo* (n 8) [86], [88].

14 *X v Minister for Immigration and Multicultural Affairs* (n 13) [34]–[41].

15 Mary Crock, 'Of Relative Rights and Putative Children' (n 10) 35.

16 In *Odhiambo* (n 8) [93–100], the Court held that responsibility for ensuring that an unaccompanied child has legal representation in tribunal or court proceedings falls to the tribunal or court not the Minister as their guardian.

17 *WACA v Minister for Immigration and Multicultural Affairs* (2002) 121 FCR 463.

18 *Plaintiff M168/10, A Minor, by His Litigation Guardian Sister Brigid (Marie) Arthur v The Commonwealth* [2011] HCA 25. This case was an application for interlocutory relief, seeking the release from detention of the plaintiff, who arrived in Australia as an unaccompanied minor from Afghanistan.

19 *Plaintiff M70/2011 v Minister for Immigration and Citizenship; Plaintiff M106 of 2011 v Minister for Immigration and Citizenship* (2011) 244 CLR 18. For further discussion of the case, see Tamara Wood and Jane McAdam, 'Australian Asylum Policy All at Sea: An Analysis of Plaintiff M70/2011 v Minister for Immigration and Citizenship and the Australia–Malaysia Arrangement' (2012) 61 *International and Comparative Law Quarterly* 274; Michelle Foster, 'The Implications of the Failed Malaysian Solution: The Australian High Court and Refugee Responsibility Sharing at International Law' (2012) 13 *Melbourne Journal of International Law* 395.

In *M70/2011*, so far as that decision related to unaccompanied children, solicitors for a 16-year-old Afghan unaccompanied child sought an injunction from the High Court restraining the Minister for Immigration and Citizenship (as he then was) from removing him to Malaysia without the Minister's written consent under the *IGOC Act*. That case, thus, involved consideration of whether and to what extent the conferral of power on an officer to take an 'offshore entry person' from Australia to a declared third country (Malaysia, in this instance) under the *Migration Act* needed to be informed by the Minister's obligations as guardian under the *IGOC Act*.

20 *IGOC Act* s 6A.

21 Explanatory Memorandum, the *Migration Legislation Amendment (Regional Processing and Other Measures) Bill 2012* (Cth) [270–271].

22 The government first introduced the *Migration Legislation Amendment (Offshore Processing and Other Measures) Bill 2011* (Cth), which did not gain the support of the Coalition, Greens and the required number of independents in October 2011. On 13 October 2011, the government announced it would not pursue the amendments. However, it was subsequently reintroduced and passed as the *Migration Legislation Amendment (Regional Processing and Other Measures) Act 2012*, receiving Royal assent on 18 August 2012.

23 *IGOC Act* ss 8(1) and 8(3). However, whether any scope remains for argument that the sections in the *IGOC Act* prescribing the Minister's guardianship obligations to unaccompanied child asylum seekers still have some work to do remains untested. The Minister must still presumably consider their duties as guardian when making discretionary decisions under the *Migration Act.*

24 These powers include removals pursuant to Section 198 or 199 of the *Migration Act*, taking them to an offshore processing country pursuant to Section 198AD of the *Migration Act*, deporting them pursuant to Section 200 of the *Migration Act* or taking them to a place outside Australia pursuant to Section 245F(9)(b) of the *Migration Act.* The amending Act also repealed the old subsection 6A(4), which had provided that Section 6A did not affect the operation of any other law regulating the departure of persons from Australia.

25 Accordingly, the Minister is the guardian of unaccompanied child asylum seekers awaiting transfer to a regional country for processing, but once they are transferred, they are subject to the guardianship arrangements, if any, in those jurisdictions.

26 Mary Crock, 'Lonely Refuge: Judicial Responses' (n 10) 129.

27 Commonwealth and Immigration Ombudsman, *Suicide and Self-Harm in the Immigration Detention Network Report 02/2013* (Commonwealth Government, 2013) [7.20]–[7.21].

28 *Immigration (Guardianship of Children) Delegation 2013* (Cth) sch 2.

29 Australian Human Rights Commission, *The Forgotten Children: National Inquiry into Children in Immigration Detention* (Commonwealth Government, 2014) 169 (*The Forgotten Children Inquiry Report*).

30 Department of Immigration and Border Protection, Submission to the *Forgotten Children Inquiry* (30 May 2014) <https://www.humanrights.gov.au/sites/default/files/Submission%20No%2045%20-%20Department%20of%20Immigration%20and%20Border%20Protection.pdf>.

31 Australian Human Rights Commission, *The Forgotten Children Inquiry Report* (n 29) 171.

32 Commonwealth and Immigration Ombudsman, *Suicide and Self-harm in the Immigration Detention Network Report 02/2013* (2013), [7.20].

33 This was in addition to not having automatically appointed legal representation, as discussed in Sections 6.3.2.2 and 6.3.2.3 of Chapter 6.

34 Note that there are potentially additional obligations for States in which an unaccompanied minor is a victim of trafficking or has a disability or there are additional factors of vulnerability. Under Article 39 of CRC, States are obliged to take all appropriate measures to promote physical and psychological recovery and social reintegration of child victims of 'any neglect, exploitation, or abuse; torture or any other form of cruel, inhuman or degrading treatment or punishment; or armed conflicts'. The health, self-respect and dignity of the child should dictate the environment in which the recovery and reintegration takes place. Moreover, under Article 23 of the CRC, mentally or physically disabled children have the right to enjoy a full and decent life in conditions that ensure dignity, promote

self-reliance and facilitate active participation in the community, and Article 1 of the CRPD obliges States to 'promote, protect and ensure the full and equal enjoyment of all human rights and fundamental freedoms by all persons with disabilities, and to promote respect for their inherent dignity'.

35 See the discussion in Chapter 3 in Sections 3.3.2.2 and 3.3.3.1.

36 See, for example, Australian Churches Refugee Taskforce, *All the Lonely Children: Questions for Policy Makers Regarding Guardianship for Unaccompanied Minors* (Australian Churches, 2013); Mary Crock and Mary Anne Kenny, 'Rethinking the Guardianship of Refugee Children after the Malaysian Solution' (2012) 34(3) *Sydney Law Review* 437. In 2012, the Parliamentary Joint Select Committee on Australia's Immigration Detention Network recommended that the Minister for Immigration should not be the legal guardian of unaccompanied minors in immigration detention. See Parliamentary Joint Select Committee on Australia's Immigration Detention Network, *Final Report* (Commonwealth Government, 2012) [5.95–5.96].

37 The AHRC found that:

> In the event of any conflict between guardianship obligations and migration policies, the Minister and the delegated guardians are required to give priority to their roles under the Migration Act. In August 2012 the *Immigration (Guardianship of Children) Act 1946* (Cth) was amended to make clear that the Minister or his delegated guardians can only exercise 'the same rights, powers, duties, obligations and liabilities as a natural guardian' of an unaccompanied child in immigration detention to the extent that those duties do not affect the performance or exercise of any function, duty or power under the migration law. In some instances, the law or the policies relating to immigration detention are in direct conflict with the best interests of the child.

See Australian Human Rights Commission, *The Forgotten Children Inquiry* (n 29) 167–168.

38 Ibid 171.

39 Commissioner for Children and Young People Bill 2010 (Cth); *Guardian for Unaccompanied Children Bill 2013* (Cth).

40 See the discussion of Australia's international obligations examined in Section 3.3.3 in Chapter 3.

41 See, for example, the Netherlands, Austria, Germany and Italy.

42 See, for example, Belgium – the Guardianship Service; and Sweden – the Chief Guardian.

43 See, for example, Austria, Germany, Lithuania and Spain.

44 See, for example, France, the Netherlands and Poland.

45 See, for example, Belgium (professional non-government employees and volunteers) and the Czech Republic (child protection departments and NGOs).

46 European Migration Network, 'Policies on Reception, Return and Integration Arrangements for, and Numbers of, Unaccompanied Minors – An EU Comparative Study' (EMN, 2010) <http://ec.europa.eu/dgs/home-affairs/what-we-do/networks/european_migration_network/reports/docs/emn-studies/unaccompanied-minors/0._emn_synthesis_report_unaccompanied_minors_publication_sept10_en.pdf>.

47 UN Committee on the Rights of the Child *General Comment No. 6 (2005), Treatment of Unaccompanied and Separated Children Outside Their Country of Origin,* UN Doc.CRC/GC/2005/6, [33]–[38].

48 See Paul Rigby et al., *Responding to Unaccompanied Minors in Scotland: Policy and Local Authority Perspectives* (University of Stirling, October 2018) <https://www.scottishinsight.ac.uk/Portals/80/SUIIProgrammes/Asylum%20Seeking

%20Children/Responding%20to%20Unaccompanied%20Minors%20-%20Policy %20and%20LA.pdf>. See also ISMU *At a Crossroads. Unaccompanied and Separated Children in Their Transition to Adulthood in Italy* (IOM, 2019) 22.

49 *Law No. 47/2017 on Provisions on Protective Measures for Unaccompanied Children in Italy* [*Disposizioni in materia di misure di protezione dei minori stranieri non accompagnati*].

50 European Union Agency for Fundamental Rights and AGIA, *Guardianship for Unaccompanied Children in Italy* (EUAFR, 2018) <https://fra.europa.eu/en/news/2018/innovative-italian-legislation-updates-approach-guardianship>.

8 Scope to expand the application of the mitigating vulnerability framework to other contexts

8.1 Prising open space to respond to unaccompanied child asylum seekers

There has been a longstanding and vigorous debate in Australia between academics, political commentators, politicians and refugee advocates about the appropriate balance between national security based on tight border protection and the humane treatment of asylum seekers. This often-fraught debate is framed between two polarities. One side has expressed strong and longstanding condemnation of the treatment of asylum seekers and the disconnect between this treatment and Australia's human rights obligations.[1] On the other side, successive governments have asserted that Australia's national security interests can only be met by the retention of punitive border control policies. In the middle, political 'pragmatists' contend that Australia has a moral responsibility to settle asylum seekers stranded on Nauru. However, they argue that 'it is inconceivable that in the next few years any Australian government – either Coalition or Labor – will be willing to … cease offshore processing of asylum claims and to abandon the policy of naval interception and turn-back to the point of departure'.[2] They call on opponents of the government's 'ring of naval steel' policy to accept that 'the only realistic position from the political point of view is one involving the retention of turn-back',[3] contending that the 'political unrealism and unwillingness to compromise' of countervailing view holders have contributed to the current impasse.[4] Robert Manne colourfully argued in 2017 that 'it is as certain as anything in politics can ever be that no government that has a chance of being elected in Australia in the next few years will return to the position … where offshore processing and turn-backs were both abandoned'.[5]

I disagree.

History has shown that, on the contrary, Australians do respond to principled and informed leadership on this issue.[6] In relation to unaccompanied children seeking asylum, the bipartisan commitment to a border-driven rhetoric has obscured our capacity to respond to their triple vulnerabilities and permitted egregious harms. Principled leadership could focus on a broader context than the border: the key drivers of flight by sea towards Australia and the lack of effective protection for refugees and people seeking asylum in the Asia-Pacific region. It

DOI: 10.4324/9781003260134-9

could also lead debate about obvious priorities for reform: first, expanding opportunities for the safe entry of unaccompanied child asylum seekers by increasing the size of Australia's resettlement program and improving access to alternative migration pathways; and second, developing alternative regional responses that focus on their protection rather than deterrence strategies. Both would enhance recognition of the common humanity and dignity of these children, enhance protection for unaccompanied children fleeing persecution in accordance with our international human rights obligations and be an effective and sustainable means of preventing flight by sea. Unfortunately, current Australian policy only seeks to prevent arrivals.

This principled leadership could also expand the political debate that has contracted to whether governments are unelectable with policies that can be portrayed as opening Australia to unauthorised boat arrivals and that loosen its iron-clad maritime borders to, instead, lead the discussion about Australia's responsibility for unaccompanied children as a 'special case' because of their triple vulnerability. It could point to the clear and unequivocal publicly available evidence examined in Chapters 5–7 about the damage wrought on these children, especially those held in mandatory immigration detention on the mainland and those sent to Nauru. Their triple burden of vulnerability as children who have experienced persecution or serious harm in their State of nationality, seeking protection in a State where their entry is unauthorised, and while separated from their parents or guardians has not only been obscured. The hardening of laws and policies prioritising border securitisation over humanitarian obligations has also exacerbated their acute vulnerabilities.

There are very real complexities in Australian migration law and policy. However, they do not justify Australia further harming these children. Genuine guardianship, care and protection could easily be extended to them without seriously threatening Australia's borders. It is one of the more remarkable paradoxes in Australian law that the functions of the Minister, who is the statutory legal guardian of unaccompanied children – to the exclusion of any others who might effectively perform that role – are subject to the exercise of that Minister's functions under the *Migration Act*. Guardians stand in the parents' shoes for an unaccompanied child with no adult carer. Guardians and parents have an overriding obligation to act in the child's best interests while discharging their duties for that child to survive and thrive. It should be a requirement under State law and policy for a statutory guardian to do so. After the amendments to the *IGOC Act* in 2012–2014, not only is acting in the best interests of these children – who are subject to transfer to Nauru and to Boat Turnbacks and Takebacks – not a requirement, but it is also no longer possible. This State response proactively pathogenises the triple vulnerability of these children. Australia's treatment of these children is a deliberate policy choice. As Italy's example shows, the damage inflicted on unaccompanied children by Australian law and policy is neither necessary nor inevitable. Italy's *Law 47/2017* demonstrates that it is possible to not generate occurrent harms and pathogenic sources of vulnerability by granting unaccompanied children a residence permit; facilitating their representation in, and expedited access to, resolution of their protection claims; and appointing an independent guardian. In fact, as Italy's *Law 47/2017* has shown, it is possible to also ameliorate their situational vulnerabilities.

Principled leadership can address the complexity of the security *and* the human impact of Australia's policies without a diminution of the protection extended to these children. The momentum in Australia connecting increasing border control and diminishing protection of unaccompanied children must be halted if Australia is to comply with either its moral obligations to stop harming proximate vulnerable children or its international human rights obligations.

By interrogating the vulnerabilities of unaccompanied child asylum seekers and the impact of a series of Australian legislative amendments between 2012 and 2014 on those vulnerabilities, this book is positioned as an 'interrupter' to the current political trajectory. It not only critiques the disconnect between human rights and State practice but proposes a reconceptualisation of States' responsibilities to respond to that vulnerability and provides a new imperative for prioritising and formulating new law and policy responses. To this end, this book has asked and answered five questions. Are unaccompanied children vulnerable in a way that generates a moral obligation for the State to respond to, not exacerbate, their vulnerability, an obligation that supplements international law obligations? How effectively does international human rights law respond to their acute vulnerability? How did amendments to Australian laws and policies in 2012, 2013 and 2014 respond to the vulnerabilities of these children? In what ways was this response inadequate? How should Australian law and policy be reformed to respond to their vulnerability?

In answering these questions, this book has argued that this reconceptualisation is urgently required for two reasons: the acute and specific vulnerability of unaccompanied child asylum seekers and the as-yet unfulfilled potential of human rights law, particularly in Australia. It also argued that vulnerability theory should be expanded to extend to these proximate vulnerable children and that it provides the ethical imperative for reframing legal and policy responses to ensure States *do not further harm* children seeking their protection. Connecting theory and practice, this book proposed a three-stage process to identify a mitigating vulnerability framework in different contexts. It applied that method to evaluate the impact of amendments between 2012 and 2014 to the *Migration Act* and the *IGOC Act* on these children.

8.2 The acute vulnerability of unaccompanied child asylum seekers

This book has argued that unaccompanied children are vulnerable in a way that generates a moral obligation that supplements international law obligations to respond to, not exacerbate, their vulnerability. Unaccompanied child asylum seekers experience an intersecting and intertwined 'triple burden' of vulnerability that characterises their specific dependence on the State: their minority, alienage (asylum-seeking and unauthorised presence in the territory), and separation from their parents. They have distinct needs arising from their minority, including to be cared for, given opportunities to develop and to be protected from physical or mental violence, foreseeable harm and neglect. Both their legal precariousness and unauthorised presence likewise generate a distinct need not to be refouled or refused access to an RSD procedure. Similarly, their separation from their parents gives rise to a specific need for a legal guardian with legislative and functional responsibilities to act in the child's best interests.

Understanding that 'childhood' is simultaneously a period and a state and that a 'child' is simultaneously a becoming person and an extant being has been shown in this book to be central to properly comprehend the rationale for determining the proper extent of States' obligation to respond to unaccompanied children. As Chapter 2 demonstrated, viewing childhood holistically brings into sharp focus that children need care and protection both as their current selves to be psychologically well in the present and simultaneously to develop age-appropriate developmental benchmarks and psychological maturity milestones in their futures. Unaccompanied children arrive in States at their specific stage of development, with their specific care and protection needs, as well as the embodiment of all the potential for growth and development they possess. Whether their care, protection and development needs are adequately responded to, for example, through providing appropriate custodial care, appropriate psychological care to enable recovery from past trauma or additional educational services to remediate disruptions to education, is crucially important. Comprehending children and childhood in this way is critical to understanding the real impact of the amendments between 2012 and 2014 to the *Migration Act* and the *IGOC Act* examined in Chapters 5–7.

8.3 Human rights compliance as the long game

This book has argued that, to date, international human rights law has ultimately been ineffective at compelling an adequate Australian State response to the acute vulnerability of these children. The existing normative response to the acute vulnerability of unaccompanied child asylum seekers is grounded in States' extensive human rights obligations. These obligations *ought* to provide an effective counterbalance to the punitive laws, policies and securitisation rhetoric. However, the dispersal of these obligations across the core international human rights legal instruments and the Refugee Convention obscures both their extensive nature and a holistic conception of how the obligations pertain to unaccompanied child asylum seekers. I addressed this by correlating States' dispersed human rights obligations to these children with each of the three sites of vulnerability identified in Chapter 2 (their minority, alienage, and separation from their parents). I then examined the scope and content of these human rights obligations to demonstrate that, if States so conceptualised and then fully realised them, unaccompanied asylum-seeking being/becoming children would be adequately protected.

Chapter 3 went on to argue that, despite the adequacy of human rights in principle, they have been inadequate protection against 'securitised' policies in Australia in practice. They have proven incapable of preventing real harms being perpetrated on these acutely vulnerable children. This chapter detailed how especially in legal systems such as Australia, where treaty ratification does not create domestic legal obligations unless the provisions are incorporated into domestic law, State practice routinely falls far short of human rights legal standards. I argued that the unfulfilled potential of human rights law is particularly evidenced by the progressive degrading of treatment of unaccompanied children seeking asylum by boat under Australian law in the past two decades. Australia is responsible in international law for fully discharging its duties, having ratified all core human rights treaties and the Refugee Convention. And yet, over the past 20 years, apart from brief periods in which child asylum seekers have been released into the community while their claims have been processed, laws and policies implemented by both of Australia's dominant political parties have increasingly hidden child asylum seekers from view and repudiated their need for special assistance. These children were initially detained in remote and inhospitable places on the Australian mainland before being further consigned to the background on remote Australian island outposts. This was followed by their individual treatment and any corresponding harms being completely obscured when sent to other States to process their claims for asylum. Lastly, in the most emphatic repudiation, Australia has refused to receive them at all by turning back the boats taking them to seek asylum. These successive responses to asylum seekers each represent watershed moments in which lines of fundamental human rights standards were crossed. Australian contemporary law and policy deliberately disowns the abject vulnerability of these children. Analysis of the extensive and egregious human rights breaches caused by Australia's harsh, punitive and rejecting response to these children illustrates how human rights law has not provided the necessary break for these children on the excesses of securitised responses in successive regressive changes in law and policy.

Australia should continue to strive to realise the totality of its international human rights obligations. Its policies, legislation and regulations ought not undermine the fundamental normative human rights standards in global human rights instruments, conventions and other internationally agreed commitments that Australia has ratified. While advocacy will, and should, continue urging legal and policy changes that balance border control priorities with human rights obligations, urgent interim changes to law and policy are required that respond to the particular vulnerability of unaccompanied asylum-seeking children and the substantive evidence of the considerable and lasting harm that Australian laws and policies are causing them. Behind the catalogues of breaches of Australia's human rights obligations are children whose lives have been indelibly marked because of Australian laws and policy, together with the actions of, and failure to act by, their legal guardian. Further inaction until Australia makes sufficient progress in realising its human rights obligations will inflict additional harm and cannot be justified.

8.4 The novelty of an expanded vulnerability theory in identifying the content of, and prioritising the rollout of, an acute response

As a basis for a supplementary approach to human rights, this book has argued that vulnerability theory offers a new way of delineating the precise nature of the vulnerabilities of particular groups, the significance of the role of the State in ameliorating those vulnerabilities, the impact of State practice and the changes required to laws and policies to redress vulnerability. Since Fineman's work, along with other mainstream vulnerability scholarship on domestic themes, implicitly restricts the scope of States' obligations on account of vulnerability to citizens as liberal subjects, vulnerability theory, as traditionally conceived, falls short of providing a normative theory that includes unaccompanied non-citizen children within its protective scope. Unaccompanied child asylum seekers fall between the gaps of human rights and vulnerability theory. They miss out on the protections of an international human rights system that does recognise extensive State obligations owed to them *because they are non-citizen asylum-seeking children*, but that does not guarantee the creation of equivalent domestic legal obligations. They are then overlooked by vulnerability theory, which provides a normative framework for holding States to account for their role in ameliorating or exacerbating people's vulnerabilities but excludes these children *because they are non-citizen asylum-seeking children.*

Chapter 4 argued for the radical application of vulnerability theory outside of the traditional context of nation-state obligations to citizens. Developing Fineman's neglected acknowledgement that non-citizens 'should be afforded equality on the same terms as citizens if they … have *some other connection* that would make placing state responsibility for them and their situation appropriate',[7] it argued that unaccompanied child asylum seekers have this requisite *other connection* as 'proximate vulnerable children'. This is because of the convergence of their urgent need to have their acute 'triple burden' of vulnerability responded to *and* their spatial, temporal and relational proximity to the State.

The chapter contended further that a State's obligations to these children, while they are seeking asylum, are not to fully ameliorate their vulnerabilities but, rather, that responsibility will fall on the State in which they are ultimately settled. Yet, the urgency and acuteness of their vulnerability, as well as the potential sequential impacts of maltreatment by potentially successive receiving and asylum processing States, necessitates a response by *each* State that does not exacerbate their vulnerabilities and that specifically avoids generating new vulnerabilities for the period that the child is physically or relationally proximate to the State.

Fineman's vulnerability theory does not reach to determining what constitutes a response that neither exacerbates nor generates new vulnerabilities in practice. This book, therefore, drew on the conceptual work by Mackenzie, Rogers and Dodds to distinguish between inherent, situational, occurrent and pathogenic vulnerabilities.[8] It then articulated a three-stage process to identify the requisite mitigating vulnerability response to avoid exacerbating existing inherent or situational vulnerabilities or generating new occurrent or pathogenic ones in specific contexts. First, it examined the operation of laws and policies governing the relationship between the proximate vulnerable child and the State in a specified context and time period to understand the legal context resulting from government choices regarding laws and policies in practice. Second, it discerned the impact of those laws and policies on unaccompanied children's minority, alienage, and separation from their parents to identify which changes have ameliorated vulnerabilities or generated occurrent or new pathogenic vulnerabilities. Third, it identified the impacts that can be addressed by legislative and policy change and proposing the content of those changes and priorities for reform to first address impacts that create occurrent or new pathogenic vulnerabilities.

8.5 Roadmap for reform

This book argues for two immediate reform priorities to create an environment of care for unaccompanied children that does not generate occurrent or pathogenic vulnerabilities. The first priority is limiting mandatory immigration detention of all unaccompanied children to no longer than 72 hours in purpose-built child-friendly reception centres before transferring them into foster care, or a sponsorship arrangement or, as a last resort, to community detention on the Australian mainland while their asylum claim is processed. The second priority is providing them access to trauma remediation services while their asylum claim is processed. Neither of these proposed reforms requires legislative changes.[9] It also proposed progressive practice improvements in community detention arrangements. Finally, it recommended that *if* the government persists with offshore processing on Nauru RPC in the future, no unaccompanied child should be transferred there until a mitigating vulnerability assessment has been conducted and facilities and services are in place to effectively respond to their complex care needs.[10]

This book argues for five urgent priorities for reform to avoid existing occurrent and pathogenic vulnerabilities generated by Australia's response to these children's alienage. Three can be implemented immediately. First, the Minister should make a Section 198AE (1) *Migration Act* declaration that the Section 198AD transfer to a regional processing country requirement does not apply to unaccompanied child asylum seekers,[11] preferably permanently, but at least until such time as the UN declares that transferring children to Nauru does not constitute refoulement. Second, all unaccompanied children should be provided with specialist legal assistance from reception until finalisation of their protection claim by expanding the funding of existing service providers. Third, the processing of protection claims of unaccompanied children should be expedited, and custodial carers of the Legacy Caseload cohort in community detention group homes should be trained to identify cases of 'lethal hopelessness' and be provided with appropriate referral points.

The fourth and fifth reforms proposed in the book entail amending the *Maritime Powers Act 2013* and the *Migration Act* to reverse the changes made by the *Resolving the Asylum Legacy Caseload Act 2014* to re-invoke Australia's non-refoulement obligations in full and exempt unaccompanied children from on-sea enhanced screening and Boat Turnbacks and Takebacks. Unaccompanied children should, instead, be transferred to the mainland for assessment of their claim.

The book also proposes longer term priorities for legislative reform:

- Full merits review of primary protection decisions by the Migrant and Refugee Division of the AAT should be reintroduced, ensuring that status determinations for unaccompanied child asylum seekers comply with international norms.
- Should transfers to offshore processing resume, ensure that the pre-transfer Best Interest Assessment is a genuine and individualised assessment with the possibility that the child not be transferred, and
- Continue cooperation to build a regional processing system in Bali Process countries with consistent and timely access to the RSD process, merits review and durable solutions and, if bipartisan government policy continues to refuse the prospect of settlement in Australia, ensure that there are realistic 'third country' settlement options.

Lastly, the book recommends the appointment of an independent guardian. This is crucial if Australia is to even minimally discharge its guardianship obligations to unaccompanied children. The roadmap for reform proposed the development of a Guardianship Bill. This Bill would comply with Australia's six core obligations to respond to the complex vulnerabilities of these children through the provision of an effective guardianship framework. The Bill would also acknowledge the critical importance of the guardian's dual role as gatekeeper, both being in a relationship with the child *and* mediating the child's relationship of proximity with the State.

The roadmap for reform recommended that Australia should also look to the global context for models that comprehensively respond to these children's vulnerability. For example, on its terms, Italy's *Law 47/2017* presents as a lighthouse model for Australia to draw on in developing a human rights compliant and mitigating vulnerability-informed Guardianship Bill.[12] *Law 47/2017* codified the prohibition on forced returns of unaccompanied children, introduced child-friendly assessment and determination procedures, enabled their simultaneous application for international protection (with rights to be heard, to legal assistance and to prioritised examination of their application) and the automatic granting of a residence permit for unaccompanied and/or separated children. It permits them to convert that permit to a residence permit for study, work or job-seeking when they turn 18. It also provides for transitional arrangements for their continued care and protection, irrespective of legal status, and the provision of social services until the age of 21.[13] Finally, it regulates appointment of the child's legal guardian under three normative guardianship models and the scope of their legal responsibilities (including safeguarding their best interests and ensuring legal representation). As examined in Section 7.4, in the medium and longer term, the Italian volunteer guardian model discharges each of the six best practice requirements for guardians in international law.

8.6 The utility of the mitigating vulnerability framework in other contexts

This book has demonstrated the three-pronged utility of the mitigating vulnerability framework. It enables comprehension of the complex vulnerability of a specific group of people in a given context by identifying sites of State responsibility in which State interventions either support resilience or expose people to a probability of having their vulnerabilities exacerbated and their dependencies manifested. It provides a normative framework for action by precisely articulating the impact of consequences of laws and policies when States fail to respond to that vulnerability. And it clarifies the imperative for components of and the rationale for prioritising necessary reforms.

This book disrupts embedded political discourse that legitimises State actions that treat groups of individuals punitively without regard to States' extensive human rights obligations to them. Drawing on childhood studies, human rights, vulnerability theory and philosophy, this book has proposed principled criteria by which children can be characterised as having sufficient connection with the State to compel the State to implement a mitigating vulnerability response in addition to the States' human rights obligations. It has illustrated the value of correlating the precise scope of States' obligations that may be dispersed across multiple treaties with identifiable sites of vulnerability that arise in a given context. It has proposed a universally applicable three-stage process that embeds a taxonomy for identifying types and severity of harms to arrive at a mitigating vulnerability framework in any given context. This book demonstrates the utility of applying the mitigating vulnerability framework by applying it to examine Australia's treatment of unaccompanied asylum-seeking children. However, the methodology could be similarly applied in different jurisdictions and contexts wherever there are key existing gaps between the promise of human rights protection and treatment in practice. A mitigating vulnerability framework based on specific vulnerabilities of minority, separation from parents and susceptibility to imminent violence could, for example, be applied to internally displaced refugee children in conflict corridors. Other contexts could include, for example, children experiencing forced migration due to starvation, water shortages and flooding as a result of climate change; children who are trafficked; and children experiencing statelessness.

The mitigating vulnerability framework brings together international human rights law, childhood studies and vulnerability theory to provide a comprehensive interdisciplinary framework for comprehending the complex and specific vulnerabilities of different groups. The three-stage mitigating vulnerability framework, with its embedded taxonomy for articulating the gravity of harm, provides a valuable resource for governments, practitioners, NGOs, advocates and the general public seeking a methodology for analysing the operation and real-world impact of laws on vulnerable populations and for prioritising reforms. This book also paves new ground for multidisciplinary advocacy by refugee and climate change advocates, human rights lawyers and children's rights advocates seeking to examine and challenge the operation and impact of laws and policies that harm children and to propose concrete recommendations for law and policy reform that minimise identifiable harms.

By applying the mitigating vulnerability framework to assess the effects of law and policy in other contexts and identify the specific sites where law and policy fail to respond to the situational vulnerabilities of children or generate new occurrent and pathogenic vulnerabilities, we can illuminate the correlation between the relative degree of vulnerability of children and the egregiousness of harm caused to the being/becoming child by State laws and policies in a way that human rights law does not.

By focusing on reforms that can end these children's exposure to occurrent and pathogenic vulnerabilities, the mitigating vulnerability framework identifies a reform roadmap identifying the specific law and policy sites requiring urgent responsive action to respond appropriately to these children. Implementing this reform roadmap will prevent these children from being subjected to further harm until States fully realise the human rights obligations they have voluntarily assumed in international law. In the meantime, these reforms would move States closer to compliance with those obligations.

Finally, the mitigating vulnerability framework also has the potential to be utilised to identify potential sites of occurrent or pathogenic vulnerabilities when new laws and policies are announced, or when new crises arrive that impact a particular group, to pre-empt responses to avoid preventable and predictable harms occurring. For example, the embedded taxonomy could have been used to identify the sites likely to generate occurrent or pathogenic vulnerabilities for groups of children impacted by the COVID pandemic, such as children losing access to education for extended periods because they lack the equipment to access remote or virtually delivered education. In this way, the mitigating vulnerability framework can be used proactively to create protective responses and transparency and accountability mechanisms from the moment a crisis arises, rather than retrospectively analysing harms.

This book, ultimately, offers both hope and pragmatism regarding the promise and limits of human rights law to deliver to those who need its protection the most. Children are resilient, but government policy can and does create wounds that are long and deep and potentially indelible. Our urgent goal must be to put an immediate stop to foreseeable ineffaceable harm. Implementing the mitigating vulnerability framework set out in this book can achieve this end.

Notes

1 These advocates argue that Australia has voluntarily undertaken legal obligations in international law by ratifying the Refugee Convention and that Australia is prohibited from refouling, imposing penalties based on a refugee's mode of arrival and expelling a refugee who is lawfully in Australia except on the grounds of national security or public order. See, for example, Anne Mcnevin et al., 'Beyond Deterrence: Reframing the Asylum Seeker Debate' *Inside Story* (online

at 13 October 2014) <https://insidestory.org.au/beyond-deterrence-reframing-the-asylum-seeker-debate/>.

2 For example, Robert Manne, Frank Brennan, Tim Costello and John Menadue, 'A Solution to Our Refugee Crisis' *Pearls and Irritations* (online at 13 August 2016) <https://johnmenadue.com/robert-manne-frank-brennan-tim-costello-john-menadue-a-solution-to-our-refugee-crisis/>; Frank Brennan et al., 'Boat Turnbacks and Medical Transfers' *Pearls and Irritations* (online at 15 February 2019) <https://johnmenadue.com/frank-brennan-tim-costello-robert-manne-john-menadue-boat-turnbacks-and-medical-transfers/>.

3 Robert Manne, 'Seeking a Workable Solution for Asylum' *The Monthly* (online at 24 August 2017) <https://www.themonthly.com.au/blog/robert-manne/2017/10/2017/1491808388/seeking-workable-solution-asylum-seekers#mtr>. Subject to the proviso that the turnbacks are 'lawful, transparent and conducted in such a way that the asylum seekers lives are not put in peril'.

4 Ibid.

5 Ibid.

6 See Claire Higgins's discussion of the policy debates in the 1970s, which considered, but rejected, implementing Boat Turnbacks and mandatory detention of asylum seekers arriving by boat. Claire Higgins, *Asylum by Boat: Origins of Australia's Refugee Policy* (University of New South Wales Press, 2017).

7 Martha Fineman, 'The Vulnerable Subject and the Responsive State' (2010) 60(2) *Emory Law Journal* 251, 256.

8 Catriona Mackenzie, Wendy Rogers and Susan Dodds 'Why Bioethics Needs a Concept of Vulnerability' (2012) 5(2) *International Journal of Feminist Approaches to Bioethics* 11, 24–25.

9 As noted in Section 5.4 in Chapter 5, the Minister can achieve the first by revoking their guideline directing that residence applications for asylum seekers arriving after 19 July 2013 not be referred for consideration unless there are exceptional reasons or the Minister has requested it. The second requires funding for these children to be able to access existing specialist services.

10 Although, as shown in Chapter 6, even if the government could ensure that expert wrap-around allied healthcare services and specialist custodians were provided, the legitimacy of offshore processing, as an Australian but not a regional solution, still needs to be justified.

11 This complements the recommendation in Chapter 5 that the Minister utilise their existing discretionary power to release unaccompanied children from mandatory immigration detention for processing under a residence determination.

12 See Paul Rigby, Maria Fotopoulou, Ashley Rogers and Andriana Manta, *Responding to Unaccompanied Minors in Scotland: Policy and Local Authority Perspectives* (University of Stirling, 2018). See also ISMU Foundation, *At a Crossroads: Unaccompanied and Separated Children in Their Transition to Adulthood in Italy* (November 2019) 22.

13 As discussed in Chapter 5, appropriate arrangements are critical for unaccompanied young people leaving group community detention living arrangements to ensure that they have the necessary support and skills to transition safely and effectively to living independently.

Bibliography

Articles/books/reports

Amnesty International, *Nauru Offshore Processing Facility Review 2012* (Amnesty, 2012)

Amnesty International, *Island of Despair: Australia's "Processing" of Refugees on Nauru* (Amnesty, 2016)

Ansell, Nicola, *Children, Youth, And Development* (Routledge, 2005)

Appiah, Kwame, 'Cosmopolitan Patriots' in Martha Nussbaum and Joshua Cohen (eds), *For Love of Country?* (Beacon Press, 1996)

Archard, David, 'Philosophical Perspectives on Childhood' in Julia Fionda (ed), *Legal Concepts of Childhood* (Hart, 2001)

Archard, David, *Children: Rights and Childhood* (Routledge, 2nd ed, 2004)

Arendt, Hannah, *The Origins of Totalitarianism* (Harcourt Brace, 1951)

Arnold, Samantha, Martine Goeman and Katja Fournierr, 'The Role of the Guardian in Determining the Best Interest of the Separated Child Seeking Asylum in Europe: A Comparative Analysis of Systems of Guardianship in Belgium, Ireland and the Netherlands' (2014) 16 *European Journal of Migration and Law* 467

Australian Churches Refugee Taskforce, *All the Lonely Children: Questions for Policy Makers Regarding Guardianship for Unaccompanied Minors* (Australian Churches, 2013)

Australian Human Rights Commission, *The Forgotten Children: National Inquiry into Children in Immigration Detention* (Commonwealth Government, 2014)

Australian Human Rights Commission, *Lives on Hold: Refugees and Asylum Seekers in the 'Legacy Caseload'* (Commonwealth Government, 2019)

Australian National Audit Office, *Offshore Processing Centres in Nauru and Papua New Guinea: Procurement of Garrison Support and Welfare Services* (ANAO, 2016)

Babacan, Alperhan and Hurriyet Babacan, 'Detention Downunder: New Directions in the Detention of Asylum Seekers in Australia' (2008) 4(15) *Review of International Law and Politics* 137

Babacan, Alperhan and Linda Briskman (eds), *Asylum Seekers: International Perspectives on Interdiction and Deterrence* (Cambridge Scholars Publishing, 2009)

Bacon, Wendy, Pamela Curr, Carmen Lawrence, Julie Macken and Claire O'Connor, *Protection Denied, Abuse Condoned: Women on Nauru at Risk* (Australian Women in Support of Women on Nauru, 2016) (online 22 July 2016) <https://www.asrc.org.au/2016/07/22/protection-denied-abuse-condoned-women-on-nauru-at-risk-report/>

Basham, Jennifer, *Protecting the Lonely Children* (Australian Churches Refugee Taskforce, 2012)

Bauböck, Rainer, *Transnational Citizenship: Membership Rights in International Migration* (Edward Elgar, 1994)

Bauböck, Rainer, 'Stakeholder Citizenship: An Idea Whose Time Has Come?' in Bertelsmann Stiftung, European Policy Centre and Migration Policy Institute (eds), *Delivering Citizenship* (The Transatlantic Council on Migration, 2008)

Bayefsky, Anne, *The UN Human Rights Treaty System: Universality at the Crossroads* (Kluwer Law International, 2001)

Bean, Philip and Joy Melville, *Lost Children of the Empire* (Unwin Hyman, 1989)

Bean, Tammy, Ilse Derluyn, Elisabeth Eurelings-Bontekoe, Eric Broekaert and Philip Spinhoven, 'Comparing Psychological Distress, Traumatic Stress Reactions and Experiences of Unaccompanied Refugee Minors with Experiences of Adolescents Accompanied by Parents' (2007) 195(4) *Journal of Nervous and Mental Disease* 288

Becker, Rise and Derrick Silove, 'Psychiatric and Psychosocial Effects of Prolonged Detention on Asylum-Seekers' in Mary Crock (ed), *Protection or Punishment: The Detention of Asylum Seekers in Australia* (Federation Press, 1993)

Beier, J. Marshall (ed), *The Militarization of Childhood* (Palgrave Macmillan, 2011)

Beiter, Klaus, *The Protection of the Right to Education by International Law* (Martinus Nijhoff, 2006)

Bem, Kazimierz, Nina Field, Nic Maclellan, Sarah Meyer and Tony Morris, *A Price Too High: The Cost of Australia's Approach to Asylum Seekers: The Australian Government's Policy of Offshore Processing of Asylum Seekers on Nauru, Manus Island and Christmas Island* (A Just Australia and Oxfam Australia, 2007) <http://pandora.nla.gov.au/pan/76526/20070910-1523/www.oxfam.org.au/media/files/APriceTooHigh.pdf>

Benhabib, Seyla, *The Rights of Others: Aliens, Residents and Citizens* (Cambridge University Press, 2004)

Berg, Laurie, 'At the Border and Between the Cracks: The Precarious Position of Irregular Migrant Workers under International Law' (2007) 8(1) *Melbourne Journal of International Law* 1

Berg, Laurie, *Migrant Rights at Work: Law's Precariousness at the Intersection of Immigration and Labour* (Routledge, 2016)

Berger, Kathleen, *The Developing Person Through the Life Span* (Worth Publishers, 7th ed, 2006)

Bhabha, Jacqueline and Mary Crock, *Seeking Asylum Alone: A Comparative Study: Unaccompanied and Separated Children and Refugee Protection in Australia, the UK and the US* (Federation Press, 2007)

Bhabha, Jacqueline and Nadine Finch, *Seeking Asylum Alone: United Kingdom* (Harvard University Press, 2006)

Bhabha, Jacqueline, Christine Bohne, Vasileia Digidiki, Elizabeth Donger, Rochelle Frounfelker, Jeff Glenn, Alexandra Lancaster, Susan Lloyd McGarry, Nevena Milutinovic and Shanoor Seervai, *Children on the Move: An Urgent Human Rights and Child Protection Priority* (Harvard University, 2016)

Bielefeld, Shelley, 'Cashless Welfare Transfers for 'Vulnerable' Welfare Recipients: Law, Ethics and Vulnerability' (2018) 26 *Feminist Legal Studies* 1

Biggeri, Mario, Jerome Ballet and Flavio Comin (eds), *Children and the Capability Approach* (Palgrave Macmillan, 2011)

Billings, Peter, 'Operation Sovereign Borders and interdiction at sea: *CPCF v Minister for Immigration and Border Protection*' (2016) 23(2) *Australian Journal of Administrative Law* 76

Bosniak, Linda, 'Membership, Equality, and the Difference that Alienage Makes' (1994) 69 *New York University Law Review* 1047

Bosniak, Linda, 'Citizenship Denationalized' (2000) 7 *Indiana Journal of Global Legal Studies* 447

Bosniak, Linda, *The Citizen and the Alien: Dilemmas of Contemporary Membership* (Princeton University Press, 2006)

Bosniak, Linda, 'Being Here: Ethical Territoriality and the Rights of Immigrants' (2007) 8(2) *Theoretical Inquiries in Law* 389

Bosniak, Linda, 'Persons and Citizens in Constitutional Thought' (2010) 8(1) *International Journal of Constitutional Law* 9

Brighouse, Harry, 'What Rights (If Any) Do Children Have?' in David Archard and Colin Macleod (eds), *The Moral and Political Status of Children* (Oxford University Press, 2002)

Briskman, Linda, Susie Latham and Chris Goddard, *Human Rights Overboard* (Scribe, 2008)

Broad, Bob and Ian Robbins, 'The Wellbeing of Unaccompanied Asylum Seekers Leaving Care' (2005) 2(4) *Diversity in Health & Social Care* 271

Brough, Mark, Robert Schweitzer, Jane Shakespeare-Finch, Lyn Vromans and Julie King, 'Unpacking the Micro–Macro Nexus: Narratives of Suffering and Hope among Refugees from Burma Recently Settled in Australia' (2012) 26(2) *Journal of Refugee Studies* 207

Brown, Kate, Kathryn Ecclestone and Nick Emmel, 'The Many Faces of Vulnerability' (2017) 16 *Social Policy and Society* 497

Brownlie, Ian and Guy Goodwin-Gill (eds), *Brownlie's Documents on Human Rights* (Oxford University Press, 2010)

Burman, Erica, *Deconstructing Developmental Psychology* (Palgrave, 2nd ed, 2008)

Buti, Antonio, 'The Early History of the Law of Guardianship of Children: From Rome to the Tenures Abolition Act 1660' (2003) 7(1) *University of Western Sydney Law Review* 92

Butler, Judith, *Precarious Life: The Powers of Mourning and Violence* (Verso, 2004)

Butler, Judith, *Frames of War: When Is Life Grievable?* (Verso, 2009)

Butler, Judith 'Rethinking Vulnerability and Resistance' in Judith Butler, Zeynep Gambetti and Leticia Sabsay (eds), *Vulnerability in Resistance* (Duke University Press, 2016)

Cameron, Matthew, 'From "Queue Jumpers" to "Absolute Scum of the Earth": Refugee and Organised Criminal Deviance in Australian Asylum Policy' (2013) 59(2) *Australian Journal of Politics and History* 241

Carens, Joseph, 'Aliens and Citizens: The Case for Open Borders' (1987) 49 *Review of Politics* 251

Carens, Joseph, 'The Case for Amnesty: Time Erodes the State's Right to Deport' (2009) 34(4) *Boston Review* 7

Carney, Terry, 'Vulnerability: False Hope for Vulnerable Social Security Clients?' (2018) 41(3) *University of New South Wales Law Journal* 783

Carr, Andrew, 'The Engagement Pendulum: Australia's Alternating Approach to Irregular Migration' (2016) 40(3) *Journal of Australian Studies*, 319

Castles, Stephen and Alastair Davidson (eds), *Citizenship and Migration: Globalization and the Politics of Belonging* (Macmillan, 2000)
Chase, Elaine, 'Security and Subjective Wellbeing: The Experiences of Unaccompanied Young People Seeking Asylum in the UK' (2013) 35(6) *Sociology of Health & Illness* 858
Chetail, Vincent, 'The Human Rights of Migrants in General International Law: From Minimum Standards to Fundamental Rights' (2013) 28(1) *Georgetown Immigration Law Journal* 225
Clapham, Andrew, *Human Rights Obligations of Non-State Actors* (Oxford University Press, 2006)
Clough, Beverley, 'Disability and Vulnerability: Challenging the Capacity/Incapacity Binary' (2017) 16 *Social Policy and Society* 469
Coffey, Guy, Ida Kaplan, Robyn Sampson and Maria Tucci, 'The Meaning and Mental Health Consequences of Long-Term Immigration Detention for People Seeking Asylum' (2010) 70 *Social Science & Medicine* 2070
Cohen, Cynthia, *Jurisprudence on the Rights of the Child, Volumes 1–4* (Transnational Publishers, 2005)
Coldrey, Barry, *Good British Stock: Child and Youth Migration to Australia* (National Archives, 1999)
Cornall, Robert AO, *Review into Allegations of Sexual and Other Serious Assaults at the Manus Regional Processing Centre* (Department of Immigration and Border Protection, 2013)
Cornall, Robert AO, *Review into the Events of 16–18 February 2014 at the Manus Regional Processing Centre* (Department of Immigration and Border Protection, 2014)
Correa-Velez, Ignacio, Sandra M Gifford and Sara J Bice, 'Australian Health Policy on Access to Medical Care for Refugees and Asylum Seekers' (2005) 2 *Australia and New Zealand Health Policy* 23
Crawley, Heaven and Ravi Kohli, *She Endures with Me: An Evaluation of the Scottish Guardianship Service Pilot* (Centre for Trust, Peace and Social Relations, 2013)
Crock, Mary (ed) *Protection or Punishment: The Detention of Asylum Seekers in Australia* (Federation Press) 1993
Crock, Mary, *Immigration and Refugee Law in Australia* (Federation Press, 1998)
Crock, Mary, 'You Have To Be Stronger than Razor Wire': Legal Issues Relating to the Detention of Refugees and Asylum Seekers' (2002) 10 *Australian Journal of Administrative Law* 33
Crock, Mary, 'In the Wake of the Tampa: Conflicting Visions of International Refugee Law in the Management of Refugee Flows' (2003) 12 *Pacific Rim Policy Journal* 49
Crock, Mary, 'Lonely Refuge: Judicial Responses to Separated Children Seeking Refugee Protection in Australia' (2005) 22(2) *Law in Context* 128
Crock, Mary, *Seeking Asylum Alone: A Study of Australian Law, Policy and Practice Regarding Unaccompanied and Separated Children* (Themis Press, 2006a)
Crock, Mary, 'Seeking Asylum Alone: The Treatment of Unaccompanied and Separated Children in Australia's Refugee Determination Process' (2006b) 42 *Australian Children's Rights News* 1.
Crock, Mary, 'Of Relative Rights and Putative Children: Rethinking the Critical Framework for the Protection of Refugee Children and Youth' (2013) 20 *Australian International Law Journal* 33

Crock, Mary and Ben Saul, *Future Seekers: Refugees and the Law in Australia* (The Federation Press, 2002)

Crock, Mary and Daniel Ghezelbash, 'Do Loose Lips Bring Ships? The Role of Policy, Politics and Human Rights in Managing Unauthorised Boat Arrivals' (2010) 19(2) *Griffith Law Review* 238

Crock, Mary and Jacqueline Bhabha, *Seeking Asylum Alone: Unaccompanied and Separated Children and Refugee Protection in Australia, the UK and the US* (Themis Press, 2007)

Crock, Mary and Laurie Berg, *Immigration, Refugees and Forced Migration: Law, Policy and Practice in Australia* (Federation Press, 2011)

Crock, Mary and Lenni Benson (eds), *Protecting Migrant Children: In Search of Best Practice* (Edward Elgar Publishing, 2018)

Crock, Mary and Mary-Anne Kenny, '*Rethinking the Guardianship of Refugee Children after the Malaysia Solution*' (2012) 34 *Sydney Law Review* 437

Crock, Mary, Ben Saul and Azadeh Dastyari, *Future Seekers Future Seekers II: Refugees and Irregular Migration in Australia* (Federation Press, 2006)

Crock, Mary, Laura Smith-Khan, Ron McCallum and Ben Saul, *Legal Protection of Refugees with Disabilities: Forgotten and Invisible?* (Edward Elgar Publishing, 2017)

Crock, Mary, Kate Bones, Daniel Ghezelbash, Jemma Hollonds and Mary Anne Kenny, *Children and Young People in Asylum and Refugee Processes: Towards Best Practice in the Management of Children Seeking Asylum* (Federation Press, 2020)

Dastyari, Azadeh, 'Detention of Asylum Seekers in Nauru: Is Deprivation of Liberty by any Other Name Just as Unlawful?' (2015) 38(2) *UNSW Law Journal* 669

Dauvergne, Catherine, *Making People Illegal: What Globalization Means for Migration and Law* (Cambridge University Press, 2008)

Davies, Sara, 'Protect or Deter? The Expert Panel on Asylum Seekers in Australia' (2013) 32(2) *Social Alternatives* 26

Del Gaudio, Eleonora and Stephen Phillips, 'Detention of Child Asylum Seekers in the Pursuit of State Interests: A Comparison of the Australian and EU Approaches' (2018) 36(1) *Nordic Journal of Human Rights* 1

Department of Immigration and Citizenship, *Annual Report 2011–12* (Commonwealth of Australia, 2012)

Department of Immigration and Citizenship, *Annual Report 2012–13* (Commonwealth of Australia, 2013)

Department of Immigration and Border Protection, *Annual Report 2013–2014* (Commonwealth Government, 2014)

Department of Immigration and Border Protection, *Annual Report 2014–2015* (Commonwealth Government, 2015)

Department of Immigration and Border Protection, *Annual Report 2015–2016* (Commonwealth Government, 2016)

Derluyn, Ilse and Eric Broekaert, 'Different Perspectives on Emotional and Behavioural Problems in Unaccompanied Refugee Children and Adolescents' (2007) 12(2) *Ethnicity & Health* 141

Derluyn, Ilse, Valesca Lippens and Tony Verachtert, 'Minors Travelling Alone: A Risk Group for Human Trafficking?' (2009) 48(4) *International Migration* 164

Dickey, Anthony, *Family Law* (Law Book Co, 4th ed, 2002)

Dixon, Jo and Jim Wade, 'Leaving 'Care'? Transition Planning and Support for Unaccompanied Young People' in Ravi Kohli and Fiona Mitchell (eds), *Working with Unaccompanied Asylum Seeking Children* (Palgrave MacMillan, 2007)

Dixon, Rosalind and Martha Nussbaum, 'Children's Rights and a Capability Approach: The Question of Special Priority' (2011–2012) 97 *Cornell Law Review* 549

Dodds, Susan, 'Depending on Care: Recognition of Vulnerability and the Social Contribution of Care Provision' (2007) 21 *Bioethics* 500

Dudley, Michael, Zachary Steel, Sarah Mares and Louise Newman, 'Children and Young People in Immigration Detention' (2012) 25(4) *Current Opinion in Psychiatry* 285

Durkheim, Emile, 'Childhood' in William Stuart Frederick Pickering (ed), *Durkheim: Essays on Morals and Education* (Routledge, 1979)

Durocher, Evelyne, Ryoa Chung, Christiane Rochon and Matthew Hunt, 'Understanding and Addressing Vulnerability Following the 2010 Haiti Earthquake: Applying a Feminist Lens to Examine Perspectives of Haitian and Expatriate Health Care Providers and Decision-Makers' (2016) 8(2) *Journal of Human Rights Practice* 219

Eekelaar, John, '*What Are Parental Rights?*' (1973) 89 *Law Quarterly Review* 201

Eekelaar, John, 'The Emergence of Children's Rights' (1986) 6 *Oxford Journal of Legal Studies* 161

Emerton, Patrick and Maria O'Sullivan, 'Rethinking Asylum Seeker Detention At Sea: The Power To Detain Asylum Seekers At Sea Under *The Maritime Powers Act* 2013 (Cth)' (2015) 38(2) *UNSW Law Journal* 695

European Parliament, *Report on the Situation of Unaccompanied Minors to the European Parliament on 26 August 2013* (European Parliament, 2013) <http://www.europarl.europa.eu/sides/getDoc.do?type=REPORT&reference=A7-20130251&language=EN>

European Union Agency for Fundamental Rights, *Separated, Asylum-Seeking Children in European Union Member States: Comparative Report* (2011) <http://fra.europa.eu/sites/default/files/fra_uploads/1692-SEPAC-comparative-report_EN.pdf

Evenhuis, Mark, 'Child-Proofing Asylum: Separated Children and Refugee Decision Making in Australia' (2013) 25(3) *International Journal of Refugee Law* 535

Feinberg, Joel, 'The Child's Right to an Open Future' in William Aiken and Hugh LaFollette (eds), *Whose Child?* (Rowman and Littlefield, 1980)

Fineman, Martha Alberston, *The Autonomy Myth: A Theory of Dependency* (The New Press, 2004)

Fineman, Martha Alberston, 'The Vulnerable Subject: Anchoring Equality in the Human Condition' (2008) 20(1) *Yale Journal of Law and Feminism* 1

Fineman, Martha Alberston, 'The Vulnerable Subject and the Responsive State' (2010) 60(2) *Emory Law Journal* 251

Fineman, Martha Alberston, 'Grappling with Equality: One Feminist Journey' in Martha Albertson Fineman (ed), *Transcending the Boundaries of Law: Generations of Feminism and Legal Theory* (Routledge, 2011)

Fineman, Martha Alberston, 'Equality, Autonomy, and the Vulnerable Subject in Law and Politics' in Martha Albertson Fineman and Anna Grear (eds), *Vulnerability: Reflections on a New Ethical Foundation for Law And Politics* (Ashgate 2013)

Foster, Michelle, 'The Implications of the Failed Malaysian Solution: The Australian High Court and Refugee Responsibility Sharing at International Law' (2012) 13 *Melbourne Journal of International Law* 395

Freeman, Michael (ed), *Children's Rights: Progress and Perspectives* (Martinus Nijhoff, 2011)

Freeman, Michael, *Article 3: The Best Interests of the Child* (Martinus Nijhoff, 2007a)

Freeman, Michael, 'Why It Remains Important to Take Children's Rights Seriously' (2007b) 15 *International Journal of Children's Rights* 5

Freeman, Michael, 'The Human Rights of Children' (2010) 63 *Current Legal Problems* 1

Freeman, Michael, 'Towards a Sociology of Children's Rights' in Michael Freeman (ed), *Law and Childhood Studies* (Oxford University Press, 2012)

Freeman, Michael and Philip Veerman (eds), *The Ideologies of Children's Rights* (Martinus Nijhoff, 1992)

Gammeltoft-Hansen, Thomas, *Access to Asylum: International Refugee Law and the Globalisation of Migration Control* (Cambridge University Press, 2013)

Gammeltoft-Hansen, Thomas and Nikolas Tan, 'The End of the Deterrence Paradigm? Future Directions for Global Refugee Policy' (2017) 5(1) *Journal on Migration and Human Security* 28

Gelber, Katherine and Matt McDonald, 'Ethics and Exclusion: Representations of Sovereignty in Australia's Approach to Asylum Seekers' (2006) 32(2) *Review of International Studies*, 269

Gheaus, Ancus, 'Unfinished Adults and Defective Children: On the Nature and Value of Childhood' (2015) 9(1) *Journal Of Ethics & Social Philosophy* 21

Gibney, Mark, 'Introduction' in Mark Gibney (ed), *Open Borders? Closed Societies? The Ethical and Political Issues* (Greenwood Press, 1988)

Gill, Alan, *Orphans of the Empire: The Shocking Story of Child Migration to Australia* (Random House, 1998)

Gleeson, Madeline, *Offshore: Behind the Wire on Manus and Nauru* (UNSW Press, 2016)

Goodnow, Jacqueline, 'Refugees, Asylum Seekers, Displaced Persons: Children in Precarious Positions' in Gary Melton, Asher Ben-Arieh, Judith Cashmore, Gail Goodman and Natalie Worley (eds), *The Sage Handbook of Child Research* (Sage, 2014)

Goodnow, Jacqueline and Jeanette Lawrence, 'Children and Cultural Contexts' in Marc Bornstein and Tama Leventhal (eds), *Handbook of Child Psychology and Developmental Science* (Wiley, 2015)

Goodwin-Gill, Guy and Jane McAdam, *The Refugee in International Law* (Oxford University Press, 3rd ed, 2007)

Graham, Anne, Jenni Whelan and Robyn Fitzgerald, 'Progressing Participation: Taming the Space between Rhetoric and Reality' (2006) 16(2) *Children, Youth and Environments* 231

Grear, Anna, 'Vulnerability, Advanced Global Capitalism and Co-Symptomatic Injustice: Locating the Vulnerable Subject' in Martha Fineman and Anna Grear (eds), *Vulnerability: Reflections on a New Ethical Foundation for Law And Politics* (Ashgate 2013)

Grosz, Elizabeth, *The Nick of Time: Politics, Evolution and the Untimely* (Duke University Press, 2004)

Habermas, Jürgen, Ciarin Cronin and Pablo De Greiff (eds), *The Inclusion of the Other: Studies in Political Theory* (MIT Press, 1998)

Hamburger, Keith AM, *Nauru Review 2013: Executive Report of the Review into the 19 July 2013 Incident at the Nauru Regional Processing Centre* (Knowledge Consulting, 2014)

Hamilton, Carolyn, Kirsten Anderson, Ruth Barnes and Kamena Dorling, *Administrative Detention of Children: A Global Report* (UNICEF, 2011).

Heikkilä, Mikaela, Hisayo Katsui and Maija Mustaniemi-Laakso, 'Disability and Vulnerability: A Human Rights Reading of the Responsive State' (2020) 24(8) *The International Journal of Human Rights* 1180 <https://doi.org/10.1080/13642987.2020.1715948>

Hek, Rachel, 'Using Foster Placements for the Care and Resettlement of Unaccompanied Children' in Ravi Kohli and Fiona Mitchell (eds), *Working with Unaccompanied Asylum Seeking Children: Issues for Policy and Practice* (Palgrave MacMillan, 2007)

Held, David, *Democracy and the Global Order: From the Modern State to Cosmopolitan Governance* (Polity Press, 1995)

Helmholz, R. H, 'The Roman Law of Guardianship in England, 1300–1600' (1978) 52 *Tulane Law Review* 223

Herring, Jonathan, *Vulnerable Adults and the Law* (Oxford University Press, 2016)

Herring, Jonathan, 'Foreword' (2018a) 41(3) *University of New South Wales Law Journal* 624

Herring, Jonathan, *Vulnerability, Childhood and the Law* (Springer, 2018b)

Higgins, Claire, *Asylum by Boat: Origins of Australia's Refugee Policy* (University of New South Wales Press, 2017)

Hodes, Matthew, Daljit Jagdev, Navin Chandra and Anna Cunniff, 'Risk and Resilience for Psychological Distress Amongst Unaccompanied Asylum Seeking Adolescents' (2008) 49(7) *Journal of Child Psychology and Psychiatry* 723

Hodgkin, Rachel and Peter Newell, *Implementation Handbook for the Convention on the Rights of the Child* (UNICEF, 2002)

Hodgson, Douglas, 'The Child's Right to Life, Survival and Development' (1994) 2 *International Journal of Children's Rights* 369

Houston, Angus, Michael L'Estrange and Paris Aristotle, *Report of the Expert Panel on Asylum Seekers* (Commonwealth Government, 2012)

Human Rights and Equal Opportunities Commission, *A Last Resort? Report of the National Inquiry into Children in Immigration* (Commonwealth Government, 2004)

Human Rights Watch and Amnesty International, *Australia: Appalling Abuse, Neglect of Refugees on Nauru: Investigation on Remote Pacific Island Finds Deliberate Abuse Hidden Behind Wall of Secrecy* (online at 2 August 2016) <https://www.hrw.org/news/2016/08/02/australia-appalling-abuse-neglect-refugees-nauru>

Humphreys, Margaret, *Empty Cradles* (Transworld, 2009)

International Federation of Red Cross and Red Crescent Societies, *Alone and Unsafe: Children, Immigration and Sexual and Gender-Based Violence* (IFRC, 2018)

James, Allison, 'Competition or Integration? The Next Step in Childhood Studies?' (2010) 17 *Childhood* 485

James, Allison and Adrian James, *Constructing Childhood: Theory, Policy and Social Practice* (Palgrave Macmillan, 2004)

James, Allison and Alan Prout, 'Re-Presenting Childhood: Time and Transition in the Study of Childhood' in Allison James and Alan Prout *Constructing and Reconstructing Childhood* (Routledge, 2nd ed, 1997)

James, Allison, Chris Jenks and Alan Prout, *Theorizing Childhood* (Teachers College Press, 1998)

Jensen, Tine, Envor Skårdalsmo and Krister Fjermestad, 'Development of Mental Health Problems: A Follow-Up Study of Unaccompanied Refugee Minors' (2014) 8 *Child Adolescent Psychiatry and Mental Health* 29

Jensen, Tine, Ane-Marthe Skar, Elin Andersson and Marianne Skogbrott Birkeland, 'Long-Term Mental Health in Unaccompanied Refugee Minors: Pre- and Post-Flight Predictors' (2019) 28(12) *European Child & Adolescent Psychiatry* 1671

Johnson, Sarah, Robert Blum and Tina Cheng, 'Future Orientation: A Construct with Implications for Adolescent Health and Wellbeing' (2014) 26(4) *International Journal of Adolescent Medicine & Health* 459

Katz, Ilan, Geraldine Doney and Effie Mitchell, *Evaluation of the Expansion of the Community Detention Program: Client and Service Provider Perspectives* (Social Policy Research Centre, 2013a)

Katz, Ilan, Geraldine Doney and Effie Mitchell, *Evaluation of the Expansion of the Community Detention Program: Final Report SPRC 12/13 to the Department of Immigration and Citizenship* (DIAC, 2013b)

Keles, Serap, Oddgeir Friborg and Thormod Idsoe, 'Resilience and Acculturation among Unaccompanied Refugee Minors' (2016) 42(1) *International Journal of Behavioural Development* 52

Kenny, Mary Anne and Maryanne Loughry, '"These Don't Look Like Children to Me": Age Assessment of Unaccompanied and Separated Children' in Mary Crock and Lenni Benson (eds), *Protecting Migrant Children: In Search of Best Practice* (Edward Elgar Publishing, 2018)

Kesby, Alison, *The Right to Have Rights: Citizenship, Humanity, and International Law* (Oxford University Press, 2012)

Kirby, Michael, 'Domestic Implementation of International Human Rights Norms' (1999) 5(2) *Australian Journal of Human Rights* 109

Klein, Natalie, 'Assessing Australia's Push Back the Boats Policy Under International Law: Legality and Accountability For Maritime Interceptions Of Irregular Migrants' (2014) 15 *Melbourne Journal of International Law* 1

Kneebone, Susan, 'The Pacific Plan: The Provision of 'Effective Protection'? (2006) 18 *International Journal of Refugee Law* 696

Kneebone, Susan, 'The Bali Process and Global Refugee Policy in the Asia-Pacific Region' (2014) 27(4) *Journal of Refugee Studies* 596

Kohli, Ravi and Rosie Mather 'Promoting Psychosocial Well-Being in Unaccompanied Asylum Seeking Young People in the United Kingdom' (2003) 8(3) *Child and Family Social Work* 201

Kohn, Nina, 'Vulnerability Theory and the Role of Government' (2014) 26 (1) *Yale Journal of Law & Feminism* 2014

Lansdown, Gerison, *The Evolving Capacities of the Child* (Save the Children and UNICEF, 2005)

Lawrence, Jeanette, Agnes Dodds, Ida Kaplan and Maria Tucci, 'The Rights of Refugee Children and the UN Convention on the Rights of the Child' 2019 8(3) *Laws* 20

Lee, Nick, *Childhood and Society: Growing Up in an Age of Uncertainty* (Open University Press, 2001)

LeVine, Robert A. and Rebecca New (eds), *Anthropology and Child Development: A Cross cultural Reader* (Blackwell Publishing, 2008)

Linklater, Andrew, 'Cosmopolitan Citizenship' (1998) 2(1) *Citizenship Studies* 23

Lomasky, Loren, *Persons, Rights and the Moral Community* (Oxford University Press, 1987)

Mackenzie, Catriona, Wendy Rogers and Susan Dodds 'Introduction: What Is Vulnerability and Why Does it Matter for Moral Theory?' in Catriona Mackenzie, Wendy Rogers and Susan Dodds (eds), *Vulnerability: New Essays in Ethics and Feminist Philosophy*, (Oxford Publishing, 2014)

Mackenzie, Catriona, Wendy Rogers and Susan Dodds 'Why Bioethics Needs a Concept of Vulnerability' (2012) 5(2) *International Journal of Feminist Approaches to Bioethics* 11

MacLeod, Colin, 'Primary Goods, Capabilities and Children' in Ingris Robeyn and Harry Brighouse (eds) *Measuring Justice: Primary Goods and Capabilities* (Cambridge University Press, 2010)

Mainwaring, Cetta and Noelle Brigden 'Beyond the Border: Clandestine Migration Journeys' (2016) 21(2) *Geopolitics* 243

Marr, David and Marian Wilkinson, *Dark Victory: The Military Campaign to Re-Elect the Prime Minister* (Allen & Unwin, 2003)

Mathew, Penelope, 'Australian Refugee Protection in the Wake of the *Tampa*' (2002) 96 *American Journal of International Law* 661

Mathew, Penelope and Tristan Harley, *Report From the Colloquium on Refugees, Regionalism and Responsibility* (Australian National University, 2013)

Mathew, Penelope and Tristan Harley, *Refugee Protection and Regional Cooperation in Southeast Asia* (Australian National University, 2014)

Mayall, Berry, *Towards a Sociology of Childhood: Thinking From Children's Lives* (Open University Press, 2002)

McAdam, Jane, 'Leading on Protection' in Bob Douglas and Jo Wodak (eds), *Refugees and Asylum Seekers: Finding a Better Way: Essays by Notable Australians* (2013)

McAdam, Jane and Fiona Chong, *Refugees: Why Seeking Asylum Is Legal and Australia's Policies Are Not* (UNSW Press, 2014)

McAdam, Jane and Fiona Chong, *Refugee Rights and Policy Wrongs: A Frank, Up-To-Date Guide by Experts* (UNSW Press, 2019)

McAdam, Jane and Kate Purcell, 'Refugee Protection in the Howard Years: Obstructing the Right to Seek Asylum' (2008) 27 *Australian Year Book of International Law* 87

McCrudden, Christopher, 'Human Dignity and Judicial Interpretation of Human Rights' (2008) 19 *European Journal of International Law* 655

McMaster, Don, *Asylum Seekers: Australia's Response to Refugees* (Melbourne University Press, 2001)

McNevin, Anne, 'The Liberal Paradox and the Politics of Asylum in Australia' (2007) 42(4) *Australian Journal of Political Science* 611

Mead, Margaret, *Coming of Age in Samoa: A Psychological Study of Primitive Youth for Western Civilisation* (Penguin Books, 1943)

Mead, Margaret and Martha Wolfenstein (eds), *Childhood in Contemporary Cultures* (University of Chicago Press, 1955)

Miller, David, 'The Ethical Significance of Nationality' (1988) 98 *Ethics* 647

Montgomery, Heather, *An Introduction to Childhood* (Wiley-Blackwell, 2009)

Moreno-Lax, Violeta, 'Seeking Asylum in the Mediterranean: Against a Fragmentary Reading of EU Member States' Obligations Accruing at Sea' (2011) 23 *International Journal of Refugee Law* 174
Moss, Phillip, *Review into Recent Allegations Relating to Conditions and Circumstances at the Regional Processing Centre in Nauru Final report* (Department of Immigration and Border Protection, 2015)
Multicultural Youth Advocacy Network, *Unaccompanied Humanitarian Minors in Australia: An Overview of National Support Arrangements and Key Emerging Issues* (MYAN, 2012) <http://www.myan.org.au/file/file/MYAN%20UHM%20Policy%20Paper%20Sept%202012.pdf>
Murphy, Ann, 'Corporeal Vulnerability and the New Humanism' (2011) 26(3) *Hypatia* 575
Newman, Louise, Nicholas Procter and Michael Dudley, 'Seeking asylum in Australia: Immigration Detention, Human Rights and Mental Health Care' (2013) 21(4) *Australasian Psychiatry* 316
Nielson, Harriet, 'The Arrow of Time in the Space of the Present: Temporality as Methodological and Theoretical Dimension in Child Research' (2016) 30 *Children and Society* 1
NIDOS, *Annual Report* (NIDOS, 2007) <http://www.nidos.nl/~/media/annual%20report%202007.ashx>
NIDOS Foundation and Refugium, *Towards a European Network of Guardianship Institutions, ENGI-Project Report* (NIDOS, 2011) <http://www.epim.info/wp-content/uploads/2011/02/ENGIReport-Towards-a-European-Network-of-Guardianship-Institutions.pdf>
Nowak, Manfred, *Article 6: The Right to Life, Survival and Development* (Martinus Nijhoff, 2005)
Nussbaum, Martha, *Creating Capabilities: The Human Development Approach* (Harvard University Press, 2011)
O'Doherty, Kieran and Martha Augoustinos, 'Protecting the Nation: Nationalist Rhetoric on Asylum Seeker and the Tampa' (2007) 18 *Journal of Community and Applied Social Psychology* 576
O'Sullivan, Maria, 'Best Interests of Asylum-Seeker Children: Who's Guarding the Guardian' (2013) 38(4) *Alternative Law Journal* 224
Oppedal, Brit and Thormod Idsoe, 'The Role of Social Support in the Acculturation and Mental Health of Unaccompanied Minor Asylum Seekers' (2015) 56(2) *Scandinavian Journal of Psychology* 203
Orchard, Phil, *A Right to Flee: Refugees, States, and the Construction of International Cooperation* (Cambridge University Press, 2014)
Peer, Sophie, Caroline deCosta and Emma Adams, *Visit to Darwin Alternative Places of Detention December 6th–8th, 2013: Darwin Detention: Damaging Children (Research Findings Report)* (ChilOut, 2013) <http://media.virbcdn.com/files/11/7ab4e1dd0c5ca616DarwinReportF.pdf>
Peleg, Noam, 'What Do We Mean When We Speak About Children's Right to Development?' in Farhad Malekiam and Kerstin Nordlöf (eds), *The Sovereignty of Children in Law* (Cambridge Scholars Publishing, 2012)
Penovic, Tania, 'Immigration Detention of Children: Arbitrary Deprivation of Liberty' (2003) 7 *Newcastle Law Review* 56
Penovic, Tania, 'The Separation of Powers: *Lim* and the 'Voluntary' Immigration Detention of Children' (2004) 29 *Alternative Law Journal* 222

Penovic, Tania and Adiva Sifris, 'Children's Rights through the Lens of Immigration Detention' (2006) 20 *Australian Journal of Family Law* 12

Piaget, Jean, *The Child's Conception of the World* (Routledge, 1929)

Pittaway, Eileen, Linda Bartolomei and Richard Hugman, 'Stop Stealing Our Stories': The Ethics of Research with Vulnerable Groups' (2010) 2(2) *Journal of Human Rights Practice* 229

Pogge, Thomas, 'Cosmopolitanism and Sovereignty' (1992) 103(1) *Ethics* 48

Proctor, Nicholas, Diego De Leo and Louise Newman, 'Suicide and Self-Harm in Immigration Detention' (2013) 199(11) *The Medical Journal of Australia* 730

Procter, Nicholas, Suresh Sundram, Gillian Singleton, Georgia Paxton and Andrew Block, *Physical and Mental Health Subcommittee of the Joint Advisory Committee for Nauru Regional Processing Arrangements: Nauru Site Visit Report'* (Nauru Site Visit Report, 30 May 2014) <http://www.theguardian.com/world/interactive/2014/may/29/nauru-family-health-risks-report-infull>

Proctor, Nicholas, Mary Anne Kenny, Heather Eaton and Carol Grech, 'Lethal Hopelessness: Understanding and Responding to Asylum Seeker Distress and Mental Deterioration' (2018) 27 *International Journal of Mental Health Nursing* 448

Prout, Alan, *The Future Of Childhood* (Routledge, 2005)

Prout, Alan and Alison James, 'A New Paradigm for the Sociology of Childhood? Provenance Promise and Problems' in Alison James and Alan Prout (eds), *Constructing and Reconstructing Childhood* (Routledge, 2nd ed, 1997)

Qvortrup, Jens, Marjatta Bardy, Giovanni Sgritta and Helmut Wintersberger (eds), *Childhood Matters: Social Theory, Practice and Politics* (Ashgate, 1994)

Raghallaigh, Muireann, 'The Causes of Mistrust amongst Asylum Seekers and Refugees: Insights from Research with Unaccompanied Asylum-Seeking Minors Living in the Republic of Ireland' (2013) 27(1) *Journal of Refugee Studies* 82

Rothwell, Donald and Tim Stephens, *The International Law of the Sea* (Hart, 2010)

Rubenstein, Kim, *Australian Citizenship Law in Context* (Lawbook Co, 2002)

Sarantou, Elina and Angeliki Theodoropoulou, *Children Cast Adrift: The Exclusion and Exploitation of Unaccompanied Minors (UAMs) in Greece, Spain and Italy* (Rosa Luxemburg Stiftung, 2019).

Schildkrout, Enid, *People of The Zongo* (Cambridge University Press, 1978)

Schloenhardt, Andreas, 'Deterrence, Detention and Denial: Asylum Seekers in Australia' (2002a) 22 *University of Queensland Law Journal* 54

Schloenhardt, Andreas, 'To Deter, Detain and Deny: Protection of Onshore Asylum Seekers in Australia' (2002b) 14 *International Journal of Refugee Law* 302

Schloenhardt, Andreas and Colin Craig, 'Turning Back the Boats: Australia's Interdiction of Irregular Migrants at Sea' (2015) 27(4) *International Journal of Refugee Law* 536

Seginer, Rachel, *Future Orientation: Developmental and Ecological Perspectives* (Springer, 2009)

Sen, Amartya, *Inequality Reexamined* (Harvard University Press, 1992)

Sen, Amartya, 'Capabilities and Well-Being' in Martha Nussbaum and Amartya Sen (eds), *Quality of Life* (Oxford University Press, 1993)

Sen, Amartya, *Development as Freedom* (Oxford University Press, 1999)

Sen, Amartya, 'Human Rights and Capabilities' (2005) 6 *Journal of Human Development* 151

Sen, Amartya, 'Children and Human Rights' (2007) 1 *Indian Journal of Human Development* 235

Senate Community Affairs References Committee, *Lost Innocents: Righting the Record* (Commonwealth Government, 2001)

Senate Legal and Constitutional Affairs Committee, *Conditions and Treatment of Asylum Seekers and Refugees at the Regional Processing Centres in the Republic of Nauru and Papua New Guinea* (Commonwealth Government, 2016a)

Senate Legal and Constitutional Affairs Committee Inquiry, *Conditions and Treatment of Asylum Seekers and Refugees at the Regional Processing Centres in the Republic of Nauru and Papua New Guinea*, Interim report (Commonwealth Government, 2016b)

Senate Select Committee, *Taking Responsibility: Conditions and Circumstances at Australia's Regional Processing Centre in Nauru* (Commonwealth Government, 2015)

Serpell, Robert, 'How Specific Are Perceptual Skills? A Cross-Cultural Study of Pattern Reproduction' (1979) 70(3) *British Journal of Psychology*, 365–380

Seymour, John, 'Parens Patriae and Wardship Powers: Their Nature and Origins' (1994) 14 *Oxford Journal of Legal Studies* 159

Shearer, Ivan, 'Problems of Jurisdiction and Law Enforcement against Delinquent Vessels' (1986) 35 *International and Comparative Law Quarterly* 320

Shelton, Dinah (ed), *Commitment and Compliance: The Role of Non-Binding Norms in the International Legal System* (Oxford University Press, 2000)

Siegel, Harvey (ed), *The Oxford Handbook of Philosophy of Education* (Oxford University Press, 2009)

Silove, Derrick, Philippa McIntosh and Rise Becker, 'Risk of Retraumatisation of Asylum-Seekers in Australia' (1993) 27 *Australian and New Zealand Journal of Psychiatry* 606

Silverstein, Jordana, 'I Am Responsible: Histories of the Intersection of the Guardianship of Unaccompanied Child Refugees and the Australian Border' (2016) 22(2) *Cultural Studies Review* 65

Soldatic, Karen, Kelly Somers, Anna Buckley and Caroline Fleay, '"Nowhere to Be Found": Disabled Refugees and Asylum Seekers within the Australian Resettlement Landscape' (2015) 2(1) *Disability and The Global South* 501

Steel, Zachary and Derrick Silove, 'The Mental Health Implications of Detaining Asylum Seekers' (2001) 175 *Medical Journal of Australia* 596

Steel, Zachary, Derrick Silove, Robert Brooks, Shakeh Momartin, Bushra Alzuhairi and Ina Susljik, 'Impact of Immigration Detention and Temporary Protection on the Mental Health of Refugees' (2006) 188(1) *The British Journal of Psychiatry* 58

Tanaka, Yoshifumi, *The International Law of the Sea* (Cambridge University Press, 2012)

Taylor, Julie, 'Guardianship of Child Asylum-Seekers' (2006) 34 *Federal Law Review* 185

Taylor, Savitri, 'The Pacific Solution or a Pacific Nightmare?: The Difference between Burden Shifting and Responsibility Sharing' (2005) 6 *Asian-Pacific Law and Policy Journal* 1

Tobin, John, 'Understanding a Human Rights Based Approach to Matters Involving Children: Conceptual Foundations and Strategic Considerations' in Antonella Invernizzi and Jane Williams (eds), *The Human Rights of Children. From Visions to Implementation* (Ashgate, 2011)

Tobin, John, 'Understanding Children's Rights: A Vision beyond Vulnerability' (2015) 84 (2) *Nordic Journal of International Law* 155

Tully, Stephen and Michael Smith, 'Operation "Sovereign Borders": The High Court of Australia Considers Implications of International Law' (5 June 2015) 19(12) *American Society of International Law* <https://www.asil.org/insights/volume/19/issue/12/operation-sovereign-borders-high-court-australia-considers-implications>

Turner, Bryan, 'Personhood and Citizenship' (1986) 3 *Theory Culture Society* 1

Turner, Bryan, *Vulnerability and Human Rights* (Pennsylvania State University Press, 2006)

UNICEF, *A Child Is a Child: Protecting Children on the Move from Violence, Abuse and Exploitation* (UNICEF, 2017)

United Nations High Commissioner for Refugees, *Mission to the Republic of Nauru, 3 to 5 December 2012: report* (UNHCR, 2012)

United Nations High Commissioner for Refugees, *Monitoring Visit to Manus Island, Papua New Guinea, 11–13 June 2013* (UNHCR, 2013a)

United Nations High Commissioner for Refugees, *Monitoring Visit to Manus Island, Papua New Guinea: 15–17 January 2013* (UNHCR, 2013b)

United Nations High Commissioner for Refugees, *Monitoring Visit to the Republic of Nauru 7 to 9 October 2013* (UNHCR, 2013c)

United Nations High Commissioner for Refugees, *Monitoring Visit to Manus Island, Papua New Guinea 23–25 October 2013* (UNHCR, 2013d)

United Nations High Commissioner for Refugees, *Refugee Global Trends* (UNHCHR, 2017)

United Nations High Commissioner for Refugees, *Refugee Global Trends* (UNHCHR, 2019)

United Nations High Commissioner for Refugees, UNICEF and IOM, *Refugee and Migrant Children in Europe: Overview of Trends* (UNHCR, 2017)

Uprichard, Emma, 'Children As "Being and Becomings": Children, Childhood and Temporality' (2008) 22 *Children & Society* 303

Van Acker, Elizabeth and Robyn Hollander, 'Protecting Our Border: Ministerial Rhetoric and Asylum Seekers' (2003) 25(2) *Australian Journalism Review* 103

Van Bueren, Geraldine, *The International Law on the Rights of the Child* (Martinus Nijhoff, 1995)

Veerman, Philip, *The Rights of the Child and the Changing Image of Childhood* (Martinus Nijhoff, 1992)

Vervliet, Marianne, Melinda Meyer Demott, Marianne Jakobsen, Eric Broekaert, Trond Heir and Ilse Derluyn, 'The Mental Health of Unaccompanied Refugee Minors on Arrival in the Host Country' (2014) 55(1) *Scandinavian Journal of Psychology* 33

Vogl, Anthea, 'Seeking Asylum: Human Smuggling and Bureaucracy at the Border' (review) (2012) 27(1) *Canadian Journal of Law and Society* 159

Vogl, Anthea, 'Over the Borderline: A Critical Inquiry Into the Geography of Territorial Excision and the Securitisation of the Australian Border' (2015) 38(1) *UNSW Law Journal* 114

Walzer, Michael, *Spheres of Justice* (Basic Books, 1983)

Weisner, Thomas, 'Culture, Context, and Well-Being' in Asher Ben-Arieh, Ferran Casas, Ivar Frones and Jill Korbin (eds), *Handbook of Child Well-Being* (Springer, 2014)

Weissbrodt, David and Mary Rumsey (eds), *Vulnerable and Marginalised Groups and Human Rights* (Edward Elgar Publishing, 2011)

Wells, Karen, *Childhood in a Global Perspective* (Polity Press, 2009)

Wernesjö, Ulika, 'Unaccompanied Asylum-Seeking Children: Whose Perspective?' (2011) 19(4) *Childhood* 495

Wood, Tamara and Jane McAdam, 'Australian Asylum Policy All at Sea: An Analysis of Plaintiff M70/2011 v Minister for Immigration and Citizenship and the Australia-Malaysia Arrangement' (2012) 61 *International and Comparative Law Quarterly* 274

Woodhead, Martin, 'Child Development and the Development of Childhood' in Jens Qvortrup, William, Corsaro and Michael-Sebastien Honig (eds), *The Palgrave Handbook of Childhood Studies* (Palgrave Macmillan, 2009)

Woodhead, Martin, Dorothy Faulkner and Karen Littleton (eds), *Cultural Worlds of Early Childhood* (Routledge, 1998)

Wyness, Michael, *Childhood and Society* (Palgrave Macmillan, 2006)

Yuval-Davis, Nira, 'The "Multi-Layered Citizen": Citizenship in the Age of "Glocalization"' (1999) 1(1) *International Feminist Journal of Politics* 119

Zulfacar, Diane, *Surviving Without Parents: Indo-Chinese Refugee Minors in NSW* (Government Printing Office, 1984)

Zulfacar, Diane, 'Alternative Forms of Care for Unaccompanied Refugee Minors: A Comparison of US and Australian Experience' (1987) 30(1) *International Social Work* 61

Zwi, Karen and Sarah Mares, 'Stories from Unaccompanied Children in Immigration Detention: A Composite Account' (2015) 51(7) *Journal of Paediatrics and Child Health* 659

CASES

'AYX18 v Minister for Home Affairs' (2018) *FCA* 283

'Clay v Clay' (2001) 202 *CLR* 410

'CPCF v Minister for Immigration and Border Protection & Anor' (2015) *ALJR* 207

'D7 v Minister for Immigration and Border Protection' (2016) *FCA* 1331

'FRX 17 as Litigation Representative for FRM17 v Minister for Immigration and Border Protection' (2018) *FCA* 63

'Hospital Products Ltd v United States Surgical Corporation' (1984) 156 *CLR* 41

'Minister of State of Immigration and Ethnic Affairs v Teoh' (1995) 183 *CLR* 273

'Mr BF on Behalf of Master BG v Cth of Australia (DIBP)' (2017) *Aus HRC* 114

'Ms BK, Ms CO and Mr DE on Behalf of Themselves and Their Families v Commonwealth Department of Home Affairs' (2018) *AusHRC* 128

'Namah v Pato' (2016) *PGSC* 13

'Odhiambo v Minister for Immigration and Multicultural Affairs' (2002) 122 *FCR* 29

'Plaintiff M68–2015 v Minister for Immigration and Border Protection' (2016) 257 *CLR* 42

'Plaintiff M70/2011 & Plaintiff M106/2011 by his Litigation Guardian v. Minister for Immigration and Citizenship' (2011) 244 *CLR* 144

'Plaintiff M147/2016 v Minister for Immigration and Border Protection (2018) *HCA* 18

'Plaintiff M168/10, A Minor, by His Litigation Guardian Sister Brigid (Marie) Arthur v The Commonwealth' (2011) *HCA* 25

'Plaintiff S99/2016 v Minister for Immigration and Border Protection' (2016) 243 *FCR* 17

'Plaintiff S156/2013 v Minister for Immigration and Border Protection & Anor' (2014) 254 *CLR* 28

'Secretary, Department of Health and Community Services v JWB and SMB' (1992) 175 *CLR* 218
'Trevorrow v South Australia (No.5)' (2007) 98 *SASR* 136
UN Human Rights Committee, *Van Alphen v. The Netherlands, Communication No. 305/1988 U.N. Doc. CCPR/C/39/D/305/1988* (23 July 1990)
UN Human Rights Committee, *A v Australia, Communication No. 560/1993 U.N. Doc. CCPR/C/59/D/560/1993* (30 April 1997)
UN Human Rights Committee, *C v Australia U. N. Doc. CCPR/C/76/D/900/1999* (13 November 2002)
UN Human Rights Committee, *Baban v Australia U. N. Doc CCPR/C/78/D/1014/2001* (18 September 2003)
'WACA v Minister for Immigration and Multicultural Affairs' (2002) 121 *FCR* 463
'Wedd v Wedd' (1948) *SASR* 104
'X v Minister for Immigration and Multicultural Affairs' (1999) 92 *FCR* 524

Legislation

Asylum Seekers (Regional Processing Centre) Act 2012 (Nauru)
Australian Border Force Act 2015 (Cth)
Australian Human Rights Commission Act 1986 (Cth)
Commissioner for Children and Young People Bill 2010 (Cth)
Guardian for Unaccompanied Children Bill 2013 (Cth)
Guardian for Unaccompanied Children Bill 2014 (Cth)
Immigration (Guardianship of Children) Act 1946 (Cth)
Immigration (Guardianship of Children) Amendment Bill 1993 (Cth)
Legislation Amendment (Miscellaneous Measures) Act 2019 (Cth)
Maritime Powers Act 2013 (Cth)
Migration Act 1958 (Cth)
The Migration Amendment Act 1992 (Cth)
Migration Amendment (Detention Arrangements) Act 2005 (Cth)
Migration Amendment (Designated Unauthorised Arrivals) Bill 2006 (Cth)
Migration Amendment (Excision from Migration Zone) Act 2001 (Cth)
Migration Amendment (Excision from Migration Zone) (Consequential Provisions) Act 2001 (Cth)
Migration Amendment (Repairing Medical Transfers Act) 2019 (Cth)
Migration Amendment (Unauthorised Maritime Arrivals and Other Measures) Act 2013 (Cth)
Migration and Maritime Powers Legislation Amendment (Resolving the Asylum Legacy Caseload) Act 2014 (Cth)
Migration Legislation Amendment Act 1989 (Cth)
Migration Legislation Amendment (Offshore Processing and Other Measures) Bill 2011 (Cth)
Migration Legislation Amendment (Offshore Processing and Other Measures) Act 2012 (Cth)
Migration Legislation Amendment (Regional Processing and Other Measures) Act 2012 (Cth)
Migration Reform Act 1992 (Cth)

Treaties

Convention on the Elimination of All Forms of Discrimination Against Women, opened for signature 18 December 1979, 1249 *UNTS* 13 (entered into force 3 September 1981)

Convention on the Elimination of All Forms of Racial Discrimination, opened for signature 21 December 1965, 660 *UNTS* 195 (entered into force 4 January 1969)

Convention on the Law of the Sea, opened for signature 10 December 1982, 1833 *UNTS* 396 (entered into force 16 November 1994)

Convention on the Rights of Persons with Disabilities, opened for signature 13 December 2006, 2515 *UNTS* 3 (entered into force 30 March 2008)

Convention Relating to the Status of Refugees, opened for signature 28 July 1951, 189 *UNTS* 137 (entered into force 22 April 1954)

International Convention on Civil and Political Rights, opened for signature 19 December 1966, 999 *UNTS* 171 (entered into force 23 March 1976)

International Convention on Economic, Social and Cultural Rights, opened for signature 16 December 1966, 993 *UNTS* 3 (entered into force 3 November 1976)

International Convention on the Rights of the Child, opened for signature 20 November 1989, 1577 *UNTS* 3 (entered into force 2 September 1990)

Vienna Convention on the Laws of Treaties, opened for signature 23 May 1969, 1155 *UNTS* 331 (entered into force 27 January 1980)

Declarations and Resolutions

United Nations General Assembly, *Universal Declaration of Human Rights, G.A res. 217 A (III)* (10 December 1948)

United Nations General Assembly, *Declaration of the Rights of the Child G.A. res. 1386 (XIV)* (20 November 1959)

General Comments

UN Committee on the Rights of the Child, *General Comment Number 4 Adolescent Health and Development in the Context of the Convention on the Rights of the Child UN Doc CRC/GC/4/2003* (1 July 2003a)

UN Committee on the Rights of the Child, *General Comment Number 5 General Measures of Implementations of the Convention on the Rights of the Child UN Doc CRC/GC/5/2003* (27 November 2003b)

UN Committee on the Rights of the Child, *General Comment Number 6 Treatment of Unaccompanied and Separated Children Outside Their Country of Origin UN Doc CRC/GC/2005/6* (1 September 2005)

UN Committee on the Rights of the Child, *General Comment Number 8 The Rights of the Child for Protection from Corporal Punishment and other Cruel or Degrading Forms of Punishment UN Doc CRC/GC/8* (2 March 2007a)

UN Committee on the Rights of the Child, *General Comment Number 9 The Rights of Children with Disabilities UN Doc CRC/C/GC/9* (27 February 2007b)

UN Committee on the Rights of the Child, *General Comment Number 12 The Rights of the Child to Be Heard UN Doc CRC/C/GC/12* (20 July 2009)

UN Committee on the Rights of the Child, *General Comment Number 13 The Right of the Child to Freedom from All Forms of Violence UN Doc CRC/C/GC/13* (18 April 2011)

UN Committee on the Rights of the Child, *General Comment No. 14 The Right of the Child to Have His or Her Best Interests Taken as a Primary Consideration UN Doc CRC/C/GC/14* (29 May 2013)

UN Human Rights Committee, *General Comment No. 18 Non-Discrimination, UN Doc CCPR/C/21/Rev.1/Add. 1* (10 November 1989)

UN Human Rights Committee, *General Comment No. 31 The Nature of the General Legal Obligation Imposed on States Parties to the Covenant, CCPR/C/21/Rev.1/Add.13* (26 May 2004)

Guidelines

UN General Assembly, *Guidelines for the Alternative Care of Children* (resolution adopted 24 February 2010) A/RES/64/142 <https://www.refworld.org/docid/4c3acd162.html>

UN High Commissioner for Refugees, *Refugee Children: Guidelines on Protection and Care* (UNHCR, 1994) <https://www.refworld.org/docid/3ae6b3470.html>

UN High Commissioner for Refugees, *Guidelines on Policies and Procedures in Dealing with Unaccompanied Children Seeking Asylum* (United Nations, 1997) <http://www.unhcr.org/3d4f91cf4.html>

UN High Commissioner for Refugees, *Annexes to UNHCR Guidelines on Formal Determination of the Best Interests of the Child* (United Nations, 2008a) <https://www.refworld.org/docid/4bfe92b32.html>

UN High Commissioner for Refugees, *Guidelines on Determining the Best Interests of the Child* (United Nations, 2008b) https://www.refworld.org/docid/48480c342.html

UN High Commissioner for Refugees, *Handbook on Procedures and Criteria for Determining Refugee Status UN Doc HCR/1P/4/ENG/REV. 3* (2011)

UN High Commissioner for Refugees, *Guidelines on the Applicable Criteria and Standards relating to the Detention of Asylum-Seekers and Alternatives to Detention* (United Nations, 2012)

Other

Abbott, Tony, *Joint Press Conference, Hamilton Island* (Media Release, 21 March 2015)

Alford, Peter, 'Jakarta Fires Shot across PM's Bow' *The Australian* (26 September 2013)

Alford, Peter, 'ABC Navy Brutality Reports Unravel' *The Australian* (online at 1 February 2014) online at: <http://www.theaustralian.com.au/news/abc-navybrutality-reports-unravel/story-e6frg6n6-1226815392921>

Alford, Peter and Paul Maley, 'Asylum Tide Swamping Solution' *The Australian* (21 August 2013)

Allard, Tom, 'Nauru's Move to Open Its Detention Centre Makes It 'More Dangerous' for Asylum Seekers' *Sydney Morning Herald* (online at 9 October 2015) <http://www.smh.com.au/federal-politics/political-news/naurus-move

-to-open-its-detention-centre-makes-it-more-dangerous-for-asylum-seekers-20151008-gk4kbt.html>

Amnesty International, *Malaysia Refugee Swap: Trading in Human Lives* (Amnesty International, 2011) <http://www.amnesty.org.au/news/comments/25763/>

Anonymous Unaccompanied Child, Submission 146, Australian Human Rights Commission, *The Forgotten Children: National Inquiry into Children in Immigration Detention* (AHRC, 2014)

Ash, Houston, 'The High Court Upholds the 'PNG Solution': Plaintiff S156/2013' *Opinions on High* (University of Melbourne, 11 July 2014) <https://blogs.unimelb.edu.au/opinionsonhigh/author/hash/>

'Asylum Seekers Arriving in Australia by Boat To Be Resettled in Papua New Guinea', *ABC News* (online at 20 July 2013) <http://www.abc.net.au/news/2013-07-19/manus-island-detention-centre-to-beexpanded-under-rudd27s-asy/4830778>

Australian Churches Refugee Taskforce, *All the Lonely Children: Questions for the Incoming Government Regarding Guardianship of Unaccompanied Minors Discussion Paper* (ACRT, 2013)

Australian Human Rights Commission, *Submission to the Joint Select Committee on Australia's Immigration Detention Network* (AHRC, 2011) <http://www.humanrights.gov.au/australian-humanrights-commission-submission-joint-select-committee-australia-s-immigration#s3>

Australian Human Rights Commission, *Tell Me About: The 'Enhanced Screening Process* (Commonwealth Government, 2013) <https://www.humanrights.gov.au/our-work/asylum-seekers-and-refugees/publications/tell-me-about-enhanced-screening-process>

Bachelard, Michael, 'Bali Process Grinds On with No Sign of Results', *Sydney Morning Herald* (online at 4 April 2013) <https://www.smh.com.au/politics/federal/bali-process-grinds-on-with-no-sign-of-results-20130404-2h7yz.html>

Bachelard, Michael, 'Investigation: "Burned Hands" on the High Seas' *Sydney Morning Herald* (online at 7 February 2014) <http://www.smh.com.au/world/investigation-burned-hands-on-the-high-seas-20140206-hvbdl.html#ixzz2salkUX2y>

Bhabha, Jacqueline, *Independent Children, Inconsistent Adults: International Child Migration and the Legal Framework*, Innocenti Discussion Paper (UNICEF Innocenti Research Centre, 2008)

Brennan, Frank 'High Court Fails High Seas Detainees' *Eureka Street* (online at 1 February 2015) <https://www.eurekastreet.com.au/article/high-court-fails-high-seas-detainees>

Brennan, Frank, Tim Costello, Robert Manne and John Menadue, 'Boat Turnbacks and Medical Transfers' *Pearls and Irritations* (online at 15 February 2019) <https://johnmenadue.com/frank-brennan-tim-costello-robert-manne-john-menadue-boat-turnbacks-and-medical-transfers/>

Brewster, Kerry and Deb Richards, 'Manus Island Riot: Asylum Seeker Speaks of Witnessing Reza Berati's Death' *ABC News* (online at 4 April 2014) <https://www.abc.net.au/news/2014-04-04/manus-island-asylum-seekers-witness-statements-reza-berati-death/5367118?nw=0>

Buckmaster, Luke and Jonathon Guppy, 'Australian Government Assistance to Refugees: Fact Versus Fiction' in *Research Paper Series 2014–15* (Commonwealth Parliamentary Library, 2015)

Burke, Tony, Minister for Immigration, Multicultural Affairs and Citizenship Minister for the Arts, 'Split in the Opposition's Asylum Seeker Policy; Asylum Seeker Policy' in Transcript of Press Conference (7 July 2013)

ChilOut, Submission No 168, Australian Human Rights Commission, *The Forgotten Children Inquiry* (May 2014) <https://humanrights.gov.au/sites/default/files/Submission%20No%20168%20-%20ChilOut.pdf?_ga=2.120120769.878436188.1589764716-644388670.1588671908>

Clark, Martin, 'CPCF v Minister for Immigration and Border Protection' in *Opinions on High* (University of Melbourne, 28 January 2015) <https://blogs.unimelb.edu.au/opinionsonhigh/tag/migration-act-1958-cth/>

Clark, Martin, 'Plaintiff M68/2015 v Minister for Immigration and Border Protection' *Opinions on High* (University of Melbourne, 3 February 2016) <https://blogs.unimelb.edu.au/opinionsonhigh/2016/02/03/plaintiff-m68-2015-case-page/>.

Commonwealth, *Parliamentary Debates* (House of Representatives, 18 November 1948)

Commonwealth, *Parliamentary Debates* (House of Representatives, 16 March 1982)

Commonwealth, *Parliamentary Debates* (House of Representatives, 3 March 1994)

Commonwealth, *Parliamentary Debates* (House of Representatives, 25 September 2014)

Council of the European Union, 'Resolution on Unaccompanied Minors who are Nationals of Third Countries' (19 July 1997) *Official Journal C* 221 <https://eur-lex.europa.eu/legal-content/EN/ALL/?uri=CELEX%3A31997Y0719%2802%29>

Defence for Children International, *Core Standards for Guardians of Separated Children in Europe* (DFCI, 2014) <http://www.corestandardsforguardians.eu/images/22/335.pdf>

Department of Home Affairs, *The Home Affairs Portfolio* (November 2017) <https://www.scribd.com/document/385531200/FA180200897-Document-Released>

Department of Immigration and Border Protection, *Procedures Advice Manual 3* (Commonwealth Government, 2016a)

Department of Immigration and Border Protection, Submission No. 18, *Senate Legal and Constitutional Affairs Committee Inquiry into the Conditions of Treatment of Asylum Seekers and Refugees at the Regional Processing Centres in the Republic of Nauru and Papua New Guinea* (March 2016b) <https://www.aph.gov.au/DocumentStore.ashx?id=fabbe9e5-2ed3-47cd-86c2-f313a6f1b7e8&subId=411483>.

Department of Immigration and Border Protection, Transcript of Second Public Hearing of Australian Human Rights Commission, *Forgotten Children Inquiry* (2 July 2014) <http://www.humanrights.gov.au/our-work/asylum-seekers-and-refugees/national-inquiry-children-immigration-detention-2014-1>

Department of Immigration and Border Protection Website, *Australian Government, FAQ's: How Do We Care for Unaccompanied Minors Until Their Immigration Status Is Resolved?* (online at 16 March 2015) (Commonwealth Government, 2014a) <https://www.immi.gov.au/FAQs/Pages/how-do-we-care-for-unaccompanied-minorsuntiltheir-immigration-status-is-resolved.aspx>

Department of Immigration and Border Protection Website, '*How Does the Minister's Guardianship Work?*' (online at 19 March 2015) (Commonwealth Government, 2014b) <https://www.immi.gov.au/FAQs/Pages/how-does-theministers-guardianship-work.aspx>

Department of Immigration and Border Protection Website, *Status Resolution Support Services Policy Advice Manual* (online at 18 November 2018) (Commonwealth Government, 2016) <https://www.border.gov.au/AccessandAccountability/Documents/20161006_FA160700108_documents_released.pdf>

Doherty, Ben, 'Nauru Asylum Seekers Sew Lips Shut in Protest over Cambodia Transfer', *The Guardian* (online at 2 October 2014) <http://www.theguardian.com/world/2014/oct/02/nauru-asylum-seekers-sew-lips-shut-protest-cambodia-transfer>

Employees of Save the Children Australia in Nauru (names withheld), Submission No 183, Australian Human Rights Commission, *Forgotten Children Inquiry* (n.d.) <https://humanrights.gov.au/sites/default/files/Submission%20No%20183%20-%20Names%20withheld%20-%20Employees%20of%20Save%20the%20Children%20Australia%20in%20Nauru_0.pdf?_ga=2.77504988.878436188.1589764716-644388670.1588671908>

Executive Committee of the High Commissioner's Programme, *Non-Refoulement* (12 October 1977) No. 6 (XXVIII) <https://www.refworld.org/docid/3ae68c43ac.html>

Executive Committee of the High Commissioner's Programme, *Refugee Children* (2 October 1987) No. 47 (XXXVIII) <https://www.refworld.org/docid/3ae68c432c.html>

Farrell, Paul, Nick Evershed and Helen Davidson, 'The Nauru Files: Cache of 2,000 Leaked Reports Reveal Scale of Abuse of Children in Offshore Detention' *The Guardian* (online at 10 August 2016) <https://www.theguardian.com/australia-news/2016/aug/10/the-nauru-files-2000-leaked-reports-reveal-scale-of-abuse-of-children-in-australian-offshore-detention>

Forum of Australian Services for Survivors of Torture and Trauma, Submission No 210, *Australian Human Rights Commission, The Forgotten Children Inquiry* (13 June 2014) <https://humanrights.gov.au/our-work/asylum-seekers-and-refugees/submissions-made-inquiry>

Gillard, Julia, *Joint Statement with the Prime Minister of Malaysia* (Media Release, 7 May 2011a) <http://pmtranscripts.dpmc.gov.au/release/transcript-17843>

Gillard, Julia, 'Asylum Seekers; Malaysia Agreement; Commonwealth Ombudsman' in Transcript of Joint Press Conference (13 October 2011b) <http://www.pm.gov.au/ press-office/transcript-joint-press-conference-canberra-17>

Gleeson, Madeline, 'Glimmers of Hope for Detained Asylum Seekers in the High Court's Nauru Decision' *The Conversation* (online at 3 February 2016a) <https://theconversation.com/glimmers-of-hope-for-detained-asylum-seekers-in-the-high-courts-nauru-decision-54036>

Gleeson, Madeline, 'PNG Court Decision Forces Australia to Act on Manus Island Detainees' *The Conversation* (online at 27 April 2016b) <https://theconversation.com/png-court-decision-forces-australia-to-act-on-manus-island-detainees-58439>

Grattan, Michelle, 'Malaysia Angry over Australian Criticism' *Sydney Morning Herald* (online at 13 August 2012) <http://www.smh.com.au>

Hall, Bianca, 'Human Misery of Transferred Asylum Seekers Turns into Big Business' *Sunday Age* (23 February 2014)

Hashan, Nicole, 'High Court Finds Offshore Detention Lawful' *Sydney Morning Herald* (online at 3 February 2016) <http://www.smh.com.au/federal-politics/politicalnews/ high-court-finds-offshore-detention-lawful-20160202-gmk5q6.html>

International Committee of the Red Cross, *Inter-Agency Guiding Principles on Unaccompanied and Separated Children* (International Committee of the Red Cross, 2004) <https://www.icrc.org/en/publication/1101-inter-agency-guiding-principles-unaccompanied-and-separated-children>

Karlsen, Elibritt, 'High Court gets Another Chance to Have the Final Word on Regional Processing' *Flagpost* (Parliamentary Library blog, 18 June 2014) <https://www.aph.gov.au/About_Parliament/Parliamentary_Departments/Parliamentary_Library/FlagPost/2014/June/High_Court_gets_another_chance_to_have_the_final_word_on_regional_processing>

Karlsen, Elibritt, 'Australia's Offshore Processing of Asylum Seekers in Nauru and PNG: A Quick Guide to Statistics and Resources' *Research Paper Series 2016–17* (Commonwealth Parliamentary Library, 2016a)

Karlsen, Elibritt, 'Refugee Resettlement to Australia: What Are the Facts?' *Research Paper Series 2016–17* (Commonwealth Parliamentary Library, 2016b)

Laughland, Oliver, 'Doctors Concerned by 48-Hour Turnaround Target for Asylum Seekers' *The Guardian* (online at 25 September 2013) <http://www.theguardian.com/world/2013/sep/25/doctors-concerned-asylum-seeker-health>

Laughland, Oliver and Ben Doherty, 'Nauru Staff Report Persistent Child Abuse and Self-Harm, Leaked Documents Show' *The Guardian* (online at 4 October 2014) <http://www.theguardian.com/australia-news/2014/oct/04/nauru-detention-centre-staff-persistent-child-abuse-self-harm>

Manne, Robert, Frank Brennan, Tim Costello and John Menadue, 'A Solution to Our Refugee Crisis' *Pearls and Irritations* (online at 13 August 2016) <https://johnmenadue.com/robert-manne-frank-brennan-tim-costello-john-menadue-a-solution-to-our-refugee-crisis/>

Manthorpe, Michael, 'Transcript of Evidence to Senate Standing Committee on Legal and Constitutional Affairs Committee' *Senate Estimates* (Parliament of Australia, 25 May 2015) <https://parlinfo.aph.gov.au/parlInfo/search/display/display.w3p;db=COMMITTEES;id=committees%2Festimate%2F0c5973fa-5b41-457f-af39-57df2971a205%2F0004;query=Id%3A%22committees%2Festimate%2F0c5973fa-5b41-457f-af39-57df2971a205%2F0000%22>

Mcnevin, Anne, Damir Mitric, Klaus Neumann, Savitri Taylor and Peter Mares, 'Beyond Deterrence: Reframing the Asylum Seeker Debate' *Inside Story* (online at 13 October 2014) <https://insidestory.org.au/beyond-deterrence-reframing-the-asylum-seeker-debate/>

Medhora, Shalailah, 'Asylum Seekers: 23 Vessels Turned Back but Coalition Stays Silent on Payments' *The Guardian* (online at 5 February 2016) <https://www.theguardian.com/australia-news/2016/feb/05/asylum-seekers-23-vessels-turned-back-but-coalition-stays-silent-on-payments>

Memorandum of Understanding between the Government of the Independent State of Papua New Guinea and the Government of Australia, Relating to the Transfer to, and Assessment and Settlement in, Papua New Guinea of Certain Persons, and Related Issues, signed 3 August 2013

Memorandum of Understanding between the Government of the Kingdom of Cambodia and the Government of Australia Relation to the Settling of Refugees in Cambodia, signed 26 September 2014

Memorandum of Understanding between the Republic of Nauru and the Commonwealth of Australia, Relating to the Transfer to and Assessment of Persons in Nauru, and Related Issues, signed 3 August 2013

Morrison, Scott (Minister for Immigration and Border Protection), *Operation Sovereign Borders Update* (Transcript of Press Conference, 8 November 2013)

Murphy, Kerry, 'High Court Backs Ministerial Power over Asylum Seekers', *Eureka Street* (online at 19 June 2014) <https://www.eurekastreet.com.au/article/high-court-backs-ministerial-power-over-asylum-seekers>

Name Withheld (16-Year Old Detained in Nauru OPC) Submission No 91, Australian Human Rights Commission, *The Forgotten Children Inquiry* (27 May 2014) <https://humanrights.gov.au/sites/default/files/Submission%20No%2091%20-%20Name%20withheld%20-%2016%20year%20old%20detained%20in%20Nauru%20OPC.pdf?_ga=2.216574687.878436188.1589764716-644388670.1588671908>

Name Withheld (Child Detained in Nauru OPC), Submission No 95, Australian Human Rights Commission, *The Forgotten Children Inquiry* (26 May 2014) <https://humanrights.gov.au/sites/default/files/Submission%20No%2095%20-Name%20withheld%20-%20Child%20detained%20in%20Nauru%20OPC.pdf?_ga=2.24710387.878436188.1589764716-644388670.1588671908>

Name Withheld (Unaccompanied Child) Handwritten Submission No 145, Australian Human Rights Commission, *The Forgotten Children Inquiry* (n.d.) <https://humanrights.gov.au/sites/default/files/Submission%20No%20145%20-%20Name%20withheld%20-%20Unaccompanied%20child%20detained%20in%20Nauru%20OPC.pdf?_ga=2.19402353.878436188.1589764716-644388670.1588671908>

Name Withheld (Unaccompanied Child Detained in Nauru OPC), Submission No 143 to Australian Human Rights Commission, *The Forgotten Children Inquiry* (n.d.) <https://humanrights.gov.au/sites/default/files/Submission%20No%20143%20-%20Name%20withheld%20-%20Unaccompanied%20child%20detained%20in%20Nauru%20OPC.pdf?_ga=2.44082797.878436188.1589764716-644388670.1588671908>

O'Sullivan, Maria, 'Australia Can Detain Asylum Seekers on the High Seas, the High Court Decides' *The Conversation* (online at 28 January 2015) <https://theconversation.com/australia-can-detain-asylum-seekers-on-the-high-seas-the-high-court-decides-32968>

O'Sullivan, Maria, *The End of Off-Shore Detention, the Implications of the Papua New Guinea Supreme Court Decision* (Castan Centre for Human Rights Law, 27 April 2016) <https://castancentre.com/2016/04/27/the-end-of-offshore-detention/>

Olijnyk, Anna, *CPCF v Minister for Immigration and Border Protection [2015] HCA 1* (University of Adelaide Law School, 2 March 2015). <https://blogs.adelaide.edu.au/law/2015/03/02/cpcf-v-minister-for-immigration-and-border-protection-2015-hca-1/>

Pearson, Elaine, *Case Analysis: Plaintiff M68/2015 v Minister for Immigration and Border Protection* (International Law Association, 31 March 2016) <http://ilareporter.org.au/2016/03/case-analysis-plaintiff-m682015-v-minister-for-immigration-and-border-protection/>

Peleg, Noam, *The Child's Right to Development* (Doctoral Thesis, University College, London, 2013)

Phillips, Janet, 'A Comparison of Coalition and Labor Government Asylum Policies in Australia since 2001' in *Parliamentary Library Research Paper Series* (Commonwealth Parliamentary Library, 2013)

Phillips, Janet, 'Australia's Humanitarian Program: A Quick Guide to the Statistics since 1947' in *Research Paper Series 2015–16* (Commonwealth Parliamentary Library, 2017a)

Phillips, Janet, 'Boat Arrivals and Boat 'Turnbacks' in Australia since 1976: A Quick Guide to the Statistics' in *Research Paper Series 2016–17* (Commonwealth Parliamentary Library, 2017b)

Phillips, Janet, *Boat Arrivals in Australia: A Quick Guide to the Statistics* (Commonwealth Parliamentary Library, 2014)

Phillips, Janet and Harriet Spinks, 'Boat Arrivals in Australia since 1976' in *Background Note* (Commonwealth Parliamentary Library, 2013a)

Phillips, Janet and Harriet Spinks, 'Immigration Detention in Australia' in *Parliament of Australia Background Note* (Commonwealth Parliamentary Library, 2013b)

Phillips, Janet and Harriet Spinks, 'Immigration Detention in Australia' in *Parliamentary Library Research Paper* (Commonwealth Parliamentary Library, 2013c)

Phillips, Janet and Harriet Spinks, 'Boat Arrivals in Australia since 1976' in *Parliamentary Library Research Paper* (Commonwealth Parliamentary Library, 2017)

Piper, Margaret and Graham Thom, 'Removing the Stumbling Blocks: Ways to Use Resettlement More Effectively to Protect Vulnerable Refugee Minors' (University of Sydney Law School, 2014) <http://www.amnesty.org.au/images/uploads/about/Removing_the_Stumbling_Blocks_Refugees_2014. pdf>

RACS, Submission No 217, Australian Human Rights Commission, *The Forgotten Children Inquiry* (30 June 2014) <https://humanrights.gov.au/sites/default/files/Submission%20No%20217-%20Refugee%20Advice%20%26%20Casework%20Service.pdf?_ga=2.210690128.456257149.1589840532-1976784639.1520134709>

Roberts, George, 'UNHCR Interviews Asylum Seekers over Forced Return to Indonesia', *AM*(online 18 March 2014 <http://www.abc.net.au/am/content/2014/s3965710.htm>

Royal Children's Hospital Melbourne, Submission to the *Senate Select Committee on the Recent Allegations Relating to Conditions and Circumstances at the Regional processing Centre in Nauru* (2 April 2016) <https://www.aph.gov.au/DocumentStore.ashx?id=0de68038-5281-41ea-a567-96eb21d8e5b0&subId=412378>

Separated Children in Europe Programme, *Statement of Good Practice* (SCEP, 4th ed, 2009) <http://www.refworld.org/docid/415450694.html>

Spinks, Harriet, *Boat Arrivals in Australia: A Quick Guide to the Statistics since 2001* (Commonwealth Parliamentary Library, 2018)

Stooke, Gemma, *High Court Rejects Challenge to Offshore Processing* (Human Rights Law Centre, 18 June 2014) <https://www.hrlc.org.au/human-rights-case-summaries/high-court-rejects-challenge-to-offshore-processing>

Sundram, Suresh and Samantha Loi, 'Long Waits for Refugee Status Lead to New Mental Health Syndrome', *The Conversation* (online at 23 May 2012) <https://theconversation.com/long-waits-for-refugee-status-lead-to-new-mental-health-syndrome-7165>

Taylor, Lenore, 'Boys Kept in Isolation at Manus Island Detention Centre', *The Guardian* (online at 4 November 2013) <http://www.theguardian.com/world/2013/nov/03/boys-kept-in-isolation-at-manus-island-detention-centre>

Thwaites, Rayner, 'Plaintiff M68/2015: The Commonwealth Executive's Capacity to Participate in Detention in Nauru' in University of NSW Constitutional Law Conference (12 February 2016) <http://www.gtcentre.unsw.edu.au/sites/gtcentre.unsw.edu.au/files/rayner_handout.pdf>

Tinkler, Mat, 'Transcript of Evidence to Australian Human Rights Commission' *The Forgotten Children* (Inquiry, Sydney Public Hearing, 4 April 2014) <https://www.humanrights.gov.au/sites/default/files/Mr%20Tinkler_0.pdf>

UN Committee On The Rights Of The Child, *Report of the 2012 Day of General Discussion On The Rights Of All Children In The Context Of International Migration* (2012) <http://www.ohchr.org/Documents/HRBodies/CRC/Discussions/2012/DGD2012ReportAndRecommendations.pdf>

UN Conference of Plenipotentiaries on the Status of Refugees and Stateless Persons, *Final Act of the United Nations Conference of Plenipotentiaries on the Status of Refugees and Stateless Persons* (25 July 1951) UN Doc A/CONF.2/108/Rev.1

UN High Commissioner for Refugees, *Global Consultations on International Protection/Third Track: Asylum Processes (Fair and Efficient Asylum Procedures)* EC/GC/01/12 (31 May 2001)

UN High Commissioner for Refugees, *Advisory Opinion on the Extraterritorial Application of Non-Refoulement Obligations under the 1951 Convention relating to the Status of Refugees and Its 1967 Protocol* (26 January 2007) <http://www.refworld.org/pdfid/45f17a1a4.pdf>

UN High Commissioner for Refugees, *Protection Policy Paper: Maritime Interception Operations and the Processing of International Protection Claims: Legal Standards and Policy Considerations with Respect to Extraterritorial Processing* (November 2010a) <www.refworld.org/docid/4cd12d3a2.html>

UN High Commissioner for Refugees, 'Regional Cooperative Approach to address Refugees, Asylum-Seekers and Irregular Movement' Discussion Paper presented at the Bali Process Ad Hoc Group-UNHCR Regional Cooperation on Refugees and Irregular Movement Workshop (UNHCR, 2010b) <http://www.refworld.org/pdfid/4e92d7c32.pdf>

UN High Commissioner for Refugees, *Returns to Sri Lanka of Individuals Intercepted at Sea* (Media Release, 7 July 2014) <http://www.unhcr.org/afr/news/press/2014/7/53baa6ff6/returns-sri-lanka-individuals-intercepted-sea.html>

Young, Peter, 'Transcript of evidence to Australian Human Rights Commission' in *Forgotten Children Inquiry* (Sydney Public Hearing, 31 July 2014) <https://www.humanrights.gov.au/sites/default/files/Dr%20Young.pdf>

Index

Note: Page numbers in *italics* indicate figures, bold indicate tables in the text, and references following "n" refer to notes.

For Product Safety Concerns and Information please contact our EU representative GPSR@taylorandfrancis.com
Taylor & Francis Verlag GmbH, Kaufingerstraße 24, 80331 München, Germany

www.ingramcontent.com/pod-product-compliance
Ingram Content Group UK Ltd.
Pitfield, Milton Keynes, MK11 3LW, UK
UKHW020005200926
475702UK00015B/2480
* 9 7 8 1 0 3 2 1 9 6 3 0 5 *